231

D0930728

WORK AND MADNESS:
The Rise of Community Psychiatry

WORK AND MADNESS: The Rise of Community Psychiatry

by Diana Ralph

BLACK ROSE BOOKS   Montréal

Black Rose Books No. L75
Hardcover—ISBN: 0-919619-07-X
Paperback—ISBN: 0-919619-05-3

Canadian Cataloguing in Publication Data

Ralph, Diana S.
    Work and Madness: The rise of community psychiatry

Originally presented as the author's thesis
(Ph.D.—University of Regina, 1980)

ISBN 0-919619-07-X (bound).   ISBN 0-919619-05-3 (pbk.).

1. Social psychiatry   I. Title.

RC455.R34   362.2'0425   C83-090044-6

Cover design: Cliff Harper
BLACK ROSE BOOKS
3981 boul. St. Laurent
Montréal, Québec H2W 1Y5

Printed and bound in Québec, Canada

Contents

CHAPTER I
Labour and Community Psychiatry

The community psychiatry phenomenon

Community psychiatry emerged soon after World War II, in many Western nations as well as in a number of Third World countries. It has become the uncontested dominant ideology of Western psychology. Under community psychiatry, the proportion of people treated for emotional problems has expanded dramatically, chronic mental patients have been deinstitutionalized, and techniques and programmes to treat non-psychotic people have proliferated.

But the community psychiatry phenomenon is not merely a quantitative expansion in psychiatric services. It has ushered in major qualitatively different changes from pre-World War II clinical programmes.

Its central innovations include:

- Shifting from an individual clinical model of treatment to a mass public health conception of its mandate.
- Expanding the definition of mental illness to include a much broader range of relatively normal symptoms, while, for practical purposes, excluding from

treatment by mental health agencies severe organic mental damage.

- Replacing long-term, expensive hospital treatment with therapy which is cheap, accessible, non-stigmatizing, and which takes place in the community.
- Reorganizing mental health personnel to include general practitioners, non-professionals, and an assortment of highly specialized new occupations.
- Taking on "preventive consultation" with employers in businesses, public agencies, and community organizations.

The main target of community psychiatry programmes is the active and potential labour force, in sharp contrast to pre-war public psychiatry's focus on unemployable people. In the 1940's, less than half of one per cent of the Canadian and U.S. populations were treated for mental disorders, mostly unemployable people who were considered severely disturbed, retarded, or aged. By the 1970's, over 10 per cent of the populations of Canada and other Western countries were receiving explicit psychiatric treatment each year, and almost one-third of the total population was using some mood-altering prescription drugs. The overwhelming majority of these patients are relatively normal employees and housewives who are treated for relatively mild, stress-related "problems of living"—neuroses, psychosomatic illnesses, and personality and behaviour disorders. The scope of psychiatric jurisdiction has widened to include virtually any behaviour which poses a problem for individuals or for the social institutions with which they come in contact.

While psychiatric treatment of employable people has mushroomed, the number of people treated for psychotic and organic disorders, and the per capita expenditures on their care, have declined precipitously. As early as 1935, policy-makers slashed funding for mental hospitals and began advocating plans to place manageable patients with private families. In contrast to the benevolent rhetoric of the 1960's decarceration movement, these plans were intended explicitly only to save money. The tide of pressure to dump the chronic mental hospitals swelled during the 1940's and '50's, culminating in the massive deinstitutionalization movement in the '60's which cut expenditures on care of chronic patients by over 50 per cent. Although this policy eventually came to be billed as a humanitarian gesture to reintegrate the mentally ill into "the community," the move was motivated at least as much by the dramatically lower cost of boarding and nursing home care. In many cases, the decarceration movement has merely dispersed institutionalizing conditions less visibly, leaving ex-patients more isolated than they had been in the hospitals, with fewer activities, less professional care and more limited freedom.

In effect, the community psychiatry movement abandoned, as much as possible, custodial care of unemployable people which had been the mainstay of public clinical psychiatry until 1945. And simultaneously, it took on the new role of treating the "behavioural problems" of those who can work. This sudden shift in emphasis occurred throughout most of the Western world within a few years of the end of World War II.

The advent of community psychiatry has had serious implications for a broad spectrum of people. Different specialized programmes treat unemployable people (psychotic, brain damaged, elderly, and retarded patients), marginally employable people (single parents, adolescents, ethnic minorities, and displaced workers), workers (blue, white, and pink collar employees), executives and managers, and revolutionary or disruptive populations (prisoners, people being interrogated or tortured, and entire "insurgent" Third World communities). Each targeted population group receives treatment methods tailored to "adjust" patients to their respective niches within a capitalist labour force.

In other words, community psychiatry is not a simple extension of pre-war institutional psychiatry. It treats an entirely different population, for different symptoms, with different methods, in different places, using different personnel. Any connection it retains with traditional clinical psychiatry is largely vestigial.

If community psychiatry did not evolve from clinical psychiatry, then where did it come from? The purpose of this study is to explain the sudden and internationally pervasive transformation of public psychiatry, by proposing a new theory, the "labour theory." The labour theory suggests that Western states have produced a mass psychiatric industry largely to control the effects of worker alienation on productivity. It suggests that community psychiatry's consistent function has been to produce a compliant, reliable work force, and a passive, flexible supply of unemployed labour. As we shall see, rather than growing out of clinical psychiatry, community psychiatry is a direct descendant of industrial psychology, and its tradition of labour regulation. Virtually every major innovation of community psychiatry was spawned by industrial psychologists employed by large corporations or the military during periods of high labour unrest or wartime pressures to boost national productivity. Those innovations did not just "evolve." Rather, they were commissioned explicitly to complement more heavy-handed labour-busting methods such as Taylorism, yellow-dog contracts, scabbing, industrial spying, red-baiting, and armed attacks.

Ultimately, I hope that this study can help unmask the true history of community psychiatry so that we who are treated, employed by, or indirectly affected by its programmes, can fight back collectively and individually.

Scope and limits of this book

To find the roots of community psychiatry, I traced the histories of both public mental health programmes and industrial psychiatry since 1900, and examined their relationships to labour relations and to economic political trends in Western industrial countries. My conclusions were based on an extensive review of original and secondary sources, integrating the literature and statistical data since 1900 in industrial psychology, clinical psychiatry, labour-management relations, and trends in productivity, automation, unemployment, economic indicators, and social service development in Western industrial countries.

14

I focused on those countries because that is where community psychiatry and its component innovations were born. Because the United States largely led the community psychiatry movement, imposing its model on other nations, this work focuses especially on U.S. trends. Its particular history—the role of the Rockefellers, Taylor, Mayo, and U.S. military and political post-war policies—is most germane to explaining where this world-wide phenomenon came from and for what purpose.

The formative stages of community psychiatry are roughly parallel throughout Western Europe and North America. However, the particular history and situation of each nation colours its public psychiatry programmes. For example, German psychiatrists emphasize both genetic and psychoanalytic research, while Italian psychiatrists tend to focus on neurological malfunctions and to ignore psychoanalysis.[1] Europeans give more attention to existential issues than do Canadians and Americans, who tend to be more behaviouristic.[2] These philosophical differences spill over into treatment of patients, as Hoff and Arnold point out:

> If a schizophrenic lives in a certain part of the world, it is unlikely that he will escape with an intact forebrain; if he happens to live in another part of the world, he will not be declared mentally ill, but rather, disturbed in his relationships to his environment. In one locale he will become the subject of the most diverse laboratory experiments; in another, his utterances will be stifled immediately by electro-shock.[3]

However, these stylistic differences have become rather secondary since World War II. Since 1945, most Western countries have adopted widely the innovations and principles of community psychiatry.[4] Partly, this is because the United States used its enormous post-World War II influence to impose its model of community psychiatry on other countries.[5] For example, Langfeldt reports that in Scandinavia, U.S. psychiatric influence had been virtually non-existent before the war, but:

> This state of affairs has changed completely since 1945. In post-war years the majority of leading Scandinavian psychiatrists and neurologists have had one or more courses

15

of study in the United States. This has been made possible to a great extent, by generous American scholarships, especially from the Rockefeller Foundation, and by the Fulbright grants. At the same time, authorities in the Scandinavian countries have recognized the advisability of providing instruction in American psychiatric theoretic and therapeutic principles.[6]

At the same time, since World War II, most developed countries have faced similar problems of political and economic instability and of rising labour alienation. The same social forces which encouraged the United States to adopt a community psychiatry model, therefore, also made it an attractive model for other countries.

Because the book's purpose is to analyze the roots of community psychiatry—which lie in Western industrial countries—I have not dealt with psychiatric programming in either Third World countries or the Soviet Union. There are important qualitative differences between "community" psychiatry in pre- and post-revolutionary countries which are beginning to receive attention in the literature.

Pre-revolutionary Third World countries have been influenced strongly by Western (and especially U.S.) community psychiatry. Before World War II, underdeveloped countries had few public psychiatric programmes or trained personnel.[7] An early priority of the United Nations was to establish community psychiatry programmes in all nations, including those in the Third World.[8]

This study also does not address a number of issues in labour-management relations. For example, it does not discuss the consequences of internal labour divisions (e.g., craft vs. industrial unions, national vs. international unions, or union leadership vs. memberships). Nor has it dealt with the effect of racism or sexism on the labour movement and on industrial relations. On management's side, it does not explore the competing factions within business leadership (e.g., domestic vs. absentee owners, large vs. small manufacturers, financial vs. manufacturing vs. resource extraction sectors, or conservative vs. liberal political orientation).

These are all important issues. Nevertheless, for the central question of this study—why community psychiatry

16

developed—these issues are all relatively secondary. No prior research has postulated an intimate relationship between labour relations and community psychiatry, and the focus of this work is to examine this basic link. If this "labour theory" stands up, future research on the impact of these secondary conflicts can be placed in a better perspective.

CHAPTER II
Why Community Psychiatry?
Four Theories

Most attempts to explain the rise of community psychiatry have scarcely noted the discontinuity between pre- and post-World War II psychiatry. Though they vary widely in their assessment of whether or not community psychiatry is "a good thing," virtually all the theories that exist assume that community psychiatry evolved from traditional clinical psychiatry with little qualitative change in policy. From varying perspectives, these theories propose that after the war, public psychiatry simply became better, more powerful, more oppressive, or just cheaper—but *not* really different.

There are four alternative, conflicting theories about why and how community psychiatry developed: the benevolent government theory, the mental health lobby theory, the antipsychiatry theory, and the Marxist theory. Benevolent government theorists argue that community psychiatry is merely the latest development in a progressively enlightened and humane evolution of psychiatric services. The mental health lobby theorists propose that professional interest groups—psychiatrists, social workers, doctors, and pharmaceutical companies—motivated by self-interested empire building, pressured their governments to finance community psychiatry. Antipsychiatry theorists believe that community psychiatry just represents more sophisticated methods for psychiatric oppression than the old straitjackets. And Marxist theorists suggest that community psychiatry reflects a general state policy to cut public expenses for services to unemployable people, under pressure of its fiscal crises. But all four assume that community psychiatry is a variant of traditional public psychiatry, and all four fail to address key differences between pre- and post-war public psychiatry.

The benevolent government theory

Those who created and now support community psychiatry explain its existence with what could be called a "benevolent government" theory. Advocates of this approach assume that the government is a humanitarian and neutral dispenser of services for the benefit of all. This assumption steers its representatives toward an apolitical, technological explanation of community psychiatry. They perceive its growth as a consistent advance in a series of ever more enlightened scientific progressions toward "the goal of making high quality public and private mental health services available at a reasonable cost to all who need them."[9] For them, the sole motive for this "third revolution in psychiatry"[10] is the welfare of the currently and the potentially mentally ill.

Community psychiatry developed, in this view, because government leaders became more aware of mass psychiatric problems developing as side-effects of progress, and of the institutionalizing effects of mental hospitals. The first director of the U.S. National Institute of Mental Health (NIMH), for example, proclaimed that community psychiatry had a mandate both to improve care of chronic mental patients and to prevent mental illness in general:

> We have long since learned that the problem can never be solved simply by building more institutions for those persons whose abnormal behavior can no longer be ignored or neglected. Our goal must be not merely to press for better care of those mentally ill persons for whom we have failed to provide adequate treatment in time. Rather, we must adopt the positive aim of utilizing our talents and

energies to prevent such illnesses and to improve the mental health of the nation.[11]

Lawson, one of the pioneers of Canadian community psychiatry, echoed these sentiments:

> The older concept of the mental hospital as an asylum where the mentally ill could be stored out of harm's way is no longer acceptable. The mental hospital must be one of the tools used to restore the mentally ill to their place in the community and in the words of Florence Nightingale a hospital must at least "do the sick no harm." We must go further than this in our modern conception of the mental hospital for it must not only do no harm but must actively assist in the patient's cure and rehabilitation.[12]

A burst of demographic studies was funded during the 1950's and early '60's which graphically demonstrated that the prevalence of mental illness is related to social stress and that many more people are ill than are treated in mental hospitals. At the same time, Goffman's exposé of the debilitating effects of mental institutions received enthusiastic and extensive recognition.[13] These findings provided the empirical justification for policy decisions made 20 years earlier to dump the chronics. The inmates of mental hospitals were to be freed and returned to the healing, normal environments of their own communities, while all other emotional casualties of "progress" were to receive cheap, accessible treatments to cure them before they needed to go into an institution. Everyone would benefit—the mentally ill, the taxpayers, and the businesses, as services to the already mad improved and the costs of future madness to society were averted.

This perspective has some validity. Certainly a large number of liberal, humanitarian professionals have been attracted to community psychiatry out of a genuine concern for disturbed people, and with honest hopes for righting the injustices and inadequacies in their treatment.

However, as an explanation for why community psychiatry developed, this theory is extremely weak. In some ways, this is understandable since its spokespeople are usually administrators of, or lobbyists for, community psychiatry, and their interest is, therefore, more in promoting than in critically analyzing its growth. Nevertheless, the benevolent government theory suffers from multiple blind spots and inconsistencies. Among other things, it fails to address questions such as:

- Why was there such a sudden international upsurge of benevolent concern for the mad just after World War II? If professionals and administrators had these charitable urges earlier, what kept them from expressing them?
- Who else had a stake in community psychiatry besides the insane?
- How did all that charitable feeling alone motivate massive spending on psychiatric programmes, when other serious social problems were neglected?

The benevolent government theory does not analyze why so many Western governments almost simultaneously adopted community psychiatry programmes. Each country's theorists suggest local reasons, such as the Swiss democratic tradition or the prolonged exposure to welfare state policies in Britain and Norway. In the United States, President Kennedy's retarded sister had been credited as the inspiration behind the American mental health policy of the times. But this massive international phenomenon demands deeper economic and political motivation than democratic traditions, habit, or personal interests.

Nor does it examine the stake that groups other than the "mad" may have had in creating community psychiatry. The mental patients themselves and even their families never actively lobbied for these programmes. In fact, polls showed that most people preferred to have mentally ill family members treated in distant mental hospitals rather than nearby, and a number of community groups protested against deinstitutionalizing chronic mental patients.[14] On the other hand, corporations, insurance companies, military leaders, and some medical groups vociferously supported community psychiatry funding.

The benevolent government theory also ignores the links between trends in psychiatry and in other social services. These links imply a consistent, wider stimulus for community psychiatry that goes well beyond a simple concern for the mad.

It is obvious how inadequate a theory of charitable intentions is when it tries to account for community psychiatry's tendency to slash budgets and services to the chronically mentally ill. These theorists are left claiming that any inadequacies in services to ex-mental patients are nothing more than local "mistakes."

Finally, the benevolent government theorists' claim that community psychiatry is primarily a technological advance as a result of new mood-altering drugs is unconvincing, since deinstitutionalizing chronic mental patients and expanding programmes for workers began well before the drug technology was developed.

Underlying all these weaknesses is the blindness of the benevolent government theorists to the class nature of psychiatric services. Consequently, they leave out a central question: For whom is the high incidence of "mental illness" a problem and why is it a problem for them? The "problem" of mental illness, as it is defined now, is quite different from the problem as it was defined 30 years ago. The large majority of mental patients now are diagnosed for disorders which were scarcely treated and sometimes not even labelled as mental disorders before 1945. These include transient situational disorders, most personality and behaviour disorders, unaddicted and non-psychotic drug and alcohol "abuse," neurotic depression, and a variety of psychosomatic illnesses. At the same time, the number of people treated for chronic mental disorders such as organic brain damage, mental retardation, and functional psychoses had declined precipitously as a result of the decarceration movement. It is easy to see that the decline of treatment for chronic mental illness has nothing to do with lower incidence of these illnesses, but only with their changing definition from psychiatric to non-psychiatric problems. But it is harder to see the social production of the rising treatment statistics.

The rise in psychiatric treatment appears on the surface to be a response to the growing "real" incidence of mental illness in the population. We have been trained to assume, particularly in the social services, that problems exist independently of their treatment, and that the incidence and prevalence of a problem can be objectively measured. As a result, there are many attempts to study the "true" incidence of poverty (as opposed to the numbers being served by welfare), crime (as opposed to the numbers of convictions), unemployment (as opposed to the numbers receiving unemployment insurance), and so forth. Similarly, psychiatric epidemiologists have devoted impressive amounts of energy to discovering the "true" incidence of various psychiatric disorders. With widely divergent results, these studies have "confirmed" the high incidence of untreated mental illness, particularly among the poor and the oppressed.

But the measurement and the treatment of social problems are intimately related. As Dorothy Smith points out, "when you seem to be counting people becoming mentally ill, you are in fact also counting what psychiatric agencies do. The two aspects can't be taken apart. The figures can't be decontaminated."[15] Diagnosing—labelling—is a central function of psychiatric treatment, as well as of all other social services. It is the criterion by which a client's eligibility for or requirement of service is determined. The difference between actual treatment statistics and "real" incidence rates is primarily a difference in the definition of the problem, a difference between those who are treated and those who the definers of the problem believe *should* be treated. We can see the underlying political nature of the "true" incidence problem in the debate over who is to be considered unemployed. The measured rate of unemployment can vary over 300 per cent depending on what definition one employs and how rigorously one looks for cases.[16] Since the resulting number of people defined as unemployed has serious consequences, these definitions are hotly contested.

What is considered a problem reflects primarily the concerns of the definers, rather than of the people who are defined as having the problem. To be labelled and counted (and eventually processed through some official treatment), one has to pose a problem for the people who finance the labelling and treatment. For example, regular government reports are issued on the incidence of crime, inflation, union organizing and unemployment (as it affects business), but there are no official statistics on the incidence of dangerous

24

employers, un-employers, union busters, incompetent doctors, scabs, or RCMP or CIA spies.

Of course, often the people who are labelled do experience real problems, but these are not necessarily the problems that they are defined as having. Some of the miseries people experience are relatively ignored as social problems worthy of treatment. Malnutrition and infant mortality among native people, and mothers' economic powerlessness in the absence of adequate day care are prime examples. Other sources of unhappiness are explicitly not defined as problems, as in the adoption of "acceptable" levels of exposure to radiation, pollution, and noise. And some problems people experience are actively caused and supported by government policies, such as being deported, drafted, denied welfare, or arrested.

In all of these examples, the official definition of "problem" fails to include, or explicitly excludes, the individual's experience of unhappiness or discontent. On the other hand, many problems which people do *not* have *are* defined as social problems, such as the "need" for wage controls, better police intelligence operations, and treatment of "minimal brain dysfunction" in bored children, addicts, and thieves.

As we shall see, the new treatments of the new mental illnesses combine both types of error—by treating people who have real social problems for psychological problems they do *not* have, and often by producing more of the real problems they do have. For example, the recent U.S. President's Commission on Mental Health failed to propose any action to attack poverty, racism, sexism, and alienation, even though it acknowledged that these factors psychologically damage over one-third of the population. Instead, it only urged that psychiatric problems be expanded to "reach these underserved populations."[17]

The rising "incidence" of new forms of "madness" corresponds closely to the problems these people pose to business and the State. The fastest-growing diagnoses—neuroses, alcohol and drug abuse, and personality disorders—are all social diseases (to the extent that they are valid descriptions of symptoms and not just pejorative labels): reflections of aliena-

25

tion, hopelessness, frustration, and lack of dignified, useful options in life. The symptoms of these diagnoses are evidence simultaneously of personality damage and of personality repair. That is, they represent ego defenses against unbearable reality. In a sense, the problem for these people is not nearly so much their behavioural symptoms as it is the social stresses which require this distorted behaviour. People drink and take drugs largely to cope in soul-destroying situations. They repress their awareness of reality and develop "personality problems" because that is the only way they can continue to do what they must do—work or be unemployed.

But for business and for government, the psychiatric diagnoses *are* the main problem, because they pose a serious danger to profits and social order. People with these symptoms don't produce as much as they could, and they are unreliable, impulsive, and prone to accidents, work disruptions, and absenteeism. As Bertram Brown, ex-director of the NIMH, pointed out: "Mental illness is without a doubt the nation's costliest health problem and constitutes an enormous drain on the country's energies and resources."[18] This sentiment echoed an earlier statement by two prominent industrial psychologists: "The cost to industry of disruption resulting from emotional disturbance... runs into hundreds of millions of dollars annually."[19] In other words, community psychiatry *defines* potential disrupters of work and social order as "mentally ill" and as "emotional contaminants"[20] who are likely to infect others.

The definition of this new "problem" is part of the effort to control it, that is, to eliminate the danger it poses to the present social order. Many of the treatments which have been developed under community psychiatry—the mood-altering drugs, the methadone programme, the behaviour modification techniques, and psychosurgery—have little other function than to redress consciousness and emotion more than the alcohol, drugs, and ego defenses they claim to treat.

The benevolent government theory of community psychiatry basically expresses the voice of progressive business leaders under monopoly capitalism. Assuming that what is good for business is good for people logically leads these theor-

26

ists to applaud policies that adjust people to the needs of business "for their own good." If one accepts the maddening conditions of capitalist society, the only humane thing to do is to "help" people to be happy in those conditions. As Shagass, a prominent community psychiatrist, explains:

> The explicit value system [of community psychiatry] is that measures which permit people to feel comfortable, to work and to study more easily, and to get along better with others are "good."[21]

The only remaining issue is how to do that most efficiently and effectively—that is, it masks political issues with technological issues.

While these theorists offer little in direct analysis of the evolution of community psychiatry, their work is useful in clarifying the philosophical assumptions of its founders. They are well-intentioned reformers who want "the best" for people. But at the same time, they are constrained by their ideologically conditioned assumptions to define both problems and goals in terms of the priorities of a social system which is not only inequitable, but which in large measure creates the problems they are called upon to solve.

The mental health lobby theory

Mental health lobby theorists focus on the role of psychiatrists and other mental health professions in pressuring governments to expand psychiatric services. Their perspective reflects a pluralistic, dramatic conception of politics in which relatively equal, competing interest groups vie for power and money. Community psychiatrists, like other interest groups "growing out of the liberal social programs of the 1960's,"[22] capitalized on national concern over social problems and managed to convince their governments that they could prevent and cure mental illness. Other psychiatrists "followed their noses to the federal money and defined large portions of their function in the areas of community psychology and psychiatry."[23] Before long, community psychiatry became another bandwagon as psychiatrists faddishly sacrificed judgement for prestige and money. The result, these theorists claim, has been "innovation with change"; bureaucratic empire building and politicking at the expense of patients, their communities, and non-professional mental health workers. "God is dead, one has been told, 'try NIMH'."[24]

By and large, these theorists are not as concerned with analyzing the causes of community psychiatry as they are with criticizing it. Therefore, they offer little detailed investigation of the actual mechanisms by which community psychiatry managed to win such massive and sudden international political influence. Rather, they tend to avoid macro-economic and political analyses and to focus instead on the immediate political machinations of psychiatric interest groups and on the personal motivations of their leaders to expand their empires. Chu and Trotter, for example, explain the growth of the NIMH like an "Avis Rent-a-Car" ad.

> Although NIMH soon became the largest and fastest-growing component institute in NIH [National Institutes of Health], it was never completely content within the NIH fold... NIMH felt something like a second-class citizen within NIH. Perhaps fearful that psychiatry would receive short shrift within any medical agency and convinced that the rest of the medical community would not mightily promote a mental health institute, NIMH always seemed to try harder than the other institutes of health and incessantly strove to increase its own power within NIH, even after the prestige of psychiatric medicine became great.[25]

This theory that "trying harder" will reap political rewards typifies the view that growth is a result of the individual decisions of psychiatrists and agencies rather than a response to social and economic pressures.

The mental health lobby theorists fall generally into two categories: (1) conservative psychiatrists whose professional fiefdoms are threatened by community psychiatry's industrialization and state intervention, and (2) liberal social scientists who basically approve of community psychiatry, but who bemoan its unequal distributions by race, geography, and income. The conservative wing complains that community psychiatry causes too much change, and guts professional standards, while the liberals complain that little has changed,

28

and that community psychiatry is merely traditional psychiatry cloaked in a new rhetoric. But both factions agree that the professionals single-handedly created community psychiatry by legislation and clever public relations work.

This approach is useful in clarifying the internal politics of competing professional groups and their relationship to State legislative and administrative bodies. But it fails to deal with historical or class issues, and as a result, it explains little about the wider forces moulding community psychiatry or about its broad social impact. Focusing on formal administrative and bureaucratic policies, the mental health lobby theorists ignore the far greater impact of private, non-legislative forces on community psychiatry. The public sector of community psychiatry is only one highly specialized wing of a much broader and more complex phenomenon. Public mental health programmes in Canada treat less than a quarter of those receiving psychiatric diagnoses, and less than one-eighth of those who receive mood-altering drug prescriptions.

The mental health lobby theory produces a highly skewed perspective on the dynamics of community psychiatry. It recognizes only petit-bourgeois lobbyists and State policy-makers, ignoring both the impact of corporate demands and the role of labour actions in causing those demands. It cannot explain what made the psychiatric lobby, or indeed any other petit-bourgeois lobby, powerful. Clearly, the power was not inherent in the profession itself, as we can see by the rising and falling budget appropriations for community psychiatry. From 1945 to 1970, funding for psychiatric programmes rose precipitously in the United States and Canada. But beginning in 1970, mental health-related grants were frozen or cut, while criminal "justice" programmes proliferated. The mental health lobby has demonstrated little power which is independent of its ability to adapt itself to State, and ultimately to business, interests.

Like the benevolent government theorists, the lobby theorists do not address issues such as the simultaneous international upsurge of community psychiatry, the relationship of community psychiatry to other social services, or the State's motives for responding so generously to the mental health

29

lobby. As a result, they offer little insight into the causes of the evolution of community psychiatry.

They do, however, perform a useful role in discrediting the theory of the disinterested benevolent government. By analyzing the petty squabbling among professional lobby groups and by exposing the inequalities in the distribution of community psychiatric services, these theorists lay bare some of the failures of community psychiatry in its own rhetorical terms. It remains for the social control theorists to make sense of this apparent failure.

The social control theories

Social control theorists explain the rise of community psychiatry as part of a broader expansion of the social regulation of citizens. Unlike either of the previous theoretical positions, they tend to discount the government's claim about its benevolent motivations toward mental patients. They view community psychiatry as an active threat to the interests of its clients, a threat which operates "directly to enforce oppressive sex and class roles, to reinforce individualism, and to promote the idea that however oppressive your situation is, your problems are 'all in your head'."[26] As a result, far from lobbying for more and better programmes, or even for services which are more available to poor and working-class people, they oppose community psychiatry in general: "Who wants a community mental health center, even an attractive and well-staffed one, if its ultimate prescription for mental health is acquiescence to oppression?"[27]

For the social control theorists, mood-altering drugs are not a therapeutic advance, but rather a sinister progression from physical to psychological restraint of civil liberties. The widening net of psychiatric services implies for them, not improved accessibility of care, but rather forebodings of fascism. Thomas Szasz, one of the most trenchant critics of contemporary psychiatry, perceives community psychiatry as advocating an ideology that:

> ...the individual should be allowed to exist only if he is
> socially well adapted and useful. If he is not, he should be

30

"therapized" until he is "mentally healthy"—that is, uncomplainingly submissive to the will of the elites in charge of Human Engineering.[28]

For the advocates of the social control theory, deinstitutionalization is an ironic hypocrisy in light of the rapidly increasing number of people who are hospitalized and the equally institutionalizing conditions of many "community" placements. The social control theorists divide into two schools of thought on the causes of community psychiatry: antipsychiatric and Marxist. Antipsychiatrists emphasize the internal politics of therapist-patient relations, while Marxists focus on the external social and economic influences that have shaped community psychiatry.

The antipsychiatry theory

The antipsychiatry perspective grew out of the mental patients' rights movement, and it tends to reflect the specific concerns of its members who are primarily ex-mental patients and liberal mental health professionals. It focuses on the problems of those labelled psychotic, on their treatment in and out of mental hospitals, and on the professional power of therapists over their patients. The antipsychiatry theorists believe that community psychiatry is simply an expansion of a consistently oppressive psychiatric system, and they do not recognize any fundamental shift in emphasis from unemployed, chronic patients to active workers.

> The chains are gone, the beatings are less frequent and more secretive, the locked doors have been opened in many institutions, and the interior decorations have been improved. However, mental hospitals are still used primarily to confine disruptive members of the lower classes. The chains are chemical and legal, the beatings are psychological, and the locks have been replaced by members of the mental health team who guard the open doors. The rapid discharge rate, far from being an index of the "progress" of medical psychiatry, is controlling thought and behavior.[29]

31

Antipsychiatric theorists perceive the medical establishment, and particularly psychiatrists, as the principal forces for expanded social control of deviants, and they fear the threat of medical dictatorship over all of us.

> We shall have solutions for our human dilemmas proposed to us in the language of medicine, in terms of techniques for combating mental illness and promoting mental health, so that we cannot disagree unless we are wicked or mad. This can serve only those in power, who will promote their causes under the banner of medical progress. We shall have been bewitched by "experts" about our nature and our destiny. And this bewitchment will be eagerly sought by its victims—and justified and exalted "In the Name of Mental Health."[30]

Their attitude toward the non-psychiatric population is ambivalent. On the one hand, they see community psychiatry as endangering the civil liberties of everyone, and particularly of the oppressed. But on the other hand, they view all non-mental patients as the ultimate enemy, since they believe mass intolerance of deviant life-styles is the source of psychiatrists' power. From this perspective, community mental health centres are "instruments of the state employed for the involuntary confinement of persons who have offended the public sense of behavioral propriety."[31] This leaves mental patients and their allies alone in a struggle against everyone else:

> It would be a shame if the ex-patient groups now in existence lost sight of their actual political goals and adopted the line which strict Marxists like Michael Glenn... are pushing on them... Mental patients [should] see the real oppressor as being the mental health system and its practitioners... It is not the ruling class which is the enemy of mental patients. It is the community. The people who hate and fear mental patients the most are the people who insist on a system of strict controls for them, the very "masses" Glenn would have them ally with.[32]

The antipsychiatry theory offers major advantages over the benevolent government and the lobby theorists. First of all, it identifies the conflict of interests between the servers and the served in community psychiatry. Where the other theories treat all "services" as benefits, antipsychiatry theorists point out that many psychiatric "services" serve primarily the interests of the powerful and of the professionals, while they often restrict the freedom and rights of those "served." This opens up the internal politics of community psychiatry in a way that the mental health lobby theory could not. It allows antipsychiatry theorists to provide a wealth of detailed evidence on the specific mechanisms by which social control is imposed on those labelled insane. Finally, the antipsychiatry theorists offer useful descriptions of how community psychiatry helps to enforce oppressive social relations by invalidating the feelings of women, minorities, and the poor, and by treating these groups with coercive methods.

Nevertheless, the antipsychiatry theory cannot explain the rise of community psychiatry. Their emphasis on hospitalized mental patients limits their ability to examine the dramatic shift of mental health services under community psychiatry away from treating psychotics in public institutions, and toward the private sector treatment of a non-psychotic population.

Far from explaining the rise of community psychiatry, they hardly recognize it. Focusing on the internal dynamics of therapist-patient relations, they tend to ignore the wider economic and political forces impinging on community psychiatry, and to ascribe more independent power to psychiatrists than they actually possess. This leaves the antipsychiatry theory without a framework to analyze the purpose of the social control of mental patients, why this control should have expanded so rapidly since 1960, and who controls the psychiatrists. As Scull, a critic of antipsychiatric theory, explains:

> Almost exclusive attention to the impact of organizations on the individual results in only passing attention to the structure of the organizations themselves and in almost total neglect of the overarching structural context within which particular agencies of social control operate. In turn, this narrowness of vision inevitably leads to work which depicts social control as arbitrary. For want of a larger perspective, the actions of the agencies come to be seen either as free-floating and apparently perverse, or as determined simply by the immediate interests of the first line controllers [psychiatrists].[33]

One serious consequence of this omission is the tendency of antipsychiatrists to separate mental patients from the practical situations which may have caused their deviant behaviour. Antipsychiatry theorists begin their analysis at the point of deviancy labelling, ignoring and sometimes explicitly denying the existence of madness — i.e., being out of touch with one's own feelings and situation. They often treat those who are labelled insane as independent spirits or even as revolutionaries who are simply trying to assess their own individuality: "All madmen are political dissidents."[34] This romanticizing of madness alienates mental patients form their social relationships. As one ex-mental patient points out:

> But most of us... were being broken down by social conditions in our personal lives *before* psychiatry identified us as "deviants." Returning to those lives (trying to recontruct them) has placed many of us back in the frying pan — back in living situations in which we are lonely, poor, treated with no respect, and denied decent food, housing, work, and companionship. Racial and sexual discrimination are additional burdens for many of us — they are daily realities, no abstract political ideas.[35]

This asocial perspective leads antipsychiatry theorists to view non-patients as potential enemies, and to blame psychiatric power on the masses' fears of deviancy. It is difficult, however, to reconcile this position with numerous studies which indicate that the lay public has always defined madness much more narrowly than psychiatrists do, recognizing only extremely bizarre behaviour as mental illness. In fact, in spite of massive government education efforts to widen popular awareness of the new, expanded psychiatric diagnoses, the public's definition of madness has remained remarkably consistent.[36] In other words, although mass fears of severely psychotic people *may* have contributed to the creation of mental institutions, the antipsychiatrists cannot explain either the enormous expansion in the scope of treatment for non-psychotic diagnoses or the decline in treatment of psychoses which characterizes community psychiatry. Although it provides some worthwhile criticisms of psychiatric treatment — particularly the treatment of psychoses — the antipsychiatry theory does not prove a coherent explanation for the rise of community psychiatry.

34

Marxist theories

Marxist theorists have recently begun analyzing the nature and functions of public social services. Even though few of these studies focus directly on community psychiatry, they suggest solutions to some of the unanswered questions surrounding the rise of community psychiatry. They provide particularly useful insights in three areas. They clarify the social control functions of community psychiatry; they analyze the economic and political pressures which motivated the rise of community psychiatry since 1945; and they describe how these pressures may have contributed to the tendency of community psychiatry services to industrialize their methods and to shift from a public to a private emphasis.

Marxists propose that the capitalist State exists to protect the interests of big business. ("The State" as used here includes the central government, the legislatures, the civil service, the military, public corporations, central banks, the judiciary, and provincial and local governments.) In addition to mundane, relatively apolitical housekeeping functions like providing roads, currency, and sanitation services, the State actively controls the behaviour of classes, particularly of labour and the unemployed, which conflicts with business interests. These social control functions include: (1) co-opting mass grievances in order to prevent unrest and revolution; (2) using force to prevent and control "anti-social" behaviour through the police, the military, the legal structure, bureaucratic rules, and so on; (3) ideologically conditioning people through the public educational system and regulation of the mass media to cooperate with the wishes of business; and (4) moulding the current and potential labour force to fit the requirements of the job structure. Community psychiatry fulfills each of these functions to some extent.

Community psychiatry services, such as mood-altering drugs, counselling, and consultation, do help to make alienating work and living conditions more bearable, and thus to co-opt labour militancy. This co-opting role of community psychiatry explicitly was recommended by a number of management and military representatives who advocated its establishment.

35

Community psychiatry operates to control trouble-makers directly through its powers of involuntary hospitalization, and indirectly through computerized psychiatric data on individuals and groups. It also uses psychological technologies in prisons, in police intelligence operations, and in the military.

Along with other health services, community psychiatry encourages people to perceive their problems as individual and irrational, and to see their psychiatrist's advice to adjust as based on scientific authority.

Finally, and most importantly, social services in general have emerged as powerful tools in adapting workers to the faster, more degraded form of work under monopoly capitalism. Although this point has been well documented in the education, welfare, and police systems, little work has been done yet to apply this concept to community psychiatry.

Marxist theorists argue that it is not necessary to postulate that anyone consciously conspires to create these multiple social control functions. Rather, they propose, capitalist State organization implicitly assumes, depends on, and enforces capitalist values such as the "virtue" of private property, the "right" to make a profit, and the public's "need" for enlightened management. As Ehrenreich and Ehrenreich point out:

> To analyze something as a system of social control is not to view it as a conspiracy. We are not arguing that the health system is consciously designed to exercise social control, or that the social control functions of the health system somehow explain its structure and dynamics. To the contrary, we explain the social control functions as themselves a result of the institutional structure, organization, and economics of the health-care system.[37]

Nor do social control functions depend on the malevolent motives of individuals in power, as Navarro explains:

> To see these policies as a result of malevolence of individuals or the manipulation of government by certain economic groups is... limited and erroneous. Such politics respond to the need perceived by those governments that the economy, to whose health we are all supposedly tied, has to be straightened out before we can think of "other matters." And it is this behavior, and not the specific

36

motivation of individuals or manipulation of groups, which establishes these policies as capitalist policies.[38]

Panitch adds:

> The problem is not that political and bureaucratic officials *decide* to favour capitalist interests in case after case; it is rather that it rarely even *occurs* to them that they might do other than favour such interests. The problem is indeed a systemic one.[39]

Social control is not exercised uniformly on all members of a society, but rather its purpose and form are conditioned by the client's relationship to the bourgeoisie. Steven Spitzer and the Ehrenreichs make a useful distinction between control of those excluded and those included in the labour force (in Marxist terminology, the lumpen-proletariat and the proletariat, respectively). From the point of view of business, unemployable people are "social junk"; nothing more than unproductive burdens on the economy.

> The discreditability of social junk resides in the failure, inability or refusal of this group to participate in the roles supportive of capitalist society... Since the threat presented by social junk is passive, growing out of its inability ot compete and its withdrawal from the prevailing social order, controls are usually designed to regulate and contain rather than eliminate and suppress the problem. Clear-cut examples of social junk in modern capitalist societies might include the officially administered aged, handicapped, mentally ill and mentally retarded.[40]

Social services, including mental health services, directed at the unemployed tend to exercise "disciplinary social control." This form of social control is unpleasant, punitive, and exclusionary, designed to discourage workers from joining the ranks of the unproductive.

> At times, it has been used quite consciously to maintain industrial discipline in the work force. Foucault describes the combined poorhouses/insane asylums of eighteenth- and nineteenth-century Paris and London. These were maintained as *public spectacles* to remind the populace of what awaited them if they opted to drop out into pauperism or madness.[41]

This analysis helps to explain the "failure" of the decarceration movement to provide community placements for unemployable, chronic patients which are any less degrading than mental institutions. Disciplinary social control of the unemployed still requires that "social junk" be processed in the cheapest way while at the same time discouraging productive workers from dropping out.

By contrast, from the viewpoint of business, workers and potential workers threaten to become "social dynamite"— that is, to "call into question established relationships of production and domination."[42] To the extent that these people are alienated, dissatisfied, and organized, they pose a much more active threat to the social order than does "social junk." Yet, they are necessary for the success of business. This is true for the working class as a whole, of course, since capital depends on labour to produce profits. But even on an individual basis, it is expensive for employers to replace and retrain employees or to compensate for the unreliability and lower productivity of "disturbed" workers, and for their impact on the morale of other workers. "Behaviour problems" among these people tend to be subject to a quite different form of social control— "integrative"[43] or "co-optative control."[44]

"Co-optative control," unlike disciplinary social control, is attractive, accessible, and non-stigmatizing, aimed at recruiting all those with "problems" "into the fold of *professional management* of various aspects of their lives."[45] It is this aspect of community psychiatry—this expanding, dominant sector—which the antipsychiatry theorists cannot explain, because it is neither punitive, exclusive, nor stigmatizing, and as the overwhelmingly voluntary use of these services indicates, it is also not coercive. The routine, co-optative control techniques refuse to fit neatly into the paradigm of conspiracy-based, disciplinary control which the antipsychiatry theorists discuss.

The precision with which this approach differentiates the types, targets, and purposes of social control is still in an early, relatively underdeveloped state. Little of this work deals explicitly with community psychiatry. But it already suggests more useful analytic tools for explaining community psychiatry than the other approaches can offer.

In addition to the social control aspect of community psychiatry, Marxist theorists have begun to explicate its economic and political basis. Since World War II, capital has become massively centralized and the urban labour force has swollen as farms and small businesses have failed. This has required the State to intervene more directly in regulating the labour force, in guaranteeing profits in all sectors of economic life—including the social services—and in repairing or muting the damaging effects of work on labour. State intervention is "now immeasurably greater than ever before, and will undoubtedly continue to grow; and much the same is also true for the vast range of social services for which the state in these societies has come to assume direct responsibility."[46]

The social services which constitute the "welfare state" improved the living conditions of poor and working-class people, and represented concessions to mass demands. But they were organized in a way which promoted the interests of business, and they were actively supported by business leaders. Workmen's compensation, for example, serves to transfer workers' anger over unsafe working conditions to a neutral government agency and to set limits on the liability of any particular business.[47] Welfare benefits vary in direct relation to corporate needs for surplus labour.[48] Public education "is used to infuse the dominant values and ideological outlook of society," and "to meet the manpower requirements of private profit making industry."[49]

Community psychiatry was one of the best examples of the expanding intervention of the State. Federal and international government mental health agencies were created immediately after World War II, equipped with rapidly growing budgets and expanding legal and bureaucratic jurisdictions. Until the mid-1950's, the number of both psychotic and the new non-psychotic mental patients rose dramatically. Marxist theorists presumably would argue that during this era there was sufficient revenue and also sufficient demand to treat both "social junk" and "social dynamite."

However, they also suggest that this ever-increasing need for State intervention, particularly in light of the growing international pressures on capitalist economies, has become too expensive for the productive capacities of capitalist societies.

The era of cheap raw materials from Third World nations, of cheap labor in the passive colonies of major capitalist powers, and of undisturbed international relations between American and European sectors of capital is now coming to an end. As Third World nations begin to put pressure on the American capitalist class, as the price of oil and energy rises, as these same nations begin to do their *own* producing (thus beginning to compete with us), and as the socialist nations develop their own trade relations, American capitalism comes under pressure.[50]

As a result, a constant fiscal crisis of the State has developed, as governments are unable to finance the still increasing demands on them for social services. To stave off economic collapse, the State responds by cutting all expendable social services (those least useful to business), by demanding increased efficiency and productivity of those remaining (by speeding up and automating civil service jobs), and by transferring programmes to private, profit-making agencies. This seems to shift costs of social services on to clients and clients' families and to bolster business profits.

All of these responses also characterize trends in community psychiatry since 1960. The expense of services to unemployable mental patients has been slashed as much as 75 per cent through the decarceration movement.[51] Psychiatric treatment has been automated with computers capable of cutting costs on all aspects of patient care from admission, through diagnosis, therapy prescription, drug monitoring and dispensing, and discharge; not to mention payroll, record keeping, and accounting. Mood-altering drugs vastly cheapen the process of therapy, allowing expensive psychotherapy by specialists to be replaced with a five-minute prescription by a general practitioner.

These technological inventions made possible massive Taylorization of mental health manpower, by reducing the need for skilled therapists and expanding the "productivity" of unskilled and semi-skilled mental health workers. Explicit governmental policy decisions have organized the structure of mental health manpower to reduce the costs of processing patients most efficiently.

Under the guise of mounting a total crusade against illness, what does the community mental health movement really offer as a replacement for the clinical, humanistic emphasis on the unique value of each individual? *The assembly-line techniques of industry.* Assembly-line techniques borrowed, not from a therapeutic model, but from the industries they are designed to serve. Assembly-line techniques which, as presently applied, must lead to the *industrialization and dehumanization of the mental health professions.*[52]

Community psychiatry has also tended to expand primarily in the private, profit-making sector. The decarceration movement has moved ex-mental patients *en masse* from free, public institutions (however bad), into private nursing and boarding homes which operate at high rates of profit and considerable cost to patients. In effect, decarceration "transforms 'social junk' into a commodity from which various 'professionals' and entrepreneurs can extract a profit."[53] More significantly, the overwhelming bulk of growth in community psychiatry has occurred in private, out-patient care of non-psychotics, resulting in massive profits for doctors, construction companies, and especially the pharmaceutical industry. The priority which government places on these profits, sometimes (often?) at the expense of patients' best interests, is indicated by a British M.P.:

But a prosperous pharmaceutical industry does not merely help a national economy by ensuring lowered absenteeism, shorter stays in hospital and increased ability of general practitioners to treat sickness in their patients' homes. It also makes a direct contribution as a producer of wealth. This role would obviously be diminished if a harsh or unskilled curb were to be put upon its activities or doctrinaire purposes... Overall, these companies contributed 35 million [pounds] in foreign exchange in 1963...[54]

Under medicare drug plans in Canada, England, and other countries, the government explicitly subsidizes and supports the pharmaceutical companies' promotion of mood-altering drugs both locally and in Third World countries.

Through such an analysis, Marxist theories help to situate the political and economic functions, causes, and conse-

41

quences of community psychiatry. They suggest that it may be primarily a co-optative social control movement aimed largely at active workers ("social dynamite") which was motivated by the needs of business under monopoly capitalism for a reliable work force. As a result of the fiscal crisis of capitalist states since the mid-1950's, community psychiatry appears to have largely jettisoned its responsibilities for unemployable patients, industrialized its operations, and built up the profit-making aspects of its programmes as much as possible. To interpret these events, the Marxist theorists explain that it is necessary to distinguish among the different possible types of social control functions (e.g., co-optative, disciplinary, and ideological), and the different target populations (employable vs. unemployable), and that these considerations must be placed in their historical settings.

Although Marxist theorists have suggested, in broad outline, directions to explore in seeking the causes of community psychiatry, none of them has provided an adequately detailed analysis of the community psychiatry movement in particular. The most thorough work to date is Scull's book, *Decarceration*.[55] Although it is an excellent exposition of the deinstitutionalizing aspect of community psychiatry, it virtually ignores the much larger problem of the geometrical expansion in the numbers of non-psychotic people who get processed through community psychiatry programmes. This leads Scull into some awkward blind alleys. Since he argues, for example, that decarceration was a money-saving effort resulting from the fiscal crisis, he can only explain the continuing rise in government spending on mental health as evidence that bureaucratic staffs are struggling against official policy.[56] However, there is strong evidence that expanding services (and therefore expenses) *are* official policy, and that Scull has neglected to differentiate between the different forms of social control which are aimed at employed and unemployed target populations. Although the theory of the fiscal crisis of the State may help to explain the move to decarcerate mental patients, it fails to explain why the State suddenly adopted such expensive psychiatric services for the employed.

The missing link: industrial psychology

Something is missing in all these explanations. All four types of theorists assume that community psychiatry evolved directly from clinical psychiatry, and that its particular features first appeared after World War II. The benevolent government, the mental health lobby, and the antipsychiatry theorists all ignore the wider social and economic context within which community psychiatry developed. This leads them to "explain" the rise of community psychiatry *internally*, as an invention of psychiatric professionals and administrators. As we have seen, this emphasis produces serious gaps and contradictions in their analyses.

The Marxist theorists do better, since they tend to deal with social services in general in a broad social context. This allows them to analyze the economic and political pressures impinging on social services and to trace their evolution to long before World War II. But in this early stage of work, Marxist theorists have not yet defined the particular relationship of community psychiatry to these underlying social forces. Those few who do address topics in community psychiatry directly, such as Andrew Scull and the Ehrenreichs, do a good job of analyzing programmes for unemployable patients. But, because of their assumption that community psychiatry evolved from clinical psychiatry, they tend to over-generalize from the traditional function of public psychiatric care. Thus, for example, the Ehrenreichs propose that the expanding number of community mental health centres is designed to control unemployed poor people.[57] In fact, however, community mental health centres for low-income and ghetto areas are proportionally under-represented and under-funded. Similarly, Steven Spitzer's single direct reference to community psychiatry in his important paper, "Toward a Marxian theory of deviance," deals only with the decarceration of chronic, unemployable, mental patients.[58]

The largest and most rapidly growing services of community psychiatry bear little resemblance to the public, psychiatric services before World War II. Community psychiatry

43

ushered in the first public investment in massive emotional treatment of "normal" employed or employable people. With the exception of mass psychiatric screening of soldiers during the World Wars, public clinical psychiatry had confined itself, by and large, to the custodial care of unemployable psychotics and the retarded. Clinical psychiatric practitioners before World War II had focused on improving services to chronic and psychotic patients, and had shown little interest in preventive programmes or in the treatment of non-psychotic populations. Under community psychiatry, these traditional clinical services to unemployable people have been phased out as much as possible, as in the "decarceration movement." Such evidence strongly suggests that community psychiatry did not evolve from clinical psychiatry.

What, then, *is* the origin of community psychiatry? The missing link may well be the field of psychology which *has* addressed workers—industrial psychology. Industrial psychology since 1900 has specialized in improving worker adjustment and productivity. This viewpoint suggests an alternative theory, "the labour theory," which proposes that community psychiatry evolved directly from industrial psychology. This theory is an extension of the Marxist theories, and it treats community psychiatry as an example of the functions and growth of social services.

CHAPTER III
The Labour Theory of Community Psychiatry

The labour theory

Work is almost invisible as a topic in clinical psychiatry. Abnormal psychology texts hardly note where or whether "cases" are employed, much less if their jobs contribute to their problems. A recent list of mental health research grants funded in the United States includes fewer than one per cent which deal with work or occupational mental health.[59] Work is scarcely mentioned at all in the major policy documents of community psychiatry.[60] It is understandable, therefore, that work and labour regulation have been ignored in efforts to explain the rise of community psychiatry.

Nevertheless, the organization of work has had a profound impact on community psychiatry's development (as well as on the emotional condition of workers and their dependents). This chapter outlines a "labour theory" to explain why community psychiatry developed which differs sharply from existing explanations.

The labour theory proposes that community psychiatry developed primarily to control the productivity-damaging side-effects of worker alienation. It suggests that the major innovations of community psychiatry have been motivated by management's fears of labour militancy on the one hand, and worker and potential worker breakdown on the other. According to this theory, neither the welfare of mental patients nor the power of mental health professionals has motivated mental health policy decisions, although they have provided some secondary direction. Rather, the definition and treatment of mental illness has depended primarily on the economic and political priorities of business interests.

Community psychiatry's roots grow far more from industrial psychology than from public clinical psychiatry. Public psychiatry before World War II had little direct relationship to employable people. Before 1945, public psychiatric care was generally limited to isolated large mental institutions which specialized in treating patients whose employability was, at best, marginal. Although mental hospital administrators in the 19th and early 20th centuries certainly hoped to rehabilitate some of their patients, the curable patients were far outnumbered by unemployable elderly, retarded, brain damaged, and psychotic individuals. The coercive and sometimes brutal treatment of these chronic patients may also have been intended, if somewhat marginally, to deter workers from "mad" behaviour.[61] But this function was minor compared to the simple custodial care of chronically unemployable people.[62] Brenner's longitudinal data indicate that mental institutions consistently have served as dumping grounds for the unemployable, their admission rising during economic slumps and falling during periods of high employment when either the patients or their families could find work to support them.[63]

By contrast, industrial psychology, which developed early in the 20th century, has consistently focused on increasing worker productivity by eliminating "the problems of restriction of output, lack of cooperation, apathy, and worker-management conflict."[64] Industrial psychology, like community psychiatry, has focused on treating employed workers and their families, using largely non-coercive methods. Many of the innovators of community psychiatry techniques—Carl Rogers, Kurt Lewin, Raymond Cattell, Rensis Likert, and others—developed their methods under generous corporate funding and used them in industry long before they were generally applied to public clinical psychiatry. The use of the mental health team, mass psychological testing, non-professional counsellors, family involvement, and preventive psychiatry all originated in industrial psychiatry, to be incorporated as central elements of community psychiatry.

During World War II, industrial psychologists provided much of the research toward developing minor tranquilizers and mood-altering drugs designed explicitly to increase "working capacity" under stress. Prominent industrial psychologists developed a variety of other short-term therapies for use in the military which were later adopted as standard treatment for civilian employees. They also expanded the range of symptoms defined as mental illness. This new classification gave far greater emphasis to inefficient or disobedient, non-psychotic behaviours.

These links between industrial psychology and community psychiatry are not accidental. In large measure, community psychiatry represents nationalized industrial psychology. Operating at public expense, under a more neutral cover than management-run mental health programmes, community psychiatry has the resources to mass-produce and market industrial psychological techniques and to treat the labour force as a whole. In other words, community psychiatry's central task is identical with that of industrial psychology: to "help" workers and their dependents adjust to increasingly alienated, degraded, and pressured conditions, in order to prevent labour unrest.

Although individual corporations benefit from and support community psychiatry, it would not be accurate to conclude that businesses conspired to foist community psychiatry on a reluctant government. Rather, industry has functioned more as an advisor than as a lobby to government.

Since World War II, business and industry have afforded somewhat of a laboratory for social psychiatry. Intensive and extensive studies in the area of human relations in industry have yielded a body of data of importance to the general mental health field. Community mental health workers, military leaders and leaders of any human organization are looking to industry as pioneers in the area of applied action.[65]

47

Business did not have to conspire to "trick" public leaders to support community psychiatry, because the goals and well-being of business and government have always been intimately meshed. They have become increasingly more entwined since World War II, as industry has become much more centralized, and as the State has intervened far more in regulating both the economy and labour-management relations. With this growing interdependency, threats to business profits (through labour militancy or individual worker breakdowns) menace the stability of governments, and conversely, political instability threatens business profits. In self-defense, governments (with the blessing of business) have tended to expand their role in the direct production and regulation of the entire labour force. In a speech to the National Association of Manufacturers, the Director of the U.S. National Institute of Mental Health (NIMH) spelled out this mutual alliance:

> Since we live in a working society, in the largest sense, all our mental health is "occupational" mental health. It is to our mutual advantage [business and government] to promote the mental health of our population.... Our motives may stem from compassion or from a need for human productivity, but our success will profit all of us.[66]

Since 1900—and particularly since 1945—competition among businesses has grown fierce as industries, nations, and international power blocs compete in cut-throat struggles for survival and dominance. At the same time, it has become much riskier for businesses to count on exploiting Third World labour and resources. Under these dual pressures, they have relied more and more on increasing the profit extracted from their "own" national employees.

But workers resist these management pressures to raise their profitability through speed-up or automation. They realize that however attractively it is packaged, higher productivity ultimately means stress, proportionally lower pay, loss of jobs, and less bargaining power. For employers, this resistance is a serious problem:

> One of the most baffling and recalcitrant of the problems which business executives face is employee resistance to change. Such resistance may take a number of forms— persistent reduction in output, increase in the number of

"quits" and request for transfer, chronic quarrels, sullen hostility, wildcat or slowdown strikes, and of course, the expression of a lot of pseudological reasons why the change will not work. Even the more petty forms of this resistance can be troublesome.[67]

Even when they do not actively resist, workers break down emotionally (and physically) under the pressure, and exhibit a variety of "behaviours" which foil production goals. They get ulcers, headaches, and insomnia; they have accidents, stay home, drink, get irritable, daydream, and sometimes go raving mad, all of which is very costly to management. Much of the behaviour associated with either organized resistance or individual breakdown is now defined as "mental illness."

Since World War II, the economic consequences of this "mental illness," measured in lost production, property damage, and social service costs, have reached a level which threatens not only corporate profits, but also the entire economy, as a former NIMH director explains:

Mental illness is without a doubt the nation's costliest health problem and constitutes an enormous drain on the country's energies and resources. Consider the following facts:

1. Accidents, low productivity, and high personnel turnover are concrete industrial problems significantly related to mental health and mental illness.

2. Emotional problems are responsible for approximately 20 to 30 percent of employee absenteeism.

3. Personal factors cause 80 to 90 percent of industrial accidents.

4. It is estimated that from 15 to 30 percent of the work force are seriously handicapped by emotional problems...

5. At least 65 and possibly as much as 80 percent of the people who are fired in industry are dropped from their jobs because of personal rather than technical factors.

49

6. Although exact dimensions are unknown, there are considerable data which suggest that drug abuse and addiction is emerging as a serious and major problem in many work settings.[68]

As Lillian Rubin dryly points out: "When absentee and turnover rates rise, when wildcat strikes occur with increasing frequency—in short, when productivity falls off—the alienation of workers becomes a focal concern for both industrial managers and government."[69]

Equally serious is the threat which this rising alienation poses to social order. When over one million U.S. World War II army recruits were found emotionally unfit to serve, the U.S. government felt justifiably vulnerable. Even more unsettling was the rising U.S. labour militancy following the war.

> 1946 was the peak year of stoppages in our whole industrial history.... By the very contrast with the productive potentialities of American industry, labor relations appear a Pandora's box continually spilling forth new vexations—smoldering hostilities, suspicions, and fears; high turn-over, absenteeism, and strikes; discontents with wages that are the highest in the world; restrictions on output by men who are the most mechanically minded in the world—seemingly an incessant, seething ferment of dissatisfaction and discord.[70]

Government fear of this rising labour resistance was reflected in a rash of anti-union and anti-communist legislation and police actions following World War II. Leading industrial psychologists pointed in alarm to "the obvious national dangers which may result from the lack of proper safeguards and controls for maladjusted emotions."[71]

> *Collaboration* [between worker and management] *in an industrial society cannot be left to chance*—neither in a political nor in an industrial unit can such neglect lead to anything but disruption and catastrophe.... had not the emergency of the war been compelling and of personal concern to every last worker, it is questionable whether the technicians could have achieved their manifest success.... There is no active administrator of the present who does not fear that peace may see a return to social chaos.[72] (His emphasis)

50

In this embattled context, community psychiatry was born, amid a flurry of legislation, international conferences and U.N. resolutions. The philosophy of this move towards community psychiatry was summarized by Terhune:

> War and various forms of inter-social conflict are not the result only of environmental conditions, but are largely due to the mass instability of the individuals who make up society. The hope of mankind lies in *stabilizing the people who compose our society so that dissatisfaction may not spread to the point of igniting general conflagration.* Psychiatry.... can do much along these lines.[73] (Emphasis added)

In the years since 1945, labour force alienation has remained a serious problem for business. A *Harvard Business Review* survey found that U.S. industrial job satisfaction has declined steadily and steeply in the post-war years.[74] Trade union militancy and wildcat strikes grew rapidly throughout North America and Western Europe after 1960, spreading to public service employees and white collar occupations.[75] The Trilateral Commission, representing some of the largest business interests, reported recently:

> Over the last twenty years, all the European countries have witnessed similar developments. Trade unions have been encouraged by legal protection and have grown stronger; old divisions between labor organizations have become less significant, if not entirely eliminated. Collective bargaining has become more decentralized and wider in the scope of decisions covered. Management has been compelled to be less authoritarian, to disclose more information and to limit "managerial prerogative" (to decide on issues of concern to employees without consultation or negotiation) to an ever-decreasing range of decisions.[76]

Each increment in labour intransigence has been accompanied by pressures on government to control it.

In response, community psychiatry has expanded enormously along with other social (control) services. In a speech promoting community mental health centres as an "alternative to chaos," the then-Director of NIMH voiced government fears of mass alienation:

51

People.... who feel helpless to accommodate to or change an unacceptable world consciously choose to alter their own; their experience tells them that the future may be unknown but it is certainly horrible. This rejection of many goals of society makes urgent the development of new approaches to bridge these gaps. If this is not done, and if we do not focus on and try to solve the root causes of alienation, there is serious danger that large proportions of current and future generations will be embittered toward the larger society, unequipped to take on parental, vocational, and other citizen roles, and involved in some form of socially deviant behavior.[77]

The labour theory suggests that community psychiatry has two major functions. Like its antecedents in industrial psychology, community psychiatry exists primarily to increase workers' tolerance for ever more alienated and pressured work, and to reduce workers' (and their families') resistance to these alienating situations. Secondarily, it serves to pacify displaced workers and potential workers such as housewives, adolescents, and minorities, without rendering them permanently unemployable. These two population groups — the employed and the potentially employed — receive the vast bulk of and the most expensive treatment, while unemployable people have been largely diverted to the cheapest care available.[78] The central achievement of community psychiatry has been to develop the technology and organization to put industrial psychology on a mass basis.

Advantages and implications of the labour theory

The labour theory of community psychiatry offers several advantages over previous explanations. First of all, it situates community psychiatry in its historical and social context. As a result, it is able to correct the assumption that community psychiatry's roots lie exclusively in public clinical psychiatry. In fact, it demonstrates that community psychiatry owes far more to industrial psychology than it does to clinical psychiatry. Unlike the other theories, this historical rooting allows the labour theory to explain the political and

52

economic dynamics which created such strong international investment in community psychiatry after World War II, and why the most dramatic expansion of services has been aimed at employed and employable people.

Furthermore, the labour theory extends the analysis of community psychiatry beyond the issue of the personal motivations of its planners and practitioners (whether benevolent, megalomaniac, or malevolent). Instead, the labour theory suggests that corporate pressures leading to community psychiatry simultaneously *created the opportunities* for well-intentioned reformers to close the "snake pits," for mental health professionals to build empires from government grants, and for psychiatrists to expand their technological control over their clients (i.e., the benevolent government, the mental health lobby, and the antipsychiatry theories). Although all three of those theories accurately describe aspects of community psychiatry, the labour theory implies that they are all effects, rather than causes of the phenomenon. We can see their contingent quality by noting that these same corporate pressures have *closed* other options. For example, it is difficult to get funding either for lengthy treatment methods or for programmes for those considered psychotic or mentally retarded. Instead, the labour theory suggests that community psychiatry was motivated primarily by business's expanding post-war problems with labour alienation, and that it employed mainly those professionals and programmes which offered cheap solutions.

One important corollary of this point is that mental health workers are neither independent, powerful experts, nor pawns of an evil conspiracy, as the other theories imply. Rather, they are employees in an active labour-management relationship with the government. Like other workers, they vary in their commitment to their jobs and to the goals of "management." Most are able to reconcile themselves to the adjustment functions of community psychiatry, although not always without some personal conflict. For example, Bailey and Brake found that the majority of British social case workers broke regulations to help their clients.[79] Mental health workers, as employees of a social control agency, are restricted by both formal and informal pressures from providing either intensive insight therapy or social advocacy. Case loads simply are too heavy, and meaningful social action programmes are too likely to lose their funding. At the same time, however, mental health workers have been subjected to many of the same alienating trends as other workers. Psychiatry has become Taylorized with the creation of numerous gradations of auxiliary professional, sub-professional, and non-professional "careers," all of which are becoming subjected to production and efficiency ratings.[80] As a result, mental health workers, particularly those at the bottom of the hierarchy, often find themselves in situations similar to those of their clients: overworked, trapped in dead-end jobs, pressured to increase their "productivity" and to cut their wage demands, and subjected to job insecurity as a result of funding uncertainties.

> Today health workers have reluctantly concluded that deinstitutionalization means "closures, speed-ups, unemployment, and patient neglect," in the words of AFSCME President, Jerry Wurf.[81]

Frustration and exhaustion as a result of these pressures have become so common as to earn a label, "professional burnout." This conflicted position has begun to generate alliances between mental health workers and their clients, and union organizing among professional and non-professional mental health workers.

An additional advantage of the labour theory is that it helps resolve the controversy over whether or not madness is "real." Benevolent government theorists generally argue that mental illness indicates a flaw in the individual, and that the individual, and not his situation, must be changed. Conversely, antipsychiatry theorists insist that madness does not exist as an internal property of individuals, and therefore that psychiatric labelling and treatment are oppressive violations of patients' civil liberties. The labour theory, instead, argues that both these views are partially correct. Real emotional damage does indeed occur (as does physical damage), but it is caused not nearly so much by individual weakness as it is by social and occupational stress. Although genetic make-up, childhood socialization, or existential factors may influence which particular individuals break down, the consistently strong relationship between social and economic stress and emotional breakdown (regardless of individual traits) indicates that environmental pressure explains madness far better than any theory of individual flaws. Even those who assume that genetic weaknesses predispose people to break down emotionally concede that "as industry speeds in ever increasing modern technological advance, the hereditable nature of stress disorders will ensure a concomitant increase in a population sensitive to these conditions."[82] As early as 1917, Thomas Salmon, Medical Director of the National Committee for Mental Hygiene, eloquently pointed out:

> Unemployment, overwork, congestion of population, child labor, and the hundred economic factors which contribute to the stress of living for the poor are often contributing factors in the production of mental disease. Weaknesses in constitutional makeup are discovered under the stress of such conditions, that might have remained undiscovered under happier circumstances.[83]

This is particularly true of the newer non-psychotic diagnoses. Work-related stresses, in particular, cause mental breakdown. Numerous studies document the emotional damage caused by job dissatisfaction, hazardous work, competitive environments, lack of autonomy in decision-making, task ambiguity, isolation, shiftwork, job insecurity, economic worries, unemployment, and speed-up.[84] These sorts of occupational stress affect a large proportion of workers. A 1964 nationwide survey of American workers found, for example, that:

> 48 percent of workers often found themselves trapped in situations of role conflict, 45 percent complained of work overload, and 35 percent were disturbed by a lack of clarity about the scope and responsibilities of their jobs. These perceived environmental factors were found to be related to a variety of signs of psychological strain.[85]

Since the mid-1950's, there has been a steady rise in stress-related pathology among working-age adults in Canada, the United States, and many Western European countries.[86] In other words, the emotional damage—madness—is quite real, but the cause of this breakdown is *not* flawed people, but intolerable social and economic stress.

Finally, and most importantly, the labour theory reveals the defensive nature of community psychiatry. The other approaches all portray the patients and potential patients of community psychiatry as passive—either as beneficiaries or as victims of governmental and professional initiatives. The labour theory, however, argues that community psychiatry developed (along with other social services) in reaction against labour's very active role in resisting alienating and oppressive working conditions. Like the Taylorism, the mental hygiene, and the human relations movements before it, community psychiatry was created largely out of fear of labour initiatives.

This fear includes more than concern about organized union militancy. Most symptoms of the new psychiatric diagnoses reflect, at least in part, active (though not necessarily conscious) resistance on the part of the individuals who are so labelled. Drinking, drug use, quitting without notice, frequently calling in sick, talking back, and engaging in pranks, can all result in psychiatric labels—respectively, "alcoholism," "drug dependence," "occupational maladjustment," "antisocial personality," and "explosive personality." Although these actions obviously have many motives (and psychologists are fond of analyzing the irrational ones), they serve primarily to make life more tolerable and to protest non-verbally against oppressive working conditions. Barbara Garson describes workers she interviewed:

> Whether they work in factories or offices, whether their jobs are light or heavy, they toil like horses wearing blinkers. Their vision of the beginnings and the ends of their work is deliberately restricted....
>
> In this situation, the most common way of fighting back or at least retaining sanity seems to be to develop false or sub-goals within the job that is otherwise meaningless. That's the way I eventually came to understand the pastimes and oddities I encountered, like collecting dark meat from the tuna fish, working with your eyes closed, playing rhythm games with other key-punchers, or letting a line pile up so you can race to overtake the backlog. These games may in fact be essential for the flow of modern industry. For without some measurable unit of accomplishment, it is possible that leaden depression would progress to total paralysis. Indeed, it does happen

56

from time to time that a job is so designed that it becomes too fast for the human nerves, too insulting to the human spirit, or just too meaningless for the brain to comprehend.[87]

Similarly, Judson Gooding's study of blue collar workers dismisses psychological explanations of absenteeism: "By staying out, they are saying they don't like the job."[88] Even symptoms which primarily reflect emotional damage and stress—for example, depression, ulcers, and phobias—are not simply passive illnesses. They all include an inarticulate, internalized rebellion against an intolerable reality.

It is this potentially explosive rebellion which both employers and government fear because of its immediate damage to productivity, and because of the long-range threat that workers may politically unite and rebel against their maddening work conditions. The rising tide of labour militancy and individual "behaviour disorders" following World War II has posed a menace which industrial psychology, divided among separate and competing companies, was inadequate to control. This threat, far more than any intention of psychiatrists or government bureaucrats, has motivated the development of community psychiatry.

CHAPTER IV
The Industrial Parentage
of Community Psychiatry

Labour-management relations

At the heart of capitalism is the contradictory relationship between labour and capital. The interests of employers and workers are mutually dependent but also fundamentally in conflict. Workers depend on employers to provide jobs (when self-employment options are closed), and employers depend on workers to produce goods and services which can be sold at a profit. To a certain extent, therefore, "what's good for GM is also good for its employees." When business is booming, more workers tend to be hired and at higher wages, and when businesses fold, workers face hard times. Similarly, businesses prefer to keep their employees relatively content, and therefore they share some (limited) concern for worker welfare. It is this unity of interests to which employers appeal in urging worker cooperation.

But underlying this surface commonality of interests is a more fundamental conflict between employers and workers, which revolves around the division of the value which workers add to the things they work on. In general, the price of a commodity reflects the cost of labour-power expended in producing it, and variations in supply and demand tend to aver-

59

age out over time to this basic value. Although some employers may at particular times buy raw materials unusually cheaply or sell their products at unusually high prices, in general they cannot count on making profits from capital expenses or sales. The price of capital expenditures is relatively fixed (in relation to other employers). The only reliable source of profit is the value which workers add to materials by turning them into products. Both profits and wages ultimately come from this added value. Because wages and profits are both drawn from the same source, they are inversely related: one cannot rise without the other falling. This creates an implicit and irreconcilable conflict between management and labour.

To raise their profits, employers may cut directly into the workers' share by lowering wages and by hiring cheaper workers such as women, children, and immigrants. Or they may increase the productivity of workers (and thereby multiply the value each one creates while working for about the same wage) by lengthening the work day, by enforcing a "speed-up," and by mechanizing the job.

Both wage cuts and higher productivity reduce the share of added value which labour receives, at least relative to the share capital takes, and frequently in absolute terms. Wage cuts and increased productivity generally are not separate options, but two aspects of the same process. By using division of labour and mechanization, employers can simultaneously boost productivity and replace skilled workers with fewer and lower-paid employees. Often only current employees who are not displaced receive any pay increases for the resulting higher productivity, and even these raises tend to disappear as the higher output becomes general throughout the industry. In any case, the pay raises rarely equal the additional value workers produce since that would not be "cost-effective" for the employer. In addition, higher productivity that is consonant with maintaining control over labour is often achieved by making the work less tolerable: more dangerous, pressured, monotonous, and out of the worker's own control.

It is in the workers' interests, therefore, to resist management efforts to raise profits. Workers fight to raise their pay and they fight against productivity increases because the value of their extra output generally is stolen from them and used against them (for example, to lay off redundant workers, to buy machines to automate away more jobs, or to hire extra supervisory staff).

Work does not have to be organized so that higher productivity makes conditions worse, rather than better, for workers. But capitalist relations, in which employers struggle with workers over the ownership of the value workers create, inevitably produce that form of organization. As Barbara Garson points out:

> This way of organizing work is not the result of bigness, or meanness, or even the requirements of modern technology. It is the result of exploitation. When you're using someone else for your own purposes, whether it's to build your fortune, or to build your tomb, you must control him. Under all exploitative systems, a strict control from the outside replaces the energy from within as a way of keeping people working. The humiliating and debilitating way we work is a product not of our technology but of our economic system.[89]

This conflict of interests between employers and employees is an inherent characteristic of capitalism, which intensifies, rather than declines, as businesses become larger, capital more concentrated, and exploitation more global. Employers can provide temporary "progress" for some groups of workers by exploiting others even more, creating the differences in standards of living between Hong Kong and Toronto, or even between Québec and Ontario. But eventually, as the more exploited groups rebel, and as competition among economic power blocs increases, employers are forced to shift the pressures for ever-higher productivity and profits back to the relatively advantaged workers.

Taylorism and the rise of industrial psychology (1900-1919)

With the advent of monopoly capitalism in the last quarter of the 19th century, worker solidarity and resistance became a major problem for employers. Dramatic increases in industrial mechanization allowed stronger businesses to absorb weaker ones. Competition among the surviving businesses raged on a vastly expanded scale, creating tremendous pressures on employers to find ways to boost worker productivity, and therefore profits. In the United States, "between 1870 and 1900 the production of bituminous coal increased five times, of crude petroleum twelve times, of steel ingots and castings more than 140 times."[90] By 1886, this drive for greater productivity through division of labour and mechanization had already relegated three-quarters of the workers to unskilled or semi-skilled jobs, and had made factory working conditions scandalous enough to prompt national protests.

Labour reacted with militant organization. The number of unionized workers in the United States jumped over 700 per cent in one year between 1885 and 1886, and strikes, boycotts, and labour-run producers' cooperatives proliferated.[91] To control this labour upsurge, business resorted to force, using Pinkerton police, imported strikebreakers, State militia, black lists, labour spies, lock-outs, "yellow-dog" contracts and injunctions. Although these techniques succeeded in temporarily breaking the militancy of the labour movement (aided by the depression of 1893-1897), the power which labour had demonstrated seriously alarmed business. In addition, individual and group resistance to productivity hikes through "soldiering" (intentional restrictions of output) caused more immediate profit loss than that caused by strikes.[92]

At the turn of the century, even work labelled "unskilled" required practical knowledge and skill which the employer did not possess, and this gave employees some control over when and how the work would be done. In the absence of intimate knowledge of and control over the work process, employers had relatively weak leverage to enforce worker discipline. Relying on brute force was unsatisfactory because, at best, it won only grudging compliance from workers, it often disrupted production, and, worst, it strengthened the solidarity of labour against employers. As Henry Ford II later explained:

> If we cannot succeed by cooperation, it does not seem likely that we can succeed by any exercise of force. We

cannot, for example, expect legislation to solve our problems. Laws which seek to force large groups of Americans
to do what they believe is unfair and against their best
interests are not likely to succeed. In fact, such legislation
can lead to exaggeration of the very problem it is
designed to solve.[93]

Without ruling out the use of force, business leaders felt
they had to find a more effective way to prevent and control
workers' resistance to raising their output. They adopted a
succession of techniques of worker pacification which together
constitute industrial psychology.

One of the first and the most influential of these techniques was Taylorism. Frederick Winslow Taylor developed a
set of theories on how to reorganize work to give management
control over each step of the labour process and how it is
performed. Taylor argued that since it is not in the workers'
interest to raise their output, they will exercise any discretion
they have to produce as little as possible. Therefore, he proposed, management must remove all discretion in the work
process from the workers.

Under Taylorism, management divides skilled work
into its elementary component parts and redistributes it
among a number of less skilled workers, each of whom per-
forms only limited tasks in ways rigidly defined by management (or indirectly defined by controls built into the machines
they operate). In this way, Taylor demonstrated, management
could command workers to produce many times more, and at
the same time prevent them from controlling or even under-
standing how the work is done. Rather than exercising complex skills, workers under Taylorism just follow orders. As a
result, knowledge about and control over the work process
becomes the exclusive property of management, and it is
explicitly withheld from workers.

Taylorism offers three major advantages to management: (1) It increases the dependence of workers on management. Since the boss now owns not only the capital necessary
for production, but also the skills and knowledge to put it in
operation, employers have far more power to set the terms of
employment and to prevent workers from going into business

for themselves; (2) It dramatically lowers the cost of labour both because unskilled workers replace skilled, and because the control over how work is done allows management to speed up each worker's output, sometimes many times over; and (3) It weakens organized labour's bargaining power by giving management greater power to set production standards and by making it easier for it to replace trouble-making workers.

Enthusiastically adopted by industries throughout the West and even in the Soviet Union between 1880 and 1920, Taylorism has continued to spread to newly industrialized occupations. Taylorism now characterizes virtually all industrial work and an increasing proportion of clerical, service, and professional occupations.

For workers, Taylorism has been a serious blow, robbing them of the freedom to decide how and when to work, speeding up the pace of work to health-damaging levels, weakening job and income security as higher productivity allows management to lay off workers and down-grade pay, and threatening to make each worker, in the words of Taylor himself, "a mere automaton, a wooden man."[94] For many, work has become a daily struggle to maintain sanity and health. As union representatives explained in an early brief to the United States Commission on Industrial Relations:

> "Scientific management"... is a device employed for the purpose of increasing production and profits; and tends to eliminate consideration for the character, rights and welfare of the employees.
>
> It looks upon the worker as a mere instrument of production and reduces him to a semi-automatic attachment to the machine or tool.
>
> In spirit and essence, it is a cunningly devised speeding-up and sweating system, which puts a premium upon muscle and speed rather than brains; forces individuals to become "rushers" and "speeders,"... drives the workers up to the limit of nervous and physical exhaustion and over-speeds and over-strains them;... tends to displace all but the fastest workers;... is destructive of mechanical education and skill...
>
> It tends to lengthen the hours of labor; shortens the tenure of service; lessens the certainty and continuity of em-

ployment; and leads to over-production and the increase in unemployment.

It condemns the worker to a monotonous routine; tends to deprive him of thought, initiative, sense of achievement and joy in his work; dwarfs and represses him intellectually; tends to destroy his individuality and inventive genius; increases the danger of industrial accidents; tends to undermine the worker's health, shortens his period of industrial activity and earning power, and brings on premature old age.[95]

The stress, meaninglessness, and damage to self-respect of Taylorized work spills over into the workers' private lives, affecting their entire families.

In fact, any five-year-old child knows when "daddy has had a bad day" at work. He comes home tired, grumpy, withdrawn, and uncommunicative. He wants to be left alone; wife and children in that moment are small comfort. When *every* day is a "bad day," the family may even feel like the enemy at times. But for them, he may well think, he could leave the hated job, do something where he could feel human again instead of like a robot.[96]

This spillover of tension is reflected in rising rates of alcoholism, car accidents, family violence, suicides, and violent crime.[97]

Beyond its impact on individual workers, Taylorism also gave management a potent tool to use against organized labour. Organized labour's initial reaction to Taylorism, not surprisingly, was intensely and universally hostile. Taylor himself even complained of "not being able to look any workman in the face without seeing hostility there, and... feeling that every man around you is your virtual enemy."[98] But as new, unskilled workers replaced the craftsmen who had experienced the degradation of their jobs, Taylorized work became accepted as routine. By giving employers monopoly over planning, Taylorism gave business a powerful tool to second-guess worker negotiations:

The workers' struggle to get ahead of production pressures is unending—and one-sided. No victory is final. Production standards are set by engineers for management; the workers can challenge these only after they have been put into effect. If the worker and/or his union manages to score a point, management remains free to introduce still another set of production standards. Since the workers are not privy to the planning processes, they are... continually off balance when it comes to protecting their interests. "You can strike one week over standards"... reports a leader of the United Auto Workers... "and the next week they'll introduce new standards."[99]

By collapsing skilled jobs, Taylorism also made it easier for employers to eliminate troublesome workers. Many of the skilled workers displaced by Taylorism were active union members, whose passing has left unions defensively trying to "construct an ever stronger umbrella over a shrinking total number of jobs."[100]

From business's perspective, the pain Taylorism causes individuals is irrelevant, and the weapon it provides against organized labour is all to the good. But, for business, the main drawback of Taylorism was that it alienated workers from their work so much that profits suffered.

On the one hand, it was *too* successful in turning workers into passive tools. As initiative, skill, and knowledge were drained from workers, they became unable to adapt to changing job requirements. That is, they became incapable of applying the human judgement which made them necessary to employers in the first place. As Peter Drucker explains:

> Traditional Scientific Management... always increases the worker's resistance to change. Because he is being taught individual motions rather than given a job, his ability to unlearn is stifled rather than developed. He acquires experience and habit rather than knowledge and understanding. Because the worker is supposed to do rather than to know — let alone to plan — every change represents the challenge of the incomprehensible...
>
> It is an old criticism of Scientific Management that it can set up a job so as to get the most output per hour but not so as to get the most output per five hundred hours. It may be a more serious and better-founded criticism that it knows how to organize the present job for maximum output but only by seriously impairing output in the worker's next job. Of course, if the job were considered unchangeable, this would not matter... But we *know* that change is inev-

itable; it is, indeed, a major function of the enterprise to bring it about.[101]

On the other hand, workers are *not* machines. Even under the regimentation of Taylorism, they do not *act* like the passive automatons they are expected to be. They exhibit epidemic levels of "behaviour management problems," such as "absenteeism," "alcoholism," "accident-proneness," and "personality disorders." Even worse, by increasing the workers' sense of exploitation, Taylorism actually drives workers to organize against management.

The first two decades of the century were marked by severe labour unrest which rose in intensity during World War I. In order to keep pace with wartime productivity demands, employers invested heavily in finding ways to patch up these "side-effects" without sacrificing Taylorism itself.

Two of the earliest techniques were corporate welfarism and the company union. In 1915, John D. Rockefeller Jr. had been attempting to mollify national protest over the Ludlow massacre of striking miners and their families at one of his Colorado plants. He hired W.L. Mackenzie King, Canada's Minister of Labour and later Prime Minister, to come up with a plan to pacify labour.[102] The resulting "Rockefeller Plan" couched minor concessions to workers (particularly management-run company unions) in a rhetoric of "human relations" between management and worker:

> This plan in substance aims to provide a means whereby the employees of the company should appoint from their own number as their representatives men who are working side by side with them, to meet as often as may be with the officers of the corporation, sometimes in general assembly, where open discussions are participated in and any matters of mutual interest suggested and discussed; more frequently in committees composed of an equal number of employees and officers, which committees deal with every phase of the men's lives—their working and living conditions, their homes, their recreation, their religion, and the education and well-being of their children.[103]

The tactics of allowing some (highly controlled) form of worker representation through the company union and of giving paternalistic corporate welfare programmes were designed to convince workers that there is no conflict of interests between them and management. This tactic worked remarkably well at Rockefeller's Standard Oil plants, preventing any serious labour disputes there for over 30 years.

By the mid-1920's, the Rockefeller Plan and its British variant, the Whitley Plan, had become the dominant corporate ideology of American, Canadian, and British industry. As Sam Lewisohn, Chairman of the American Management Association, explained, this policy was entirely compatible with management interests:

> A large measure of autonomy and self-expression for workers in industry is not only compatible with efficiency but actually conducive to efficiency, as many experiments in employee representation and management-union co-operation have demonstrated. The point is, however, that this factor of efficiency... must be the most prominent if not the determining consideration in evolving new principles of organization.[104]

As well as supporting company unions, employers also invested heavily in two more direct aspects of industrial psychology. On the one hand, they funded research in ways to refine Taylor's techniques to develop the job organization and working conditions under which the human-machine would produce most efficiently. These studies gave birth to the fields of "human engineering," "job analysis," and psychological testing for vocational and military selection. All of these approaches assume that workers are a passive "factor of production" equivalent to the machines they operate.[105] This mechanical conception of the worker is an enduring trait of both employers and industrial psychologists, which permeates even the most "humane" approaches.

On the other hand, employers developed ways to prevent industrial unrest directly. In the United States, this research was strongly supported by the National Committee for Mental Hygiene. Originally a minor, low-budget lobby group for preventive psychiatry and reform of insane asylums, the National Committee had little money or influence. However, as strikes spread during World War I, the Rockefeller Foundation and other private philanthropies began providing substantial funding to the organization, and it suddenly leaped into national prominence. The National Committee led a highly influential lobbying and research programme whose explicit goals closely resembled those later adopted in community psychiatry:

> To work for the protection of the mental health of the public; to help raise the standard of care for those in danger of developing mental disorder or actually insane; to promote the study of mental disorders in all their forms and relations and to disseminate knowledge concerning their causes, treatment, and prevention; to obtain from every source reliable data regarding conditions and methods of dealing with mental disorders; to enlist the aid of the Federal Government so far as may seem desirable...[106]

Although these overt goals, like those of community psychiatry, are worded benignly, the central concerns of the National Committee reflected in its publications were to control labour militancy, to improve worker productivity, and to prevent crime. As a spokesman for the National Committee explained:

> Mental hygiene... presents many wider aspects. Industrial unrest to a large degree means bad mental hygiene. The various antisocial attitudes that lead to crime are problems for the mental hygienist. Dependency, insofar as it is social parasitism not due to mental or physical defect, belongs to mental hygiene. But mental hygiene has a message also for those who consider themselves quite normal, for by its aims, the man who is fifty per cent efficient can make himself seventy per cent efficient....[107]

This pioneering work by the National Committee and its grantees laid much of the foundation for the philosophy and methods of community psychiatry. It emphasized the need to isolate and treat malcontented or misbehaving workers, to train management in conciliatory skills, and to provide workers with an outlet to talk out their grievances to sympathetic-sounding listeners. Following its lead, employers began hiring psychiatrists in industry as early as 1915 specifically to control "these grudge-bearers, agitators, drinkers, fighters and lazy persons" who threaten profits.[108]

World War I, with its attendant demands for boosting industrial production, for mobilizing effective armies, and for assuring labour cooperation, provided the impetus to turn industrial psychology into a full-fledged discipline. For the first time, Western governments became actively involved in trying to "apply psychiatry on a mass basis to the armed forces."[109] In the United States, the federal government and the Rockefeller Foundation jointly funded the National Committee for Mental Hygiene to organize "neuropsychiatric units" to screen and later to treat combat soldiers. As Deutsch pointed out, the motivation for this massive psychiatric mobilization was "not to make robust citizens, to be sure, but to make more efficient fighting machines of their soldiers, present and potential."[110] Because they were treating primarily non-psychotic illnesses, the military psychiatric programmes made extensive use of both the insights and the personnel of industrial psychology.[111] And conversely, these industrial psychologists employed by the military had an ideal laboratory in which to study large numbers of people in a completely controlled environment.

As a result, the war catalyzed significant progress in industrial techniques for treating masses of non-psychotic people. On the one hand, it spurred refinements in Taylorism by promoting efficiency studies on the relationship between men and their machines and especially by encouraging the use of mass psychological testing for military selection:

> The personnel work of the psychologists in the American army and the elimination, by neuropsychiatrists supported by psychologists, of the feebleminded from the army have settled for all time the question of the applicability of skillfully [*sic*] and specially devised mental tests to groups of men.... This kind of mental-measurement psychology has come to stay. Even if we limited consideration to the personnel work of the Secretary of War's office alone, or to the work of the nervous and mental division of the Surgeon General's office alone, we should be able to demonstrate the value of these methods.... *Here was large-scale production with a vengeance. It takes but half an eye to see that many of the methods and some of the conclusions of military psychology can be carried over with due modifications into industry.*[112] (Emphasis added)

On the other hand, by requiring both government and business to control the rising tide of labour unrest in reaction against the war and to maintain military discipline, the war itself spawned dramatic advances in psychological techniques of labour pacification.

In the inter-war period, these advances were *not* applied to public psychiatry, which remained almost entirely custodial, but they *were* used extensively in industry,[113] to be incorporated into community psychiatry after World War II.

Labour militancy and industrial psychology (1919-1939)

Immediately after World War I, the problem of labour alienation became even more critical for business. The end of the war was accompanied by an unprecedented wave of labour militancy and unity. Membership in unions grew dramatically, and in the first year after the war, one-fifth of all industrial workers in the United States, both organized and unorganized, went on strike. Emboldened by the successful Russian Revolution, communist and socialist movements and militant action flourished in the West. There were general strikes in Winnipeg and Seattle in 1919, and many other major strikes across Canada, Britain and the United States to the point where authorities feared a revolution.[114] Riding this tide, workers won significant gains:

> By mid-1920 hours had been reduced to the point where... the [U.S.] nation's work week averaged fifty hours; real wages of persons engaged in manufacturing and transportation were 35 per cent higher than before the war. Politically the advance was recorded in legislation for women, improvements in workingmen's compensation, and a restrictive immigration policy.[115]

In addition to these threats to profits by organized labour, employers found the alienation of individual workers a major barrier to raising productivity. Burlingame, in a 1916 report, discovered that workers' feelings of alienation "toward their employment, their foreman and the machines were responsible for a greater loss in dollars and cents than accidents and contagion."[116] Other studies in this period claimed that 20-25 per cent of all employees were "problem workers."[117]

Needing to re-establish control to keep up with the economic boom, business and government responded to this labour threat with strong anti-union and anti-left measures, as vicious as those of the McCarthy era, which effectively broke the tide of workers' progress.

To complement this use of force, businesses began investing even more heavily in research on psychological techniques to win the cooperation of workers. Industrial psychologists began "to appear as essential factors in industrial organization."[118] In England, the Industrial Health Research Board and the National Institute of Industrial Psychology were established. In Germany:

> There is scarcely an engineering college... without its elaborately equipped psychotechnical laboratory. Governmental agencies have been active. The tramway companies, the state railways, the great steel works, the dye industries and many factories have their own psychological laboratories....[119]

In the United States, Thomas Edison exulted: "A great field for industrial experimentation and statesmanship is opening."[120] The industrially backed mental hygiene movement boomed, acquiring affiliates in 30 countries.

The most prominent psychiatric researcher of the post-World War I era was E.E. Southard. A leader of the mental hygiene movement who had consulted for the U.S. Army during the war, Southard received generous funding (both private and public) to develop techniques to control industrial unrest. Southard's research resulted in several major technical innovations for industrial psychology. He instituted the first use of family therapy, of out-patient treatment for non-psychotic patients, and of the mental health "team" (composed of a psychiatrist, a psychologist, and a psychiatric social worker).

In fact, with his associate, Mary Jarrett, Southard coined the term "psychiatric social work" and created it as a new profession. As the first auxiliary mental health workers, psychiatric social workers were the earliest stage in the Taylorization of psychiatry. They were assigned highly stratified and specialized roles, were given detailed instruction cards similar to those Taylor used on industrial workers, and were required to submit lengthy reports on their activities. The idea of the mental health team was quickly adopted both in industry and in the social services:

> Thus a working party, composed of psychiatrist, psychologist, and social worker, can already be found in advanced juvenile courts, and even in certain courts for adult cases.... Again, in schools and in various institutions for the care of children, this combined insight would penetrate many a dark corner. But industry seems to be the nearest problem to-day to the hand of mental hygiene. One is impressed by the readiness of industry for such working parties in mental hygiene.[121]

More important than his technical innovations, Southard contributed to the policy of treating problem employees on a mass basis. He pointed out that employers as a class have a mutual self-interest in treating, rather than firing, the "mentally ill" (by whom he meant people who, for example, "did not like supervision," who "resented criticism," who found the "work too hard," or who were "agitators," "drinkers," "too slow," or "insubordinate").[122] For, he argued, when each employer fired its own troublesome employees, as a group all employers actually were only circulating, rather than curing, industrial unrest, since discharged workers are re-hired elsewhere. Employers have now generally accepted this principle of corporate self-interest in treating their own "mentally ill" employees. Both Southard's technical innovations and his emphasis on a unified mass national mental hygiene programme were highly influential and were later incorporated as central parts of community psychiatry.

Nevertheless, Southard's vision was limited by his assumption that industrial unrest is an irrational trait of individuals, rather than a reasonable class reaction to oppressive conditions. His definition of irrational feelings was quite broad:

> The great majority of the causes of industrial unrest.... have their root in certain psychological conditions. Among

73

these may be mentioned lack of confidence in the government, feeling of inequality of sacrifice in army and industry,... feeling of unreliability of certain trade union offi-
cials, and feeling of the uncertainty of the whole industrial
future.[123]

This conceptualization of the problem led Southard to
exclude any analysis of organized resistance by groups of
workers:

> That portion of the unrest problem which depends not
> upon group experience, but upon individual experience,
> not upon group thought, but upon individual thought, and
> finally not upon group action, but upon individual action,
> is the proper topic for the psychiatrist.[124]

Management did not seriously address this issue of
group influence on labour unrest or on productivity for more
than a decade. By the mid-1920's, labour militancy had
declined in the United States, Canada, and Britain, at least in
part because union leaderships resisted rank and file militancy. In the years before the Great Depression, inventories
mounted, industrial productive capacity went unused, and
businesses had difficulty selling their stock. As a result, both
government and employers grew less interested in funding
new industrial psychology research either to boost worker
productivity or to prevent labour unrest. Although industrial
psychologists were hired at more companies during the period
1924-1932, they generally merely applied old techniques.

By 1934, however, rising labour militancy and radical
political organization in reaction against the Depression again
began to threaten employers in the United States, England
and Canada. This militancy was particularly evident in the
United States. Between 1934 and 1938, a series of major
strikes swept across the United States as workers defied
armed attacks on them by National Guardsmen and police.
The Congress of Industrial Organizations (CIO), formed in
1936, provided a forum for more militant organization than
had been possible under the American Federation of Labor
(AFL), and by 1939, a larger proportion of the U.S. nonagri-
cultural labour force was unionized than ever before. As a
result of this militancy, the New Deal administration in the
United States conceded significant powers to labour, includ-

ing collective bargaining rights, social security, the right to picket, minimum wage, unemployment insurance, and social welfare. Although these programmes were organized in a way which protected business interests, they were nonetheless primarily social wages granted in response to labour militancy. In Canada and Britain, where strikes were fewer during the late 1930's, similar programmes were not established until the 1940's.

To supplement their use of force against workers through the courts, the military, and both public and private police, U.S. employers again became anxious to develop new techniques to prevent labour unrest. In response to this wave of labour militancy, management interest in industrial psychology re-emerged with new urgency. Clearly, the old methods of industrial psychology had proved inadequate to control worker unrest and some new approach had to be developed to win the loyalty of the worker away from the union.

Into this gap stepped Elton Mayo, an Australian industrial psychologist who had been brought to the United States by the Rockefeller Foundation. Mayo had just published the results of his famous research at the Hawthorne plant of the Western Electric Company. His central conclusion was that workers function in groups and not as isolated individuals. He argued that management can only hope to counter worker solidarity against management by exploiting this "eager human desire for co-operative activity."[125] Mayo pointed out that earlier industrial psychologists, beginning with Taylor, had tried to break worker solidarity and treated workers individually. But, Mayo argued, this tactic is self-defeating:

> In industry... the administrator is dealing with well-knit human groups, and not with a horde of individuals. Wherever it is characteristic... that by reason of external circumstances these groups have little opportunity to form the immediate symptom is labor turnover, absenteeism, and the like.... Any disregard of [man's need to work in groups] by management or any ill-advised attempt to defeat this human impulse leads instantly to some form of defeat for management itself.[126]

Mayo's Hawthorne plant research had, he believed, provided conclusive evidence that "friendly supervision" causes greater productivity gains than either pay incentives or improved working conditions. In fact, he claimed, under friendly supervision, worker productivity continued to climb even when good working conditions, benefits, and pay incentives were removed. This "Hawthorne effect" occurred, he believed, because management had overcome the work group's *psychological* conflict between loyalty to the company and loyalty to the working group by convincing them that higher productivity was in both management's and the workers' interests, and also by giving them the *feeling* that their ideas and comfort were important to management.

> Informal organization in any organized human activity serves a very healthy function.... It gives people a *feeling* of self-respect, of independent choice, of not being just cogs in a machine. Far from being a hindrance to greater effectiveness informal organization provides the setting which makes men willing to contribute their services. Informal organization cannot be prevented; it is a spontaneous phenomenon necessary wherever co-ordinated human activity exists.... Too often management has mistakenly opposed—or what is worse—ignored this.[127] (Emphasis added)

Mayo believed that the "Hawthorne effect" demonstrated management's power to win worker cooperation on a group basis, without having to concede any costly improvements in wages or working conditions. As a result of this research, Mayo claimed to have discovered a "new method of human control."[128]

As it turned out, the Hawthorne effect was not valid. Mayo's conclusions were based on research methods which have since been widely criticized as inappropriate, inadequate, and shoddy.[129] Data which supposedly demonstrated the Hawthorne effect were based on an unrepresentative sample of only five workers, and two of those were replaced eight months into the experiment, when their productivity failed to increase, by workers whose productivity was from the start (before any exposure to "friendly supervision") much higher than any of the remaining subjects. Working conditions, pay incentives, and supervision styles were haphazardly varied, and the impact of the workers' social situation outside of the isolated work area—particularly the Depression and

Western Electric's anti-union spying—were ignored. Most important, even under these poorly controlled experimental conditions, the data still failed to support Mayo's contention that friendly supervision alone causes productivity increases. Several subsequent reviews of Mayo's data actually indicate that: (1) "Friendly" supervision had negligible impact on productivity, and, in fact, that " 'friendliness' of the supervision... was probably as much an *effect* as a *cause* of increased productivity";[130] (2) Hourly productivity dropped dramatically when rest pauses were eliminated, and only punitive, hard-line supervision kept it from falling even further; and (3) The highest increases in productivity occurred in response to pay incentives.

However, hardly anyone challenged the myth of the Hawthorne effect until the 1950's. Mayo's "discovery" of the power of "human relations" reverberated throughout the business community. It was hailed as "the single most important social-science research project ever conducted in industry,"[131] as "the first effective challenge to the prevailing theories of individual and organizational behavior,"[132] and as providing "the key to industrial peace."[133]

In other words, Mayo provided a "scientific" justification for what had already become general corporate policy. Originally funded by the Rockefeller Foundation and employed by Western Electric, he produced the expedient "discovery":[134]

> The essential ideas, as well as the very name of the [human relations] movement, were those Rockefeller had laid out in 1915: human understanding, the undesirability and eradicability of conflict, harmony of interests in the shop community, and improved communication. The only basic change was the gradual remplacement of Christ by Freud, the sloughing off of the Christian ethic and the substitution for it of a sort of group psychoanalysis.[135]

Inadvertently, however, Mayo did make one independent discovery which had enormous impact on both industrial psychology and community psychiatry. In attempting to survey workers' feelings and concerns, Mayo and his associates invented the non-directive interview. Rather than asking

77

leading questions, interviewers were instructed just to listen attentively and to comment only for clarification. The workers (apparently) responded enthusiastically to this approach, pouring out their resentments and problems in a flood that went well beyond the original purposes of survey research:

> Such comments as "This is the best thing the Company has ever done," or "The Company should have done this long ago," were frequently heard. It was as if workers had been awaiting an opportunity for expressing freely and without after-thought their feelings on a great variety of modern situations, not by any means limited to the various departments of the plant. To find an intelligent person who was not only eager to listen but also anxious to help to express ideas and feelings but dimly understood — this, for many thousand persons, was an experience without precedent in the modern world.[136]

Mayo was astute enough to recognize that the non-directive interview could be used as a potent "emotional release" of worker resentments.[137] He and his associates cited case after case in which workers' grievances evaporated after the interview even when nothing practical had been done about the problem.

> The interview has demonstrated its capacity to aid the individual to associate more easily, more satisfactorily, with other persons — fellow workers or supervisors — with whom he is in daily contact.... it also develops his desire and capacity to work better with management.... This is the beginning of a necessary double loyalty — to his own group and to the larger organization.[138]

The non-directive interview was the main practical discovery to emerge from Mayo's research. Mayo and his associates organized a massive "personnel counselling" programme at the Hawthorne plant which interviewed 20,000 employees in the first two years alone of its 14-year operation. They trained a large number of non-professional "counsellors" in non-directive interviewing skills and assigned them to interview workers whose productivity or attitude was a "problem." The workers, however, were not supposed to realize that the interviews were prompted by management's concern for productivity, and so sometimes counsellors were instructed first to conduct decoy interviews with non-problematic workers.

Management made being interviewed as convenient as possible. Workers were paid regular wages during their interviews, and they were not treated as if they were mentally ill. Rather, they were told they were merely suffering from "a defect or distortion of attitude" which could be cleared up through "communication."[139]

Although this interviewing technique was labelled "non-directive," it contained a strong, although covert, directiveness. Interviewers were instructed to concentrate on "each worker's *personal situation*"[140] and to "clarify" workers' complaints in terms which implied that the problem stemmed from the worker's unique situation rather than from valid grievances which are shared by many workers. By personalizing the worker's grievances, the "counsellor" effectively isolated the worker's problem from its class situation, and thereby established a false unity between the worker and management and a false division between the worker and other workers. Marcuse brilliantly illustrated the co-opting power of this operation, using an example from Mayo's associates, Roethlisberger and Dickson.

> A worker B makes the general statement that the piece rates on his job are too low. The interview reveals that his wife is in the hospital and that he is worried about the doctor bills he has incurred. In this case the latent content of the complaint consists of the fact that B's present earnings, due to his wife's illness, are insufficient to meet his current financial obligations.[141]

Marcuse comments:

> Such translation changes significantly the meaning of the actual proposition.... the untranslated statement established a concrete relation between the particular case and the whole of which it is a case.... This whole is eliminated in the translation.... The worker may not be aware of it, and for him his complaint may indeed have that particular and personal meaning which the translation brings out as its "latent content...."

> The translation... stops at the point where the individual worker would experience himself as "the worker," and where his job would appear as "the job" of the working class.... the worker B, once his medical bills have been

taken care of, will recognize that, generally speaking, wages are *not* too low, and that they were a hardship only in his individual situation (which may be similar to other individual situations). His case has been subsumed under another genus—that of personal hardship case. He is no longer a "worker" or "employee" (member of a class), but the worker or employee B in the Hawthorne plant of the Western Electric Company.[142]

The political content of this entire human relations programme, both Rockefeller's and Mayo's, was to *break* worker unity by *building* ties between individual workers and management, and where worker unity could not be broken, to use "friendly supervision" to win their joint cooperation, without making any tangible concessions. Workers were to be induced to perceive their grievances as unique personal problems, unions as anti-social, and management as their best ally.

The "human relations" philosophy had a tremendous impact on both industrial psychology and community psychiatry. The Rockefeller and Ford Foundations enthusiastically picked up the counselling idea and generously funded Carl Rogers to refine the technique of non-directive interviewing for general use in industry. Many corporations, already attuned to "human relations" by Rockefeller and King's earlier campaigns, enthusiastically adopted Mayo's ideas:

Mayo's system, often in vulgarized form, appealed to many employers. The levers remained solely in the hands of management; industrial conflict was condemned and avoided; government regulation was denigrated; and the level of discussion was shifted from wages to non-economic "satisfaction." Best of all, the union was eliminated. In one form or another, many American employers opted for Elton Mayo.[143]

The human relations movement dominated industrial psychology throughout the 1940's and early 1950's, as human relations schools and training programmes proliferated in the United States, Canada, and England, as well as in some areas of Europe. Kurt Lewin's concepts of management training, Bion's theories of "work enrichment," and diverse varieties of group-based wage incentive and profit-sharing schemes all rely to varying degrees on Mayo's concepts. Although refined and expanded, Mayo's strategy remains a dominant management tactic of industrial relations—to humanize Taylorism.

This corporate interest in human relations, in turn, directly influenced the philosophy of community psychiatry. Its ideological assumptions could have been written by Mayo himself:

> Among the important ethical beliefs of community psychiatry are:
>
> 1. *Good mental health services should be available to all those who need them...*
>
> 2. *Each person should control his own destiny to the greatest extent possible.* This concept of personal freedom envisions that individuals and groups of individuals will make decisions about allocation of their own resources....
>
> 3. *Close, long-term human relationships, particularly those within small groups, are valuable and to be fostered.*
>
> 4. *The strength which comes from humans banding together in social groups is to be prized and utilized....* In clinical community-oriented treatment... group therapy and the therapeutic community are major elements. So, too, are the emphasis on understanding and treating families, treating patients where they work and live, and helping the patient by changing his group or his place in the group, not by changing him or removing him from a natural group.
>
> ...The belief in the unconscious and in the powerful, long-lasting effect of childhood experience upon later life are not essential elements of community psychiatry.[144]

The entire humanistic wing of clinical psychology closely resembles Mayo's approach, particularly in its emphasis on feelings to the exclusion of practical changes, on its pseudo-equality between therapist and client, and on its concept of positive mental self-actualization as opposed to curing mental illness. Non-directive interviewing by non-psychiatrists has been institutionalized as a major counselling technique in public community psychiatry programmes.

It is important to place the human relations movement in its social context. As the Western powers geared up for World War II, employers once again needed to boost productivity to keep up with the booming sales. But they encountered a labour force far stronger than at any earlier point in history. Unions were larger, more militant, and better protected by legislation.In other words, the human relations movement was a defensive response by employers to labour strength. Forced to concede that unions and collective bargaining were here to stay, management opted for the soft sell (while maintaining the power to back up their demands with force).

> The rise of the "human relations movement" among managers coincided with the declaration by the Supreme Court of the constitutionality of the Wagner Labor Act. Management now *had* to bargain collectively with labour unions. Good human relations was seen as offering potential support for continued management control.[145]

Human relations techniques gave employers a "carrot" with which to cheaply "buy" worker cooperation. But since employers were unable to abandon their claim to profits at the expense of workers' wages and working conditions, it was a relatively weak "carrot" in comparison to the attractions of union benefits. Workers were not nearly as easily fooled by the benign rhetoric of "human relations" as employers hoped they would be. As one disenchanted union representative commented:

> Traditionally, a personnel program is simply one of management's tools for the control and direction of the enterprise. Like the others, it seeks greater efficiency and higher profits....
>
> This "humanistic" or "human relations" approach has no appeal for the trade unionist. He starts with the proposition, formulated by Emil Durkheim and popularized by the Harvard group of industrial researchers, that our society does create "a disordered dust of individuals." He goes on to seek a remedy, however, not from the open or disguised bounty of the employers but through the formation of trade unions.[146]

By the mid-1950's, when business's position was stronger, employers were more willing to scoff at "the almost panicky

82

fear of the labor union that runs through the entire work of the original Human Relations school at Harvard University."[147] But during the period 1936-1953, human relations was among the best alternatives available to employers.

In contrast to the significant expansion of industrial psychology programmes, public treatment of unemployable psychiatric patients languished in this period. During the Depression, the budgets of mental hospitals were slashed throughout the Western world. At the same time, mental hospitals were forced to accommodate many more patients — the direct and indirect casualties of the Depression. Mental hospitals became depositories for unemployable sick, elderly, and retarded people who could no longer be supported by their families, as well as for people driven mad by the economic stresses. As the Superintendent of Weyburn Psychiatric Hospital in Saskatchewan reported:

> Relatives have not always been able to take the patient home, or perhaps had no work for the patient if taken home, and in the case of patients who have no near relatives we have at times hesitated to turn them loose on recovery, realizing that parole without the prospect of employment would probably be detrimental and result in their early return to the institution.[148]

Overcrowding and inadequate funding became epidemic, destroying whatever therapeutic programmes the hospitals had been providing.

The mental hospitals never recovered. In spite of new economic growth in the late 1930's, governmental priorities had shifted away from chronic care, and policy-makers explicitly opposed increasing institutional funding. By 1945, the mental hospitals had deteriorated to the point where they "rivaled the horrors of the Nazi concentration camps."

> Hundreds of naked mental patients herded into huge, barnlike, filth-infested wards, in all degrees of deterioration, untended and untreated, stripped of every vestige of human decency, many in stages of semi-starvation.[149]

> The Weyburn Hospital stunk like something out of this world... It was crowded and all the whole basement area was a shambles, naked people all over the place, lying

83

around, incontinent. There was a lot of seclusion in use, and mechanical restraints.[150]

Innovations during the 1930's which were directed at chronic or psychotic patients were almost all intended to cheapen, rather than to improve their care. By 1935, many local government units were beginning to support plans to place manageable patients with private families. To the extent that the National Committee for Mental Hygiene (an increasingly influential, business-financed lobby) addressed the problem of mental hospitals, it favoured cutting costs of patient care by discharging them into the community. In contrast to the benevolent rhetoric of the 1960's decarceration movement, these plans were explicitly intended only to save money and to ease overcrowding for the remaining patients without additional expense.

To facilitate the management and discharge of chronic mental patients, governments supported research on a variety of technological innovations, "notably insulin therapy by Sakel in Vienna, convulsion therapy by means of drugs by Meduna in Budapest, electrical convulsion treatment by Cerletti and Beni in Rome, and the operation of prefrontal leucotomy by Egas Monez in Lisbon."[151] Generally, these biological treatments were not combined with personal counselling or psychotherapy, and after discharge these patients were generally ignored. These treatments are all hazardous to patients, resulting in high rates of brain damage, spinal fractures, and even death. Their primary benefit was to cheaply and quickly make patients more manageable.

Thus we see that in the period between World War I and World War II, psychological treatment of employed people expanded dramatically, while care of unemployable mental patients deteriorated. Treatment innovations for employable people occurred consistently in periods of economic booms (World War I and the build-up period in preparation for World War II) and of high labour militancy (1915-1921, 1934-1939). Industrial spokespersons made it explicit that the purpose of these innovations was to combat labour militancy and individual worker resistance to productivity demands. As a prominent Canadian industrial psychologist pointed out, "psychiatry in industry is no mere accident":

Its purpose is to preserve the individual while adjusting him to the central effort... It is almost axiomatic that an employee's value to his organization is in direct relation to the calm adjustment of his day to day existence.[152]

As World War II began, industrial psychology had already developed many of the central innovations which now characterize community psychiatry: mass psychological testing, the mental health team, auxiliary non-professional counsellors, family and out-patient therapy, non-stigmatizing counselling methods, and psychiatric consultation to organizations. Although these advances were primarily privately funded, British, Canadian, U.S. and other governments had begun to establish Industrial Hygiene offices which supported programmes and research in industrial psychology for both civilian and military personnel.

CHAPTER V
The Nationalization of
Industrial Psychology

World War II (1939-1945)

Like the First World War, World War II posed serious labour problems for the United States and its allies. Organized labour in these countries was in a stronger position than ever. Employers had been forced to recognize the legitimacy of unions and of collective bargaining. Booming wartime production and military mobilization created labour shortages, which, in turn, gave workers greater bargaining power. This new strength won labour grudging recognition as a "partner" in Allied war production. During the war, union membership in the United States and Canada more than doubled, and in Britain it increased by as much as a third.

Under broad government assurances that its interests would be protected, labour generally united behind the war effort, and workers accepted wage restraints, longer hours, and speed-up to raise productivity. In Britain, workers even demanded changes in industrial organization to *increase* productive efficiency. This labour effort was decisive in winning the war:

> In spite of shortages and maldistributions of manpower, production of war goods reached record proportions. By the war's end, man days of labor [in the United States]

87

> increased by 50 per cent over 1939; output increased
> nearly 100 per cent... It was this production which was the
> greatest single factor in winning the war.[153]

However, such cooperation did not at all imply the passive acceptance of employer benevolence which Mayo had advocated. Rather, it was based on labour strength and on its own commitment to defeat fascism, which was at times even stronger than that of business. Labour leaders agreed to no-strike pledges and wage restraints only in return for business and government promises of significant concessions, such as full employment after the war, maintenance of membership clauses, and price controls. Toward the end of the war, to enforce these concessions, waves of strikes grew in the United States, Canada, and England. In the U.S., there were more strikes in 1944 than ever before in American history.

As a result, in addition to the challenge of mobilizing an effective fighting force, the Allies also had to find a way to maintain worker cooperation—or what was euphemistically called "home front morale"—while conceding as few benefits as possible. Under these dual pressures, Western businesses and governments invested heavily in industrial psychology:

> The impact of World War II, with its tremendous production demands, the shortage of labor, and a consequent use of hordes of individuals not usually considered employable in factory work... enormously accentuated interest in the psychiatric approach. The problems of absenteeism, accidents, psychosomatic illness became more acutely significant, and the auditing of jobs in terms of personality requirements and vice versa was subjected to new analysis.[154]

Fritz Roethlisberger, Mayo's chief associate, was appointed to "help set up the Training Within Industrial Service of the War Manpower Commission whose goal was to 'secure maximum co-operation' from workers in essential industries."[155] His influence there helped expand "human relations" programmes in American industry. The National Committee for Mental Hygiene worked with government agencies to set up services to promote "citizen morale" and to treat civilian employees on an out-patient basis. The out-patient "community clinics" which they established were the forerunners of the community mental health centres under community psychiatry.

To help build an effective military force, the National Committee for Mental Hygiene and prominent industrial psychologists played a major role in selecting and treating soldiers. Luther Woodward of the National Committee was appointed to set up a massive psychiatric screening programme for draftees. This programme was far more detailed and exclusive than the selection procedures of World War I, as a spokesman explained:

> Few people realize how different our handling of personality placement is from that of the world war [I] conscription. They don't understand that we were then sorting out people suffering severe mental disorder, the gravely feeble-minded, and those with functional disorders which would cause them to collapse at the battle line. We are now sorting into the army with as great care as possible the people who seem peculiarly well suited to meet the demands that are necessarily associated with combat troops. *We are not merely eliminating those already broken down, but attempting to build up the armed forces from people who can scarcely be broken down by any strain they may encounter.*[156] (Emphasis added)

This new sorting procedure, therefore, implicitly extended the definition of "mental illness" to include potential, as well as actual, symptomatology.

The National Committee also helped to recruit psychiatrists, psychiatric social workers, psychiatric nurses, and ward attendants to treat emotional problems among the troops and among employees in community clinics. These mental health workers were drawn primarily from the staffs of public mental hospitals, thus further diluting the personnel available to treat chronic mental patients. As the National Committee itself pointed out:

> The maintenance of state mental hospitals... is now threatened by the diversion of professional personnel from civilian positions to service with the armed forces, and by the loss of artisans attracted to industrial defense centers... This will add to the already excessive burden borne

by our state mental hospitals in caring for the increasing number of cases among the general population.[157]

William C. Menninger and Francis J. Braceland, both prominent industrial psychiatrists, were recruited to direct, respectively, the U.S. Army and the Navy psychiatric programmes. Menninger and Braceland were members of the new Group for the Advancement of Psychiatry within the American Psychiatric Association, which lobbied for expanding preventive and community psychiatric services.

Beyond simply expanding services to employed people, the war also stimulated research to develop new techniques of industrial psychology for both military and civilian use. Organized by the National Committee for Mental Hygiene, the research directors of "seven of the country's leading industrial organizations" worked together pooling their resources "for joint action in the interests of medical and industrial research."[158] At the same time, industrial psychologists, working for the military, studied soldiers' efficiency under varying conditions of stress, and used their findings to produce many innovations which were later incorporated into community psychiatry. For example, under Menninger's direction, the American Psychiatric Association adopted a new classification system for psychopathology which gave far more emphasis to the neuroses and behaviour disorders which plagued both the military and industry. This new system became the model adopted by the World Health Organization and, with minor modifications, it has been retained ever since.

With inadequate staffs to handle the epidemic of combat fatigue, neuroses and psychosomatic illness among soldiers, the military psychiatrists tried out a variety of new therapeutic methods which were fast and cheap, and which did not require professional psychiatrists as therapists. They also applied these methods to treat the similar stress-related symptoms among civilians. These techniques became the technological foundation for community psychiatry, as a former Director of NIMH explained:

> During the war, military medicine seized its opportunity to advance the knowledge and use of a variety of short-term therapies and this experience provided a sound

basis for further development of the concepts and practice of community psychiatry...[159]

Among the war-spawned therapy techniques which have become standbys of community psychiatry were group therapy, brief talking therapies, modified electro-convulsive treatments for non-psychotic patients, and psychotropic drugs (amphetamines, narcotics, and barbiturates) designed explicitly to cheaply improve the working efficiency of *normal* people under stress. Although these methods later filtered into the treatment of chronic mental patients, they were first developed to improve the efficiency of the armed forces. German Luftwaffe pilots and Japanese war factory workers, for example, were given amphetamines, and when the Allies uncovered the reports of their improved efficiency, studies were quickly funded to duplicate and extend the Axis drug technology to Allied soldiers.[160]

To staff these new therapies, both military and industrial psychiatric programmes expanded the mental health team to include many more types of specialized mental health workers. By far the most important staffing innovation was to train general practitioners to detect early signs of emotional upset (which was defined, as in the past, as poor adjustment to work demands).

> Lowered efficiency, dissatisfaction, spoilage, vandalism, horseplay, increased labor turnover, high accident rates, continued absenteeism, excessive fatigue... these call for a general casting about for maladjusted personalities.[161]

Under community psychiatry, the role of general practitioners has expanded to constitute the key link for the early detection, treatment, and referral of mental patients.

As labour unrest increased toward the end of the war, U.S. military, business, and political leaders began to press the government to establish a national programme to treat the "mental illness" of non-psychotic employees. The problem of this "mental illness" had reached a "scale far beyond the reach of private philanthropy," and, as Foley, a psychiatric historian, has argued:

> In the 1940's it was clear to psychiatric leaders in the armed forces and their Congressional allies that there

91

was a need to develop and to organize the capacity and willingness of all relevant decision-makers... to cooperate in a broad society-wide effort to... develop new technological skills in the research and care of the mentally ill.[162]

The National Committee for Mental Hygiene, backed by business funding, lobbied extensively for a National Neuropsychiatric Institute.

Thus the war "called dramatic attention to the problem of mental disorders [among soldiers and employees], pointing up the need for a national mental health program."[163] By contrast, facilities to treat chronic mental patients had, by the end of the war, deteriorated even more than they had during the Depression. The stage had been set for public community psychiatry to supplant the custodial care of chronic mental patients.

The birth of community psychiatry (1945-1953)

If the strength of labour during the war alarmed business and government leaders, post-war labour relations appeared even more frightening to them. A frequent topic of high-level policy discussions was how to avoid revolutionary labour unrest after the war, when employment levels would drop and workers would have less patriotic incentive to curtail their demands. Soon after the war, these fears appeared well justified, as waves of strikes of unprecedented size swept the Western countries.

[U.S.] labor quickly chucked the no-strike pledge. In the last four and a half months of 1945, man-days lost due to strikes shot up to... more than double the war-time peak of 1943, when the coal strikes wracked the nation. This was but a prelude to the great strike wave of 1946.

That year set the nation on the collective-bargaining road to a new corporate welfarism. Over four and one half million workers marched on the picket lines in 1946, a half million more than the previous peak, in fateful 1919... Nationwide strikes halted production in coal, auto, electric, and steel industries; maritime and railroad transportation ground to a halt.[164]

With memberships covering the entire work forces of many basic industries, unions wielded enormous power. As one industrial psychologist pointed out:

> Certainly, none can deny the strategic power of unions speaking as sole representatives for workers in basic industries—coal, oil, steel, rubber, power, transportation, and so on. In our interdependent economy an industry-wide strike in any of these becomes, sooner or later, the equivalent of an uncalled general strike, an immediate or creeping paralysis.[165]

The power of organized labour extended to the political arena. In 1945, English workers elected the first Labour government. Strong labour unions in Denmark, Norway, and Sweden had maintained social democratic governments since the 1920's. In Canada, the social democratic Canadian Commonwealth Federation (CCF) party, with labour support, gained strength, winning one-third of the votes in Ontario in 1943 and electing a government in Saskatchewan in 1944. Although these social democratic parties were not revolutionary by any means, they forced through important social legislation and demonstrated the potential of workers to organize for more fundamental change. In 1944, for example, Canada's Mackenzie King "could argue that class conflict had reached such a point that social legislation was the only alternative to socialism."[166]

Communist parties also increased their power in European and Third World countries. In Italy, in the wake of the massive labour actions in late 1945 and early 1946, communists gained control over the Italian General Confederation of Labour and won almost a third of the seats in the 1948 elections. In France, in the fall of 1947 and again in the autumn of 1948, a strike wave of such intensity welled up as to suggest civil war rather than the give-and-take of industrial relations. Communists won representation of more than one-quarter of the electorate and challenged the rule of De Gaulle. A communist government took power in Yugoslavia, and would have also in Greece if the British had not forcibly intervened. This surge of international labour's power, of revolutions in China, Korea, and Vietnam, and threats of Soviet expansion, undermined capitalist, and particularly U.S. power.

There was a real danger that the United States might be left as an isolated island of capitalism, in a world "gone socialist." Her capitalist system, now expanded into a global empire, could not survive as an island in a non-capitalist world. Both her capitalist allies and enemies were virtually bankrupt or on the brink of collapse. Unless help was given to them quickly, to enemies and friends alike, America would herself face a massive economic depression and the peoples of these countries might well seek a solution in some form of socialist economy.[167]

In addition to organized labour actions, more individual workers than ever were passively resisting or breaking down under management productivity demands, causing a threat to profits severe enough to weaken national economies. In England, an extensive survey of industrial workers found that 30 per cent "suffered from some form of neurosis" which damaged their productivity.[168] Largely as a result of a new Taylorized work organization, absenteeism and a rapid turnover of miners in the newly nationalized British mines were so pervasive that military draftees had to be sent there to supplement the employed work force.[169] In the U.S., specific personnel problems such as alcoholism, psychosomatic reactions, "accident proneness," "absenteeism," and "habitual rule infractions" soared.[170]

Both business and governments in the United States and capitalist Europe recognized that the labour force had to be brought under control quickly. As they had in the past, Western businesses and governments reacted to this wave of labour unrest with strong anti-labour measures, including the use of police to break strikes, anti-union and anti-communist legislation, red-baiting, union spying, and vigorous public relations campaigns to discredit unions. This use of force limited new labour organization, and in the U.S. forced unions into defensive battles to protect rights previously won, such as the closed shop, union discipline of its members, and maintenance-of-membership clauses.

With the inauguration of the Cold War in 1946, attacks against communists began in earnest, sponsored by government, business, and conservative labour leaders. Communist parties were forced out of the cabinets of Austria, Belgium,

Finland, France, and Italy, and the influence of social democratic parties outside of Scandinavia weakened as they lost seats and soft-pedalled any relationship to Marxist class struggle. Red-baiting witch hunts throughout the West destroyed communist-dominated unions and forced left-wing labour leaders, intellectuals, performers, and politicians out of their jobs. As Huberman and Sweezy argued, the central function of this red-baiting campaign was not nearly so much to ensure internal security as it was to impose "thought control" over the entire labour force:

> From the point of view of effective thought control, what is needed is not the limitation of the system to areas of necessary secrecy, but on the contrary its expansion to the widest possible sector of the total employment field. What is needed is not criteria of trustworthiness, but criteria of self-regimented robotcy in the service of the status quo.[171]

As in the past, companies supported industrial psychology programmes to control labour unrest which complemented these hard-line coercive measures. But this time, business leaders demanded that the government finance and sponsor these industrial psychology measures. As U.S. House Representative Priest successfully argued in his bill for a national mental health programme, the problem of emotional control had become too large and complex for separate industries to handle:

> The mental health problem is so great that it requires the types of coordinated action by the Federal Government, the States and communities, and the professions and institutions, which has been so effective in other fields of public health. Despite the contributions of public and private organizations and of individuals, the Nation has not yet made real progress toward the goal of mental health because these efforts have been limited and have lacked coordination.[172]

In 1946, the United States passed the National Mental Health Act. This act established the National Institute of Mental Health (NIMH), with massively increased federal funding for basic research, for training psychiatric personnel (including general practitioners), and most important, for establishing out-patient clinics specifically geared to treat non-psychotic adults. The act explicitly *excluded* any aid for mental hospitals or their patients. Instead, it focused squarely on the problems of working-age adults.

> The seriousness of the mental health problem has been brought to our attention very sharply by the experiences of the Selective Service System and the armed forces during the war. The Director of Selective Service testified that about 1,767,000 men were rejected for military duty because of mental or neurological diseases or defects...
>
> The experience of the armed forces is limited largely to the male population between the ages of 18 and 37... A much larger number of people, although not hospitalized, suffer because of what their minds or emotions subtract from their otherwise normal existence or performance...
>
> ...Unless prompt and vigorous action is taken, the Nation has reason to expect during the postwar period a material increase in the volume of delinquency, suicide, homicide, and alcoholism — all of which are commonly symptoms of psychiatric disorder.[173]

Industrial and military influence dominated the formation of the NIMH. The act was drafted in close consultation with "the chief psychiatrists of two military services: Dr. William Menninger, army; Dr. Francis Braceland, navy; and Dr. Jack Ewalt, who was consultant to the air force."[174] Administrators of state mental hospital services were *not* consulted. Testimony supporting the act came primarily from military and industrial sources. The three key witnesses were General Hershey, director of the Selective Service System, Stevenson, medical director of the National Committee for Mental Hygiene, and Burlingame, a prominent industrial psychiatrist. Business control over NIMH was institutionalized in the National Advisory Mental Health Council, the policy-making overseer of the Institute. Of its first six members, at least three were industrial psychiatrists (two of whom had directed the U.S. wartime psychiatric programme), and two others were leaders of the National Committee for Mental Hygiene. Far from being a rubber-stamp, the National Advisory Council "over the next decade... assisted, checked, and in at least two instances... directed Dr. Felix [Director of NIMH] to adopt programs that he initially did not favor: the development of pharmacology and the psychiatric training program for general practitioners."[175] In addition to this formal authority, business interests worked behind the scenes to direct the focus of the NIMH:

> Key bargains struck with Mary Lasker [a philanthropist who was prominent in the National Committee for Mental Hygiene] and Mike Gorman [a lobbyist supported by the National Committee and Lasker] were necessary to obtain increased appropriations.

> Lasker pushed NIH directors to translate basic research into applied services. The fact that Felix [NIMH Director] designed and maintained a psychiatric organization that promoted applied research and demonstration services was consistent with her desires. Gorman was also sympathetic to Felix's revulsion toward traditional care in state mental hospitals. "My hidden agenda," he said recently, "was to break the back of the state mental hospital."[176]

These business interests, over Felix's objections, won Congressional appropriations of $2 million in additional funds for psychopharmacology, and over the protests of the American Psychiatric Association, won funding for training psychologists, nurses, psychiatric social workers, and general practitioners.

Following the lead of the United States (and in many cases, at its urging) many other Western countries inaugurated similar national mental health programmes, which were also oriented to treating primarily non-psychotic, working-age people. As in the United States, business and military leaders played a major role in both promoting and shaping these programmes. The industrially financed International Committee for Mental Hygiene (an offshoot of the National Committee for Mental Hygiene) created the World Federation for Mental Health in 1948 to work closely with the World Health Organization (WHO). Brock Chisholm, former Director of the Canadian Army General Medical Services, was the General Secretary of the WHO at the time, and he strongly supported this alliance. J.R. Rees, wartime chief of the British Army's psychiatric service, was elected as the first president of the World Federation, and G.R. Hargreaves, a leader of British industrial psychiatry, coordinated the WHO's Expert Committee on Mental Health.

In Canada, C.M. Hincks, founder and director of the Canadian National Committee for Mental Hygiene (an affiliate of the U.S. National Committee), strongly influenced public mental health policy. In 1946, he advised the Saskatchewan government to set up a public community psychiatric programme similar to the U.S. model. This consultation became a major stimulus for the Saskatchewan Plan for Mental Health, which, in turn, served as a model for national Canadian mental health policy. The psychiatry departments at McGill University and the University of Toronto, during the post-war years, showed "great interest in the mental health problems of industry,"[177] and worked closely with industrial relations departments of private companies, running training conferences, for example, for managers and supervisors.

The new community psychiatry programmes drew heavily on the innovations of military and industrial psychology. They emphasized early diagnostic testing and brief individual or group talking therapies (often combined with shock therapy), which were conducted in out-patient clinics or general hospitals and staffed by multi-disciplinary mental health teams. They also provided extensive free consultation to private businesses, and welcomed referrals of problem employees for treatment.

As public community psychiatry programmes took over many industrial psychology functions, the number of private industrial psychology programmes fell after the war, but private industrial research still created many of the remaining major technological innovations of community psychiatry. The Dupont and Eastman Kodak Companies, for example, launched the first alcoholism treatment programmes during the early 1940's, developing methods which have since been incorporated into public alcoholism programmes.[178] Group therapy techniques were refined by Kurt Lewin to help train business supervisors in human relations skills. And most important, private drug companies in France, Belgium, Switzerland, and the United States developed an extensive technology of mood-altering drugs.

In contrast to this booming treatment of non-psychotic, ambulatory clients, few of these programmes, either public or private, paid more than lip service to improving care of institutionalized psychotic, aged, or retarded patients. The new community mental health centres were explicitly designed to exclude chronic patients, and to treat only those who could benefit from out-patient therapy or brief hospitalization. By the early 1950's, momentum was building to move chronic patients into even cheaper, non-psychiatric facilities.[179] The vast majority of chronic patients remained seriously neglected. In England, Hargreaves reported that mental hospitals:

> all remain geographically separate, and often remote from other medical activities. They inherit buildings and equipment which would not be tolerated in general hospitals. The staffing ratios are far worse than even the chronic general hospitals and... some regional hospital boards... give the impression that they set themselves much lower standards for their mental hospitals than they do for any other medical institutions.[180]

In Canada, Richman echoed this testimony:

> It was the day of the "snake pit" hospital—bars, locks, restraints, "herding" and all the rest.

> In 1948 almost all treatment of severely ill psychiatric patients was conducted at provincial mental hospitals, often located in isolated areas. Patients were denied any legal process and retained in locked wards. Because of under-staffing and lack of funding, the emphasis was on custody rather than therapy. Patients and their families used the hospital only as a last resort.[181]

The inhabitants of the "snake pits" posed no great danger to business. Far more important was a labour unrest and alienation so severe that it threatened the economic and political future of capitalism. The problem was too widespread, and labour too well organized, for separate employers to be able to contain it. In self-defense, governments dramatically expanded their involvement in controlling and regulating the labour force, a function which until then had been by and large the domain of private employers with government support only in emergencies. One of the major products of this trend was community psychiatry.

Technological innovations (1954-1962)

By the mid-1950's, the organizational foundations for community psychiatry were well established. Government agencies had been created to conduct research, train personnel, and set up out-patient and short-term hospitalization treatment. New legislation had facilitated voluntary admissions to psychiatric treatment and increased the power of mental hospitals to discharge chronic patients.

The next task was to create a technology capable of effectively treating the 30 to 40 per cent of the labour force which was estimated to have (or to cause employers to have) problems.[182] It may be noted that this estimate is double the proportion of disturbed workers reported in 1919. This massive increase may be attributed both to the more destructive pressures of work and to the expanded definition of mental illness. As a prominent industrial psychologist explained:

> Large numbers of persons once classified as merely socially hazardous (to themselves and/or to others) have now been formally added to the ranks of the sick. This is a major advance, but [it] will not achieve its full meaning until these cases elicit... the same types of research effort which has brought other forms of illness within range of effective prevention and treatment.

> To be satisfactory, treatment for these persons... should be capable of large scale application with personnel and physical facilities which are available or easily developed. No existing method of therapy for these persons fully meets these requirements.[183]

All the treatment methods for non-psychotic emotional problems developed by 1953 required lengthy contact with trained therapists. Although both the length of treatment and the amount of training required of auxiliary workers had been significantly reduced during the war, talking therapies were still prohibitively expensive and too labour-intensive to use on a mass basis. As one industrial psychiatrist complained, talking therapies just "do not lend themselves to assembly line methods."[184] Mindus' survey of international industrial psychology programmes documented that, even with extensive government support, "psychiatric treatment is still very expensive and can seldom be given to low-salaried workers."[185] Industrial and government authorities bemoaned the monumental expense and personnel required to treat all those who "needed help."[186]

Furthermore, the results of these talking therapies were far from reliable. After all, it is hard to keep convincing people that their problems are irrational and that they must adapt if their "symptoms" occur precisely because they have been pushed past the tolerable range of adaptation. Union members were becoming even more hostile to industrial psychology programmes, which they justifiably suspected of attempting to subvert grievances and of co-opting the union's advocacy role.[187] And at the same time, workers were reluctant to use the new public psychiatric clinics because of the stigma associated with public psychiatry.

As a result, both business and government invested heavily in research to develop methods to treat large masses of people cheaply and in more neutral settings. Between 1948 and 1960, NIMH's budget increased almost 15-fold, from $4.5 million to $67.4 million. Military spending on psychiatric research also boomed. The Ford Foundation committed $15 million for research on mood-altering drugs, and other private foundations followed suit. Pharmaceutical companies, for reasons of self-interest, also were quick to invest significant amounts in developing mood-altering drugs.[188]

From this effort, two therapeutic innovations emerged in the mid-1950's which together created the technological foundation to put therapy on a mass basis: the new twin panaceas of behaviour modification and psychopharmacology.

Behaviour modification is based on the assumption that people can and should be made to adapt to a relatively unalterable "reality." Patients receive reinforcements for "appropriate" behaviour, and are not reinforced and sometimes are punished for "inappropriate" behaviour. Standards of desirable behaviour are external and arbitrary, entirely under the control of the therapist. It is a model taken almost directly from Taylorized industrial labour relations, where arbitrary production methods and goals are set by the employers, and where workers are paid ("reinforced") for meeting them and

101

are docked wages (not "reinforced") or reprimanded ("punished") for under-producing or breaking company rules. From the perspective of employers and administrators of institutionalized populations, behaviour modification was a godsend; cheaper, faster, and more reliable in eliminating symptoms than the earlier therapy methods. Training in behaviour modification is relatively easy, so "therapists" can be produced quickly and cheaply. In fact, "therapy" can be fully automated, and performed entirely with tapes. Unlike insight or client-centred therapies, behaviour modification requires no trust or intimacy between therapist and client and does not aim to improve either the patients' insight or their happiness. Instead, obedience is its only criterion of "improvement." It is the ideal management tool.

As a result, behaviour modification quickly grew popular, dominating all "talking" therapies. In 1957, the NIMH devoted only eight per cent of its "psychosocial" treatment research to behaviour modification; but by 1973 its share had grown to 55 per cent.[189] The impact of behaviour modification has been particularly strong on those defined as having "behaviour disorders." In addition to prisoners and delinquents, unreliable workers have been singled out as a prime target group. Although some voluntary behaviour modification programmes exist for middle-class patients (such as smoking and phobia clinics), the majority of behaviour modification programmes are coercive and involuntary, designed to increase the obedience of unruly populations.

Mood-altering drugs have been even more influential than behaviour modification in putting psychotherapy on a mass basis. Since World War II, researchers both in the West and in the Soviet Union had been exploring the idea of using these drugs both as weapons and as tools to improve workers' and soldiers' stress tolerance and working capacity. This research was oriented explicitly to treat "normal" subjects.[190]

The U.S. military and the CIA were "among the first large-scale users of mind-influencing drugs."[191] Their priorities included: (1) finding ways to improve the efficiency and reliability of military personnel; (2) developing hallucinogenic, incapacitating, fear-inducing, and pacifying drugs for use as weapons and as espionage tools; and (3) creating antidotes to these mind-altering drugs as defenses against both Soviet drug weapons and accidental exposure of U.S. troops. As early as 1953, the military and the CIA had experimented with inducing LSD psychoses in normal people (sometimes without their knowledge or consent), and they encouraged research to develop chlorpromazine, the first major tranquilizer, as an antidote to LSD.[192] During the late 1950's, the U.S. military Chemical Corps waged a hard-sell campaign to win public acceptance and more funding for research on mood-altering drugs:

> In one four-month period in 1959, at least nine major newspapers and magazines carried lengthy feature articles or series on the CBW [Chemical and Biological Warfare] program. Other pro-CBW articles were published in medical journals, Sunday supplements, and... periodicals... In addition Chemical Corps officers appeared before a closed Congressional hearing and later made dozens of speeches, all aimed at extolling the virtues of the psych-chemicals, and the notion that they could lead to humane warfare.[193]

In other words, much of the initial impetus for developing mood-altering drugs, including those which were used primarily to treat chronic mental patients, grew out of military interest in their use as social control agents. By 1959, the investment had paid off. Tranquilizers, barbiturates, amphetamines, anti-depressants, anti-convulsants, hormones, and a number of other categories of mood-altering drugs were being used to treat both chronic mental patients and non-psychotic, ambulatory workers.

The mood-altering drugs provided the major technological solution to community psychiatry's two problems: on the one hand, cutting public responsibility for chronic mental patients; and on the other, establishing emotional regulation of the labour force on a mass basis. Mental hospital administrators quickly recognized the potential usefulness of the major tranquilizers, chlorpromazine and reserpine, to make psychotic patients far easier to manage. These two drugs immediately halved the labour costs of in-patient, chronic, psychiatric care:

Agitation, irritability and quarrelsomeness, Dr. Salinz reported, disappeared within six to twenty-four hours after the drug had been given. As a result of the therapy, he said, the man-hours spent by psychiatric aides, nurses and doctors on such [chronic] patients was decreased by an average of 50 per cent.[194]

More important, the major tranquilizers made possible massive discharges of formerly unmanageable, chronic mental patients. In Canada, the United States, England, France and Sweden, the number of patients resident in mental hospitals dropped abruptly in 1955 when the major tranquilizers were introduced.[195] It is important to emphasize that these drugs were not the "reason" for this trend. Rather they were tools to implement an already existing policy of phasing out chronic psychiatric care. Nor were they intended to improve patient care, so much as to cut costs.

Although the major tranquilizers made patients more manageable, few claimed that they cured them or even made them happier. These drugs show high rates of seriously debilitating, and even occasionally fatal, side-effects. Even the main intentional effect of the major tranquilizers addresses the patients' manageability far more than their recovery. As John Gillis pointed out:

> Chlorpromazine [Thorazine]... may generate a kind of "cognitive dampening," a diminution in the recipient's ability to bring cognitive functions effectively to bear on any complex learning situation, whether it is social or interpersonal... On any view of psychotherapy various kinds of interpersonal learning must be involved. One member (the patient) is expected to learn something *from* the other (the therapist) about how to conceptualize, react to, or cope more effectively with his environment... The implication is straightforward—some, at least, of the psychoactive chemicals appropriately used to control psychotic *behaviors*... may nevertheless render [the patients] less susceptible to other forms of treatment...[196]

Mark Vonnegut eloquently described the dehumanizing experience of taking these drugs:

> The side effects were bad enough, but I liked what the drug was supposed to do even less. It's supposed to keep you calm, dull, uninterested and uninteresting... What

the drug is supposed to do is keep away hallucinations. What I think it does is just fog up your mind so badly you don't notice the hallucinations or much else...

On Thorazine everything's a bore. Not a bore exactly. Boredom implies impatience. You can read comic books and "Reader's Digest" forever. You can tolerate talking to jerks forever. Babble, babble, babble. The weather is dull, the flowers are dull, nothing's very impressive. Muzak, Bach, Beatles, Lolly and the Yum-Yums, Rolling Stones. It doesn't make any difference.[197]

At the same time, the minor tranquilizers — meprobamate (Equanol, Miltown) and later chlordizopoxide (Librium) and diazepam (Valium)—were revolutionizing treatment of employable people. In comparison to earlier drugs for non-psychotic people (amphetamies, barbiturates, and narcotics), the minor tranquilizers relieved tension and anxiety with far less damage to the patient's altertness, intelligence, concentration, or motor skills. With these drugs, the stress-related symptoms of workers and potential workers could be controlled on a mass basis, cheaply, quickly, and in the neutral setting of the doctor's office. They seemed the ideal treatment for making workers more efficient and less unhappy. A prominent Army researcher explained:

> It can be demonstrated that we can improve human efficiency and sense of well-being by the administration of psychotropic drugs. These facts lead to the possibility of reducing variations in efficiency of the *normal* human to a minimum around a point of optimal functioning and well-being by the use of the correct psychotropic agent or combination of agents. Possibly, the time may even come when chemicals... will be able to raise this optimal level...[198]

Other researchers predicted even more dramatic results:

> Those of us who work in this field see a developing potential for nearly total control of human emotional status, mental functioning, and will to act. These human phenomena can be started, stopped, or eliminated by the use of various types of chemical substances.[199]

Employers' interest in applying this new drug technology to workers boomed in the 1950's. Many articles appeared exhorting managers that "emotions can be dangerous," and looking hopefully to drugs to minimize "the impact of emotions on production and safety." Entire issues of industrial journals were devoted to this problem and there were many conferences among major corporate executives to discuss the mental health of their workers. The number of U.S. company-run mental health programmes jumped to over 400 by 1963.

The U.S. government cooperated with business in speeding tranquilizers onto the market. The Food and Drug Administration relaxed regulations requiring safety and double-blind studies, and allowed the pharmaceutical companies to mount a massive publicity campaign which made highly inflated claims about the appropriate use and safety of tranquilizers.[200] In 1959, NIMH set up a psychiatric training programme for general practitioners aimed at making mood-altering drug prescriptions by family doctors the main source of treatment for employable people.[201]

Under these pressures, the number of people who received mood-altering drugs increased by leaps and bounds. In 1957, U.S. patients received 35 million prescriptions for mood-altering drugs. Ten years later, the number had risen to 160 million, and by 1976 they accounted for 250 million prescriptions per year! By 1972, Valium and Librium, two minor tranquilizers, were the first and the third most frequently prescribed drugs in the United States, and psychotropic drugs as a class accounted for almost 30 per cent of all U.S. drug prescriptions.[202] A 1978 national survey in the United States revealed that:

> 31 million U.S. women, or 42%, have used tranquilizers, compared to 18 million, or 27% men.
>
> Sedatives have been prescribed for 21% of all women, or 16 million, compared to 17% or 11 million men.
>
> 12 million women, or 16%, have been prescribed stimulants, twice as often as the 5 million, or 8%, of men receiving such drugs.[203]

Women receive more mood-altering drugs because they tend to be more oppressed both in paid work and in the home. Their jobs are lower paid, less secure, more dead-ended and boring, and often as stressful as men's work. At home, they bear the brunt of responsibility for child care and housework, and often they face assault and harassment from husbands, employers, and acquaintances. When they complain or break down, doctors tend to label their behaviour as "mental illness" more than they do men's behaviour with the same symptoms. Nevertheless, the high proportions of *both* women and men who receive these drugs stand in sharp contrast to the pre-war levels of treatment, which were under one per cent of the population. Similar trends have been found in other Western countries where, as in the U.S., most of these drugs are prescribed by general practitioners without any additional psychotherapy.

The largest category of mood-altering drugs, the minor tranquilizers, are designed specifically to treat *normal* people "who are only temporarily disturbed by stressful environmental conditions."[204] Like the major tranquilizers, these minor tranquilizers do nothing to cure the underlying causes of patients' symptoms. Instead, their function is uncomfortably close to that which William Saroyan satirically attributed to aspirin:

It *is* helping to keep people going to work... It *is* sending millions of half-dead people to their jobs... It *is* deadening pain everywhere. It isn't preventing anything, but it is deadening pain.[205]

Like the major tranquilizers, they can cause a number of serious side-effects, including dizziness, blurred vision, lowered blood pressure, liver damage, blood diseases, hallucinations, nausea, rashes, and acute rage.

Simultaneously to the introduction of behaviour modification and psychotropic drugs, the 1950's saw refinements in electro-convulsive therapy (ECT) and psychosurgery which made these treatments relatively safer, cheaper, and more applicable to depressed or anti-social, non-psychotic patients. Although ECT is used to treat depression, many theorists deny that it has real therapeutic value other than inducing forgetfulness and docility, and they point out that shock therapy causes serious brain damage and permanent memory loss. Under the original unmodified method of ECT, patients frequently experienced compression bone fractures and afterward were unable to speak coherently. The refinements consisted primarily of giving sedatives and muscle-paralyzing drugs and shocking only the right (non-verbal) side of the brain. Although these modifications did eliminate fractures and babbling, brain damage to the non-verbal side of the brain is as severe as ever, and patients die more often from cardiac shock and respiratory failure. Many patients testify that, either way, the treatments are terrifying and that the memory loss is upsetting and debilitating. Psychosurgery operates by destroying the capacity of portions of the brain to respond emotionally. It is used particularly on prisoners and other "socially hazardous" people as an explicit social control mechanism with hardly any pretense of being "therapeutic."[206]

All of these therapeutic innovations treat patients as defective objects requiring external control; as "emotional contaminants" whose "behaviour" threatens social order. Nowadays, anyone who regularly or deeply feels unhappy, anxious, angry, or anti-social, no matter how valid these feelings, is considered "ill" and urged to get treatment. These treatments do nothing to help people deal more realistically with their alienated situations. Rather than offering either practical help or personal insight, they are designed only to minimize the "symptoms" as quickly and as cheaply as possible. At best they merely patch patients up enough to allow them to go on coping at work, behaving at school, or putting up with the tension and emptiness of unemployment or housework.

It is debatable whether these forms of treatment can properly be considered "therapy." "Therapy" which damages our ability to perceive anxiety, pain, tension, and anger ultimately reduces our ability to defend ourselves from the social causes of our disturbing feelings. Treatment which adapts us to damaging situations is not therapeutic, but only anaesthetic. Substantial research has demonstrated that suppressing stress-related symptoms may precipitate even more emotional and physical damage in the long run. And this without even considering the direct side-effects of treatments. As Eyer and Sterling conclude:

> It seems just plain inappropriate to view these [psychogenic] diseases as mere technical defects in the body's machinery rather than as dramatic evidence of the fear

and pain pervading people's lives. Even if technical advances can be developed cheaply, they are not an appropriate response... What sort of society... deals with the problems of 9 million people by destroying their capacity to *feel* tension and anxiety?[207]

In short, we see that during the period 1954-1962, public agencies and private industrial psychologists cooperated to develop a technology which could control the emotional symptoms of both working-class and unemployable people. Innovations in treating chronic mental patients were oriented primarily toward reducing the costs of their care and toward discharging them from public responsibility. On the other hand, the new treatments for working-class people were designed to increase their (short-term) tolerance for stressful working conditions. They markedly increase worker productivity by cutting down on absenteeism, alcoholism, and interpersonal friction. Counselling and drugs make workers more tolerant of dangerous working conditions and help them adjust to near-accidents. Most important, they mute labour militancy. By anaesthetizing workers individually, the new treatments prevent them from recognizing problems and acting on them collectively. They only "help" workers to bear their "madness"—alone.

Unlike earlier periods of psychological innovation in treating workers, this surge of research did *not* occur as a result of either high productive demand or labour militancy within the United States. In the wake of anti-labour and anti-left repression, labour militancy in the United States and elsewhere in the West was relatively low from 1954 to 1962. The AFL and the CIO merged in 1955 under a conservative union leadership committed to expelling communists and radical militants and cooperating as much as possible with management. As George Meany, then President of the AFL-CIO, explained:

> In the final analysis, there is not a great difference between the things I stand for and the things that NAM [National Association of Manufacturers] leaders stand for. I stand for the profit system; I believe in the free enterprise system completely. I believe in the return on capital investment. I believe in management's right to manage.

...no union can gain anything—I am speaking now of American unions, not a Communists-controlled [*sic*] union—no union can gain anything by putting the fellow out of business who fills the pay envelope. The interests of the worker and the employer must be identical... because they have both got to get their livelihood from whatever is produced by the industry.

I feel that unity of American labor, under the new AFL-CIO, presents no threat... to American management.[208]

As the AFL-CIO shied away from organizing new workers, the proportion of non-agricultural workers who belonged to unions dropped from 34.7 per cent in 1954 to 28 per cent in 1966. Strikes during this period were fairly mild and involved less than five per cent of the U.S. labour force. The resulting weakness of labour's influence was reflected in its failure either to elect the pro-labour Stevenson or to get the Taft-Hartley Act repealed.

However, this divergence from the tendency of community psychiatry innovations to occur in response to labour militancy or high productive demand does *not* imply that their social control function had ended. During the 1950's, the United States was establishing itself as the dominant world imperialist power. Between 1949 and 1959, U.S. companies more than doubled their overseas investments from $11 billion to $30 billion.

U.S. direct foreign investments alone increased more than sevenfold between 1946 and 1966—from $7.2 billion to $54.6 billion. By 1964, sales of U.S. goods abroad had tripled since 1950, and the size of the foreign market for U.S.-owned firms in 1965 was equal to approximately 40 per cent of the domestic U.S. output of farms, factories and mines. Indeed, U.S. firms abroad constituted the third largest economic unit after the U.S. and Soviet domestic economies.[209]

As a result, the labour force of U.S. business expanded to encompass workers and peasants in many other countries. In large measure, corporations financed the relative prosperity of U.S. workers during the 1950's (which contributed to their passivity) by "super-exploiting" workers in the Third World and such unorganized workers as women, immigrants,

110

and minorities in developed countries. As David Horowitz points out, this policy was adopted deliberately to protect capitalist stability:

> In the calculations of U.S. leaders—from William McKinley to Franklin Roosevelt, from Woodrow Wilson to John F. Kennedy and Lyndon Johnson—the preservation of American prosperity and institutions and of "the American way of life" has been predicated on the preservation and extension of U.S. control of foreign markets, and thus the inevitable expansion of U.S. power overseas. Viewed in this perspective, the cold war can be seen as the U.S. ruling class evidently sees it, namely, as a war for the American frontier.[210]

To squeeze high profits from these Third World workers and to prevent them from revolting, the United States financed both overt military and police expansion and covert methods to condition and pacify workers on a mass basis. The innovations of community psychiatry developed largely in this context.

Nor had community psychiatry's social control functions ended even for U.S. industrial workers. Although during the 1950's both labour unrest and productive demand were *relatively* lower than during the 1940's, they still remained significant. Most major U.S. industries recorded large increases in productivity in this decade (albeit smaller than the increases in countries recovering from World War II devastation). Steel workers, for example, increased their productivity per-man-hour by one-third and iron workers increased theirs by two-thirds between 1949 and 1961. This increased productivity was won at the expense of workers' job security and working conditions. During the 1950's, automation and Taylorization became far more intense in established industries, and spread to white collar sectors of the labour force. By the mid-1950's, evidence had begun to accumulate that workers were becoming less satisfied with their jobs and were reflecting this dissatisfaction in alarmingly high rates of "behavioural disorders." The dramatic increase in the number of corporate mental health programmes during this period reflects the importance placed by business on controlling these reactions.

111

Under the growing pressures of post-war Western economic competition, massive Soviet economic and military strength, and the threat of revolution in Third World countries, businesses became ever more committed to the dual programme of intensifying the Taylorized organization of work, and of expanding the technology with which to control the resulting dissatisfaction of the workers.

CHAPTER VI
Community Psychiatry in a Threatened Empire

The U.S. empire threatened (1962-1982)

For the past 20 years, the United States has faced growing challenges to its pre-eminent position as the major world power. The Soviet Union has posed a rising military threat, spreading its power into what the United States has considered its own sphere of influence, beginning with the Cuban missile crisis in 1962 and extending into South America, Western Europe, the Middle East, Africa, and Southeast Asia. Though offering no direct military threat, China's successes in developing a socialist society also worried U.S. leaders, since, as the U.S. Joint Chiefs of Staff explained: "The dramatic economic improvements realized by Communist China over the past ten years impress the nations of the region greatly and offer a serious challenge to the Free World."[211] Third World revolutionary movements have flourished in spite of massive military and economic attacks by the United States. With the U.S. defeat in Vietnam, and its subsequent losses in Angola, Mozambique, Zimbabwe, Nicaragua, Iran, and elsewhere, the U.S. hold over the Third World—with its markets and cheap labour—has slipped seriously.

The United States has also become increasingly vulnerable in its relations with other developed capitalist nations. The value of the U.S. dollar—and the political influence it wields—has been undermined by higher productive growth in Japan and Europe and by the creation of the European Common Market and OPEC (Organization of Petroleum Exporting Countries). Unprecedented levels of military spending, deficit financing, corporate tax subsidies, and the expansion of consumer credit all helped to stave off economic crises, but since 1966, the U.S. economy has grown dangerously unstable. The United States managed to export some of its economic weaknesses to Europe through the 1944 Bretton Woods agreement which established the U.S. dollar as the international currency, but this system collapsed during the late 1960's when Europe refused to support the U.S. dollar any longer. Debt financing of its military expenses and capital expansion has threatened not only the U.S. economy but also that of all other capitalist countries, and since 1974, the economies of major Western nations have become unstable, characterized by "stagflation," public fiscal insolvency, and resources crises.

To shore up its fortunes, U.S. business and government have turned increasingly to the domestic labour force both to staff the armed forces necessary to wage its counter-revolutionary battles, and to produce more profits to stabilize the economy at home and support military expenses abroad. But getting workers' cooperation has become ever more difficult.

During the 1960's, militant people's movements re-emerged with new vigour. Business, and the conservative AFL-CIO leadership, tried to confine labour struggles to narrow economic issues, but the civil rights, anti-war, women's and other grassroots movements generated massive political influence, which won some progressive concessions and contributed to the U.S. defeat in Vietnam. As Sweezy pointed out, "Vietnam has shown that the people of the United States are simply not prepared to support counter-revolutionary wars, nor are conscripted armies willing to fight them."[212] During the 1960's, civil unrest, riots and wildcat strikes rose in all the major Western countries, exploding in 1968 in a flood of militancy which rocked both political and economic stability.

> From 1968 until at least 1971 almost every country in Western Europe experienced its own milder variation of the turmoil that plagued French industrial relations after the student demonstrations there almost provoked a revolution.
>
> ...all saw some of their long-established institutions challenged... the unions were as much the subject of these challenges as any other bodies... It is not surprising that both unions and employers were driven to explore new ways of conducting their relations in the face of everything from unofficial and unauthorized wildcat strikes, through plant sit-ins and work-ins to enterprise seizures.[213]

Like their European counterparts, many American workers carried their protests into their work places, challenging both management's authority to run its plants and the co-opting role of union labour leaders.[214]

Besides these organized actions, the rising alienation and anomie of American workers has been expressed in mushrooming rates of individual absenteeism, alcoholism, drug use, sabotage, and other "behaviour disorders." Between 1965 and 1972, absenteeism and labour turnover more than doubled in the auto industry.[215] Nationwide, the incidence of people considered alcoholic in the U.S. jumped over 100 per cent between 1963 and 1974; employees with "an alcohol problem" now make up about 10 per cent of the work force.[216] The cost of alcoholism to "the American business community" has escalated from $2 billion a year in 1967 to $12.5 billion in 1976, and the annual cost of alcoholism to the American economy as a whole exceeds $25 billion.[217] Government authorities report that since 1960, drug addiction "has probably trebled or quadrupled."[218] Among auto assembly-line workers, 16 per cent were estimated to be addicted to heroin.[219] Epidemic alcohol and drug addiction rates in the military have called into question the effectiveness of the U.S. armed forces.[220]

115

Corporate response

In view of the growing vulnerability of the U.S. economy and the instability of its political empire, neither business nor government could accept this level of "wasted" potential labour-power. As a Vice-President of ALCOA explained:

> We have found it harder and harder to make a return on invested capital that will assure the company's continued capacity to serve people's needs for our product. Like many other industries, we are squeezed by the rising costs of labor, energy, materials, and services. To us, this underscores the importance of using wisely every resource we have, especially people.
>
> It is costly when an employee cannot do his job properly because of an emotional problem. In effect, we have lost part of an employee that we are paying for.[221]

We should note that this concept of "wasted" production assumes that workers have not *already* been driven beyond the productivity that they can tolerate, and that it is only some perversity in their constitution which prevents them from turning out what employers demand of them.

In the early 1960's, businesses began to invest much more money in programmes to treat the "emotional problems" of their workers. The dividends of these programmes in reduced absenteeism and higher productivity were significantly higher than the costs of the programmes themselves. A large proportion of what passes as treatment in these programmes is simply coercion, based on the threat of job loss or disciplinary action. As one Navy expert explained: "Managers have to learn that early intervention using job threat to create motivation, and monitoring of recovery are extremely cost-effective business practices."[222] A high proportion of employee "alcoholism" programmes are not limited to drinking problems, but treat "everyone with a deteriorating job performance."[223] The procedure described below, for example, is typical:

> The employee who has done a poor job, gone against plant policy, is always late, or has a poor attendance record would be put on record by his supervisor as being in work difficulty. Under this job threat, he would agree to see the

116

more neutral employee assistance counselor. A psychiatrist would then determine the kind of treatment most likely to improve the employee's adjustment, whether it be... lithium for hypomanic swings, an alcohol program with in-patient and out-patient therapy, or short-term individual psychotherapy to help him stop a pattern of reacting to work supervisors as to his despised father... The counselor would assist the troubled person to accept the proper treatment; he could even use some "constructive coercion" by reminding the employee of the supervisor's warning.[224]

By 1977, almost all of the 50 largest U.S. industrial corporations had established employee emotional treatment programmes, and many other major employers had followed suit.

Community psychiatry programmes of the 1960's

Even more far-reaching than these direct employee treatment programmes has been business influence over public community psychiatry policy since 1960. Business leaders recognized that more essential than rehabilitating the particular emotional casualties of each business was the need to establish a broad national programme which could treat all workers — both active and potential. For the welfare of particular businesses was becoming much more dependent on the political stability of the government and on the ability of the United States to mobilize effective armed forces. Much of the unrest of the 1960's emerged from populations which had not been part of the industrial working class — women, minorities, adolescents, university students, and the urban poor. Similarly, military draftees and recruits were drawn largely from low-income, minority youth. These populations, relatively untouched by the employee mental health programmes of large corporations, also had to be controlled. To provide "an alternative to chaos,"[225] industrial and military leaders began to press for a significantly expanded federal programme of community psychiatry.

In 1960, the National Association for Mental Health (the new name of the National Committee for Mental Hygiene) successfully pressured the Democratic Party to include a plank in its platform promising to provide "greatly increased Federal support for psychiatric research and training and community mental health programs."[226] Through Mike Gorman, a spokesman for the philanthropists, the National Association convinced President Kennedy and the U.S. Congress to support legislation which would "federalize" U.S. mental health care, and for the first time involve the national government in directly providing psychiatric treatment.

Significantly, there was no corresponding initiative on the part of the federal government to treat directly other health problems of the general population, in spite of the high rates of infant mortality, heart disease, cancer, and occupational illness which reflect the U.S. "failure to institute simple public health measures."[227] Medicare and Medicaid legislation passed in 1965 only subsidized existing medical treatment and—unlike community mental health centres—did not provide new federally funded treatment facilities. Similarly, there was no powerful lobby which favoured new funding for mental hospitals or for their unemployable clients, in spite of the well documented fact of their inadequate budgets. On the contrary, military, political, and business leaders, against the recommendation of the Joint Commission for Mental Illness and Health, explicitly opposed extending any federal support to state mental hospitals.[228] In contrast to these areas of obvious social need, there was little mass demand for community mental health centres, and, in fact, there was considerable union and community suspiciousness toward them. In other words, the high priority which government placed on community psychiatry was based neither on social need nor on popular demand, but rather on the priorities of business and military leaders.

The resulting Community Mental Health Centers Act of 1963 authorized the NIMH to: (1) provide direct federal funds for building and operating a national network of community mental health centres; (2) more than triple federal training grants for mental health personnel, especially for auxiliary workers, general practitioners, and non-professionals; (3) increase support for mental health research

118

on social problems and ways of treating them; and (4) eliminate the state mental hospital in its current form.

In effect, this legislation provided the vehicle to carry out the earlier mandate of the NIMH to shift the focus of public psychiatric treatment from chronic mental patients to "the population of entire communities."[229] The Act allowed the federal government to coerce and bribe the states to phase out chronic patient care and to establish facilities to treat employable, ambulatory patients. This "preventive" focus of the Act, on treating employable, non-psychotic people, was a prerequisite for its winning Congressional support.

In the wake of this 1963 legislation, state mental hospitals were encouraged to discharge as many unemployable, aged or chronic patients as possible, causing the decline of resident patients to accelerate dramatically. Many of these patients were discharged before any alternative plan had been formulated for their care in the community, and, as a result, instant psychiatric ghettoes sprang up in slum districts. Outraged relatives, staff members, and community leaders testified that the hospitals "had adopted a policy of discharging patients *no matter what* the situation, the patient's condition, etc.," that "social workers had a 'quota' of discharges to fill, at all costs," and that "they chalk up each discharge as if they were shooting down fighter planes."[230] This decarceration movement, in large measure, transferred the costs of caring for unemployable mental patients from the government to the patients, their families, and their local communities. Even in countries with "socialized" medicine, such as Canada, this trend holds. Although government Medicare in Canada continues to cover direct medical expenses, it does not support the costs of housing, food, maintenance, and non-nursing supervision for a large proportion of those who would have received these services free in mental hospitals. Aside from welfare and old age assistance, many of these patients are forced to rely on their own savings or on their family's generosity. For example, a Saskatchewan study of ex-mental patients who have returned home found that half of the families sampled had to keep a wage-earner home to care for the patients, and that almost 80 per cent reported other serious economic and practical consequences of providing for their care.[231]

119

Policy-makers indicated that they supported decarceration at least as much because it reduced the costs of caring for chronic patients as for any humanitarian motives. Generally, patients were placed in nursing homes, boarding homes, or back with their families which had not been able to handle them in the first place. In most cases, patient treatment "in the community" (to the extent that they can be considered "in" it) consists only of mood-altering drugs and occasional check-ups to see that the dosage is correct and that the patients are behaving. The mental health centres which were supposed to pick up their care have had neither the resources nor the incentive to meet their needs adequately.

As it was divesting itself of responsibility for most chronic patients, the U.S. government mobilized its resources to expand the treatment of employable people. In addition to funding community mental health centres—which account for about one-quarter of mental patient care—the government encouraged general hospitals to provide short-term psychiatric treatment—accounting for one-half of psychiatric admissions—and urged general practitioners to treat an increasing proportion of people with "emotional" problems. Over half of those who seek emotional help are treated by general practitioners. Between 1962 and 1972, the NIMH research budget jumped from $50 million to $112 million. Its research priorities emphasized such socially disruptive populations as juvenile delinquents, alcoholics, drug abusers, and urban residents, and treatment methods consisting primarily of more sophisticated mood-altering drugs and behaviour therapies.[232]

As social unrest mounted near the end of the 1960's, Congress massively increased NIMH funding for programmes to treat "crime and delinquency," "alcoholism," "minority group mental health," and "narcotic addiction and drug abuse." The government explicitly defined community psychiatry as a solution to social unrest:

> The national community mental health program is providing a basic framework for intervention—not only to treat and control the mental illnesses, but to extend the scope of mental health to all aspects of the human condition—in an effort to identify and ameliorate the root

causes of stress and alienation and to understand the mental health implications of a wide variety of social phenomena.[233]

In order to attack these social problems most efficiently, the U.S. government invested heavily in improving the technology of treatment and in further Taylorizing the nature of mental health work. Many of the resulting new techniques were designed to increase control over "disruptive" behaviour. For example, in contrast to effective addiction cures, methadone keeps heroin addicts off the streets, under surveillance, and dependent for life on government suppliers. Antabus (a drug which makes people nauseous if they drink alcohol), brain implantations, and aversive conditioning impose internal biological or psychological constraints on drinking and aggressive behaviour. Lithium salts, ritalin, and other mood regulators are prescribed on a long-term basis to stabilize moods at a level consistent with efficient, routine (but not creative) work.

The NIMH also has played a major role in both helping and requiring mental health agencies to computerize their operations.

> For many years, the Institute has required that the various states and federally funded community mental health centers submit statistical data which are then integrated by computer into reports describing national trends.

> In addition, NIMH provides financial support to a number of research and development projects in the automation of psychiatric records with the objectives of providing tools for improved patient care and more efficient use of personnel, developing institutional management information systems, building research data bases, and facilitating the reporting of data useful for state and national program planning and evaluation.[234]

Computers significantly aid large government agencies in monitoring trends and potential problem areas quickly and accurately. As one authority pointed out:

> Equipped with these data magnifiers, the social psychiatrist of tomorrow will be able to forecast the demographic and epidemiological characteristics of the behavior of populations at different risks. This is the wherewithal to

create a dynamic early-warning system that can tackle the problem of primary prevention.[235]

Computers also allow the government to compile detailed data on particular potentially troublesome individuals. With current levels of technology, computers can not only track patients through their psychiatric treatment, but also can link them with data related to welfare, private medical diagnoses, and, potentially, with income tax data, census records, and police files. Any two or more computer files can technically be combined. The only current protection of confidentiality is legislation, and laws are vulnerable when powerful interests are threatened. As Laska and Bank concede, "even though computerized administrative systems are usually planned with the best of democratic intentions, they do furnish the framework for mechanisms of totalitarian control in the hands of antidemocratic forces."[236] A recent study of government computer systems indicates that there is already considerable violation of confidentiality:

> The files at present contain too much information and are accessible to too many agencies, including private business concerns. Few safeguards protect legitimate rights of personal privacy or prevent use of the information in a discriminatory manner... The potential harm that they can inflict... is made even more critical by (a) the coincident development of new state-level intelligence files on civil disorders and dangerous persons that are maintained by the same agencies that administer the information files and that are accessible to participants in the national system, and (b) the rapid expansion of computerized records on individuals maintained by welfare, health, education and other public and private agencies that can be (and have been) readily interfaced with the criminal offender files.[237]

Beyond increasing control over patients, the new techniques also cheapen and expand control over mental health workers. They eliminate many of the remaining skills that go into treating and maintaining patients. ("Skills" need not necessarily be equated with training which benefits the clients. Before the advent of major tranquilizers, mental health aides had to be "skilled" in forcing violent patients into straitjackets. Business and a fiscally conscious capitalist government perceive "skills" primarily in terms of cost and not of usefulness to the patient.) The new methods allow general practitioners, nursing home aides, non-professional mental health workers, and family members to replace expensive psychotherapists. As Obers explains:

> Pyschoactive drugs... are chemicals whose effects are intended to replace the labor that would be involved in emotional support, education, job training, or natural healing. "Cost effectiveness" has become an increasing factor in medical treatment and health care organization, at times involving needless risks.[238]

Similarly, although computers eliminate some routine clerical tasks, their main cost-benefit is in replacing skilled labour and in increasing management control over the pace and quality of work:

> Computers in psychiatry have played a role in simulated interviews and in administering, scoring, and standardizing intelligence and personality tests... In terms of service delivery in mental health, computers function in the realms of data collection, psychiatric/medical record keeping, psychotropic drug monitoring, evaluation of patient treatment and goal attainments, and in the establishment of a total mental health information system.[239]

During the 1960's, under pressure from business lobbies and their representative, the National Association for Mental Health (and in opposition to the American Medical Association), the NIMH expanded its training programme from funding only professional graduate level studies to supporting training for general practitioners, occupational and recreational therapists, clergy, and non-professional psychiatric aides and mental health attendants. Under ever more Taylorized working conditions, mental health work has become increasingly sub-divided. A recent report lists 27 separate mental health occupations with education requirements minutely calibrated from more than six years of graduate school to grade 10 of high school.[240] Psychiatrists have taken on more administrative functions, delegating actual patient contact to auxiliary mental health workers.

> Someone else will see the patient and the psychiatrist will become an assembler of reports. He will, of course, con-

tinue to do research, to teach, to advise social agencies, and to talk to probation officers, first aid squads, industrial leaders, clergymen, judges, lawyers...[241]

Auxiliary professions, such as psychiatric nursing, psychiatric social work, and psychology, have also been subdivided into a wide range of skill levels, from Ph.D.'s to one-year certificate programmes. General practitioners, with minimal psychiatric training but with their power to prescribe psychotropic drugs, have been encouraged by NIMH to replace lengthy and expensive forms of psychotherapy. And finally, during the middle 1960's, the U.S. government encouraged social service programmes to use "indigenous non-professionals" (low-income, mostly minority group, local residents) as a buffer between professionals and their low-income clients. In spite of well publicized "new careers" and "career ladders" for these workers, non-professional mental health workers generally have been confined to dead-end, low-paying, routine work.[242]

The impact of this concerted public investment in community psychiatry has been widespread. About 12 per cent of the U.S., Canadian, British and other populations—overwhelmingly composed of employable people—receive an explicit psychiatric diagnosis each year, and twice that number receive psychotropic drugs.[243]

The anti-community psychiatry movement

By attempting to treat the social forces which threatened business on a mass scale, the NIMH was forced to take an ever higher profile as a social control agency, and thereby to become embroiled in the very disputes it hoped to solve. By the late 1960's, labour, community, and ex-mental patient groups for the first time began to attack federal mental health programmes in their own right. Unions of mental health workers organized to attack the excesses of the decarceration movement and to defend both their own job security and the welfare of chronic patients.[244] Non-professional minority workers at the prestigious Menninger Clinic and the Lincoln Hospital Mental Health Service staged effective work-ins and strikes to demand real career ladders, improved care for patients, and action against injustices in their communities.[245] A militant black youth gang used its NIMH funds to buy guns, sparking a scandal that jeopardized Congressional appropriations to the NIMH. Militant groups took over the podiums of professional psychiatric conferences to protest coercive, racist, and sexist psychiatric practices.[246] And a growing "antipsychiatry" movement, composed of more then 40 groups of ex-mental patients, mobilized to oppose oppressive psychiatric practices.

Government agencies managed to repress, divide, placate, and co-opt some of these protests by giving small grants to militant groups for innocuous self-help projects, and by making small concessions such as creating study groups on the ethics of brain surgery and tightening the limits on involuntary psychiatric hospitalization. Nevertheless, by 1970, community psychiatry programmes had generated so much controversy in the United States that the Nixon administration severely cut back NIMH funding, dismissed the director of the Institute, and tried to phase out the community mental health centres programme.[247] As one opponent of the programme explained:

> The CMHC [Community Mental Health Centre] has little or no expertise at its disposal that it might usefully apply to direct action in the vast sphere of urban problems...

> Moreover, as the CMHC has moved into the social action sphere, it has been increasingly the object of political maneuvering and confrontation. Its agenda is thus frequently perverted by the agenda of interest groups...[248]

Since 1970, the NIMH has retrenched into less controversial areas under a much more restricted budget. Business and political leaders have recently been pressing (so far successfully) to transfer community mental health centres to the jurisdiction of Health Maintenance Organizations (HMO's) and to re-integrate psychiatry into medicine. The purpose of this move is to transfer an even greater proportion of psychiatric care from public to private control, increasing the role of general practitioners and private hospitals, and putting psychiatric care on a more profitable "cost-efficient and manageable" footing.[249] As Phil Brown explains:

125

> Health Maintenance Organizations (HMO's) are highly
> favored by corporate interests since they promise a type
> of health delivery which receives guaranteed payments
> that can be made more profitable (or, in the case of non-
> profit concerns, can be made to better realize and circu-
> late profit to the actual profit-making sectors). This
> increased profitability comes from cost cutting (e.g. res-
> tricting patient usage, employing many nonphysicians in
> primary care) and from the monopolistic expansion of a
> single HMO to cover a huge population.[250]

Under restricted funding and regulations, community
mental health centres—the most controversial and visible
portion of the NIMH programme—have drawn back from
social intervention to focus on handling more severe emotional
problem populations—the aged, psychotics, youthful offend-
ers, minorities, addicts, and people with deep depressions.
While mental health centres treat these less profitable cases,
private doctors tend to handle employable patients with
milder symptoms. Most of these "private" patients, whose fees
are often paid with public funds, just get a prescription for
mood-altering drugs from their family doctors along with a
brief lecture on reducing life stress. Those who are admitted
for in-patient treatment generally get little more than per-
functory visits by their doctors and stronger doses of the
drugs, with or without shock treatments. Unlike the politically visible and volatile community mental health centres,
treatment by private doctors is virtually immune to public
scrutiny, and protected from demands for community control
and social responsibility.

Although the community mental health centres were
forced to withdraw from blatant social intervention, other,
less visible NIMH programmes have become more explicitly
coercive. During the past 10 years, community psychiatry
programmes have tended to merge with criminal justice
agencies and corporate mental health programmes. Mental
health personnel consult for law enforcement agencies, prisons, and businesses, helping them to apply the most up-to-
date psychiatric techniques to control "anti-social" behaviour.[251] Prisons are taking in a rising proportion of ex-mental
patients who are too disturbed to remain in the community but

who are now barred from mental hospitals.[252] The National Institute on Alcohol Abuse and Alcoholism (NIAAA) and the National Council on Drug Abuse, both offshoots from the NIMH, work closely with corporate and military mental health programmes, providing funds, consultants, and statistical data services. The more direct social control functions of the NIMH have been transferred to the Law Enforcement Assistance Administration (LEAA). At a time when the NIMH budget was being cut back for the first time (along with other social services), LEAA's funding rose more rapidly than almost any other federal agency, from $63 million in 1969 to over $1 billion in 1976. Unfettered by either the benevolent ideology of public health or the militant constituency of community psychiatry, LEAA operates as an explicit agency for social control.

In essence, then, the past 20 years have accelerated the consistent direction of, first, industrial psychology, and, since World War II, community psychiatry. Many more employable people are being treated for a much broader range of "maladjustments" in increasingly coercive ways and at far greater public expense. At the same time, the costs of services for chronic mental patients are being shifted to the patients, their families, and their local communities, and their care is being transformed into a private, profit-making commodity. As capitalist powers become increasingly more economically unstable and politically vulnerable, we can expect these trends to escalate, unless they are actively and efficiently opposed.

CHAPTER VII
Implications and Strategy

Implications of community psychiatry for different populations

On the surface, community psychiatry appears to be a relatively inoffensive and benevolent service, helping people who really are having trouble coping in a world of rising stresses, rescuing mental patients from the "snake pits," and generally increasing knowledge about how people tick and how to make them happier. Most people seek its services voluntarily (although often under informal duress from employers, family, and the courts), accepting the freely dispensed treatment to dull their pain.

We tend to view instances of over-zealous decarceration, drug side-effects, and homeless psychotics wandering the streets merely as correctable excesses of a policy which, on the whole, is a "good thing." After all, we have to keep coping to earn a living, and frequently we have no practical way out of the maddening tension. So drugs which relieve anxiety, shocks which drive away the blues, and counselling which lets us blow off steam do help to make it all bearable. If all these treatments are only "band-aids," we may reasonably argue, then it isn't fair to expect psychiatry to change the world: at least it helps to make people feel better.

This superficial perspective contains three errors. First of all, it assumes that community psychiatry is oriented to solve the problems workers experience; that if it only had the techniques, money, and manpower, community psychiatry *would* try to change the world for the better. However, as we have seen, the innovations of community psychiatry are precisely those which management adopted in order to speed up work and dissolve protest. In other words, these innovations were not designed to improve things for us, but on the contrary, they were powerful tools in making working and living conditions stressful in the first place.

Secondly, this benign interpretation assumes that anaesthetizing our reaction to oppression is helpful for us. If a patient has painful, terminal cancer, we see little wrong with drugs to take away the pain. But the analogy applies to community psychiatry only if we view ourselves as terminal: that is, as passive, beaten, and hopeless. In order to fight oppressive conditions and change things, we need our wits about us. We need to feel what is dangerously stressful, and we also need to feel the anxiety, aggression, and anger which give us the incentive to fight those conditions. Rather than "letting off steam" individually in counselling, we need to let it erupt in collective action.

And finally, it assumes that psychiatric treatments at least make patients feel better in the short run. The reality is that since the late 1960's community psychiatry has continued to become more overtly coercive and punitive, particularly in "treating" disruptive workers, both in developed countries and increasingly in the Third World where they are most exploited.

Community psychiatry has very little to do with curing rising alienation and stress-related problems. But that is not what it was intended to do. Its primary function is to create an efficient alienation-control apparatus, through which patients efficiently flow in and out for periodic "repairs" and "adjustments" like products on an assembly line. With the community focus, the whole concept of being a "mental patient" and being "discharged" from care has evaporated: we are all always potential patients.

The community psychiatry system is set up in such a way that it provides different specialized treatments to the various sectors of the population, depending on whether they are unemployable, marginally employable, or actively employed. (By and large, it does not treat the wealthy.)

Those who are unemployable—that is, those who cannot be "repaired" cheaply (the aged, the psychotic, and the retarded)—are disposed of efficiently in nursing, boarding, or group homes where, despite the dedicated efforts of an underpaid and overworked staff, they fall apart in poverty. Many have simply been discharged with no place to live at all. Major tranquilizers make them manageable enough to eliminate staff attendants, and if the social service budgets get cut or if the nursing home profits are not high enough, administrators simply raise the doses and make the patients more manageable. The resulting epidemic of tardive dyskinesia (a severely debilitating syndrome involving permanent brain stem damage) and other side-effects have been ignored.

> The side effects of these drugs are frightening. A short list includes: Parkinsonism, hypertension, jaundice, excessive weight gain, lupus, edema, breast engorgement, EKG abnormalities, seizures, amenorrhea, blindness from retinitis, and even "sudden death."
>
> Tardive dyskinesia is possibly the most alarming of these side effects since it is so prevalent. This degenerative and irreversible disease produced by phenothiazines (major tranquilizers) involves loss of muscle control, especially of the face. Tardive dyskinesia was known to the psychiatric profession two decades ago but was largely ignored. Only in the last few years have the psychiatric journals "discovered" and discussed the problem. Recent studies have shown that as many as 56 percent of inpatients show some form of tardive dyskinesia, and among outpatients who have been on phenothiazines for over one year, 43 percent have the disease.[253]

R.D. Laing captures the blithe inhumanity of this attitude toward unemployable mental patients:

The trouble with you
's you've lost a screw

I'm sorry it's you
but there's nothing to do

There'll be no abatements
there are no replacements

don't make a to-do
just say toodle-oo

I'm sorry I can't help you
you'd cost too much to redo

you'll have to be abolished
report to be demolished[254]

Potentially employable people include those who are largely "apartheided" from adequately paid mainstream jobs, such as women, adolescents, displaced men over 45, members of minority groups, and moderately handicapped people. These people receive slightly better treatment than unemployable populations, since their ability to work has to be maintained so that employers and the military can draw them in and out of the labour force fairly flexibly. Psychiatric treatments for them fulfill four main functions: (1) Mood-altering drugs such as minor tranquilizers, anti-depressants, stimulants and barbiturates numb their emotional reactions to poverty and discrimination. Women, for example—especially housewives—tend to receive far more of these drugs than comparably aged men; (2) Counselling at mental health centres socializes them to "adjust" to their situation and to blame themselves for it. The following ideology is typical:

> The great portion of the unemployed show avoidance behavior patterns or what has been referred to as "work inhibition," which implies that they are physically capable of work but are prevented from working because of psychological disabilities. The work-avoidance behavior patterns constitute *personal* obstacles to employment. The individual has developed these behaviour patterns to defend himself from all the experiences associated with the ethic "to work."[255]

(3) "Life skills" programmes provide training in "proper" work attitudes, such as punctuality, deportment, and neatness, without providing any substantive preparation for skilled

work; and (4) Methadone maintenance programmes, aversive conditioning, psychosurgery, and behaviour modification coercively try to prevent people from committing "anti-social" behaviour without addressing causes of the troublesome behaviour. These coercive programmes constitute a large proportion of what passes as "treatment" for adolescents and adults who run afoul of the law.

Active workers also receive large quantities of mood-altering drugs, self-blaming counselling, and — when they act up, or fall down on the job — coercive "therapies." But programmes oriented to treat employees focus on improving their productivity under stress, rather than merely maintaining minimal coping skills. Corporate counselling programmes have to justify their expense to employers in dollars-and-cents savings. Basically, they achieve these savings by elaborating on industrial psychology methods developed before 1945.

First of all, they screen job applicants with sophisticated psychological tests to select "people who can scarcely be broken down under any strain they may encounter" (to paraphrase the military testing procedure on which these methods are based).[256] Whether workers *should* be exposed to such severe strain is, of course, an issue primarily for workers, and not a serious concern of management.

Secondly, corporate mental health programmes provide an elaborate network to channel workers into "counselling" whenever their work deteriorates. Frequently, employers try to recruit union representatives to take on the chore of convincing or forcing workers to seek "help."[257]

At best, this technique of using union representatives encourages the targeted employees to trust that the treatment is in their interests, while at the same time it lines up the union with management and against the workers' wishes.

Treatment may be provided either by the company or by a public mental health service to which the company refers the worker. The government programmes work in explicit "partnership" with corporate programmes, and therefore, either way, workers are under heavy pressure to cooperate with the prescribed treatment and to "improve" by producing more efficiently and ceasing any disruptive behaviour.

Treatment is usually some form of mood-altering drug designed specifically to improve "working capacity." These therapies rarely explore the valid causes of the workers' diminished productivity, but merely treat the specific behavioural problem:

> Working capacity is determined by four factors: *action potential* on the physical level, *motivation* on the level of aspiration, *integration potential* on the cognitive level, and *control* on the emotional level. The central representative of these four factors in the brain is partly cortical and partly subcortical. Three emotional conditions can exercise a profoundly disorganizing effect on a person's work capacity. These are *anxiety, depression* and *indifference*. Different psychoactive drugs influence these emotional conditions in different ways.[258]

There are three serious dangers associated with these treatments. First, the mood-altering drugs all produce varying degrees of side-effects. Lithium carbonate, for example, a popular treatment for employed "manic-depressives," has a "therapeutic" level which is extremely close to the toxic level. Since the quantity of lithium in the body fluctuates constantly, patients frequently are poisoned, experiencing kidney damage, disorientation, convulsions, and even death. In addition to clear cases of poisoning, sub-clinical lithium toxicity causes permanent physical damage and can make workers act confused, which leads their friends and themselves to believe that they are indeed insane.[259] Equally serious side-effects accompany the other mood-modifying drugs. For workers, even relatively mild side-effects such as dizziness, blurred vision, and indifference can lead to dangerous accidents.

More serious than the danger of the drugs' side-effects is the way that they mask workers' awareness of occupational hazards. The drugs are used to "help" workers adjust to near-accidents and dangerous working conditions. In the late 1950's, the Medical Director of U.S. Steel, for example, cited as signs of mental illness the following complaints by workers:

> At one time four people came to me in the course of two days, all from one section, each requesting a change of job for medical reasons. One said he couldn't stand the noise on his job; it was making him tense and nervous and he

couldn't sleep at night. Another said the job was too heavy; at the end of the day his back and legs were aching. Two of them said the odors of solvents on the job were making them nauseated; they couldn't eat their dinner at night.[260]

In that era before the widespread use of minor tranquilizers, he "treated" the patients by counselling them to understand that their "real" problem was with their foreman, and not the noise, the over-heavy loads, or the solvents. Since then, drugs have made this sort of treatment easier. For example, in 1971, a group of electrical workers in Saskatchewan accidentally discovered that they all had been experiencing similar symptoms of irritability, insomnia, and shakiness for years. Because of these symptoms, they each had seen their family doctors separately and had been given tranquilizers (as well as lectures to cut back on their drinking and on union activities). However, once they got together, the workers were able to figure out, despite company attempts to cover up the evidence, that they were all suffering from chronic, job-related, mercury poisoning; they were able to get appropriate treatment (as opposed to tranquilizers), and after another three years of fighting, to win an award from workmen's compensation.[261]

Many other substances that workers are commonly exposed to also cause serious psychiatric symptoms; insecticides, formaldehyde, heavy metals, carbon disulfide, methyl bromide, pentaborane, and solvents, to list just a few.[262]

Masked by mood-altering drugs, and dismissed as individual madness, the symptoms of this kind of organic poisoning are made inaccessible and unintelligible to the worker. Employees are frequently barred from knowing the dangers of chemicals they work with, or even what chemicals they are being exposed to.[263]

Other occupational hazards, such as noise, speed-up, shift work, and vibration also cause both emotional strain and long-term physical damage.[264] Often the very symptoms for which workers are treated reflect the fact that their work makes dangerously severe demands on their tolerance. To the extent that community psychiatry treatments "help" workers to return to these conditions, they are likely to precipitate even more serious long-term damage.

Most important, community psychiatry poses a serious threat to workers as an entire class. It amplifies the effectiveness of traditional industrial psychology techniques, allowing management to speed up production, to "cool-out" protests, and to defuse "trouble-makers." The easily available mood-altering prescriptions encourage workers to seek individual relief from their family doctors rather than to organize collectively to change their working conditions. The psychiatric (and criminal justice) computer technology has invaded fields which have traditionally been confidential. It is entirely possible that employers and the police can be given access to psychiatric files for "sanity checks" just as we now have credit checks without our authorization. Treatment is becoming more coercive and compulsory, and the range of behaviour labelled "deviant" is broadening.

There is yet another category of people who are targets of psychiatric innovations: Third World workers in liberation movements. The U.S. military, police, and the CIA have adapted knowledge about brain functions and psychological techniques to forge a horrifying arsenal of weapons for espionage, torture, and social control. Pilisuk and Ober, describing U.S.-directed torture training in many countries, persuasively argue that torture and genocide are becoming major "public health" problems for the world's people:

> Scientific research in which doctors must necessarily have participated has made it possible to identify the maximum suffering that the various systems of the body can endure without resulting in death.

> ... In Montevideo, Uruguay, an entire ward has been set aside for the administration of pharmacological torture... In Northern Ireland, the application of a form of sensory deprivation to IRA prisoners is producing the severe cognitive deterioration, hallucinations, and anxiety states that psychologists understand well.

> ... In most instances, the torture seems intended less to protract a confession than to produce conformity through fear and the complete destruction of will.[265]

In other words, for all four groups—for the unemployable, the marginally employable, the employed peoples of the developed Western nations, and Third World freedom fighters—community psychiatry is not only not helpful; it is actively destructive. In return for quick addictive "fixes" to ease tensions and depressions, such people pay dearly: in reduced personal and class awareness; in the debilitating effects and side-effects of treatments; in the neglect of "disposable" friends, relatives; in the labels of "mad" or "disordered" given for behaviour never considered crazy before; in taxes and fees to feed the hungry madness business; and in the threat of severely authoritarian social control and torture in the future.

It is important to note that the problem of community psychiatry is not so much the techniques as how they are used. On the whole, the techniques of community psychiatry represent methods to extend corporate social control and profits, without consideration for either the wishes or long-term wellbeing of those who are treated. Electroshock, aversive conditioning, psychosurgery on prisoners, mass drugging of chronic patients, coercive alcohol and drug abuse treatment, and torture have very few or no redeeming qualities. They were invented solely for the benefit of those in power. Other techniques have some, limited, legitimate uses. Low doses of mood-altering drugs can help frantic people become calm enough so that they can discuss their problems realistically. In China, for example, psychotics are sometimes treated with short-term, low doses of tranquilizers in combination with a good deal of practical help, discussions, exercise, and good food. Behaviour modification has some limited uses in self-administered situations such as in relaxation training, phobia release, and smoking clinics. Non-directive counselling and encounter groups, employed in a sympathetic, non-manipulative manner, can sometimes lead to insight and greater self-acceptance. However, under most community psychiatry programmes— particularly those for working-class and unemployed people—these therapies tend to *substitute* for helping patients' practical situations or personal insight. They are used instead to *control* patients.

Community psychiatry as a locus of class struggle

We have seen that community psychiatry is intimately implicated in the class struggle between workers and business. Since the early 1900's, its methods have served management in its efforts to control labour. Industrial psychology was "nationalized" into community psychiatry after World War II because it was essential for us business to extend its control over a wider proportion of the domestic labour force, as well as over workers in other Western countries and in their Third World empires. The technology of community psychiatry has evolved to a point where it constitutes a serious danger. It is important, therefore, for us to develop strategies to oppose community psychiatry.

To do that, it is useful to review both the history of labour-management relations and the history of opposition to industrial psychology and community psychiatry. On a world scale, labour has come a long way since 1900. A large proportion of the world's people have succeeded in freeing themselves from, or at least resisting, first, overt British and European imperialism, and, later, Western economic imperialism. Labour movements in the developed countries have forced employers and the State to recognize the legitimacy of labour unions and labour's right to strike, to bargain collectively, and to have basic civil liberties and social services. In many European countries, labour has won a major voice in determining how work is organized and in developing economic and social welfare policies.

This does not imply either that the basis of class struggle is declining or that workers will easily win new concessions (or even maintain old ones) without fighting and eventually overthrowing the capitalist system. On the contrary, as the genocidal U.S. policies toward the Third World and the growing right-wing trend in the developed world vividly demonstrate, the struggle has escalated in both scope and ferocity.

But reviewing the history of labour victories does show that the capitalist class is vulnerable. Indeed, during periods of high labour unrest, business and political leaders have managed to prevent revolution only by making major concessions and by using every military, economic, and ideological weapon at their disposal.

In large measure, industrial psychology and its descendant, community psychiatry, represent defensive rather than offensive capitalist tactics. In virtually every instance, new psychological techniques to control workers emerged in response to the threat posed by high labour militancy. And each successive innovation was required because the previous ones had failed to keep the lid on labour unrest. Community psychiatry is an escalating technology because the scale of labour organization and struggles is escalating.

In the years before World War II, unions had opposed industrial psychology techniques; protesting against Taylorism, rejecting company unions, and refusing to participate in human relations-style counselling and co-optation ventures. Since industrial psychology programmes before the war were run directly by the managements of each separate business, it was easier for workers to see that their function was anti-labour, and to incorporate actions against these programmes in their general bargaining strategy.

Yet it was more difficult, at first, to perceive that community psychiatry programmes also were designed to maintain social control. And so, although labour did not especially support community psychiatry (it was scarcely consulted), it also did not oppose it. By the 1960's, however, with the decarceration movement, the expansion of community mental health clinics, and the growing use of coercive psychiatric techniques, the groups that were most directly affected began to organize to attack community psychiatry programmes.

The first to organize were ex-mental patients, who protested against inhumane treatments, pejorative labelling, and denial of mental patients' civil liberties. They were joined by newly organized unions of mental health workers, who demanded job security, career ladders, controls on the overdrugging of patients, and adequate staff-patient ratios, both in mental hospitals and in community facilities, so that they could provide responsible care. By the late 1960's, a broader range of affected groups had joined the movement. Minority group organizations in areas where community psychiatry

139

programmes were imposed staged effective protests against the fraud of "community participation," the victim-blaming medical model of treatment, the dependency and addiction caused by methadone maintenance programmes (as opposed to real cures), and government complicity in maintaining oppressive social conditions. "Indigenous non-professional" mental health workers went on strike to protest many of these same issues. Militant black, Latino, anti-war, women's, and gay groups denounced community psychiatry programmes as sexist, racist, and oppressive.

As a result of these movements, the NIMH lost much of its credibility as a benevolent, neutral, progressive agency. It was forced to abandon its most visible forays into low-income communities, to guarantee some degree of job security to mental health workers, to set higher standards of ethical behaviour toward patients and research subjects, and to grant some basic civil liberties to mental patients. Although these accomplishments did not alter the basically oppressive nature of community psychiatry, they did represent victories.

It is important to note that these victories were won by a relatively small and unorganized assortment of separate groups. Since 1970, the antipsychiatry movement, representing mostly ex-mental patients, has grown stronger and better organized, unified under the international umbrella organizations NAPA (Network Against Psychiatric Assault) and MPLF (Mental Patients Liberation Front). The women's, gay, and minority group movements also have matured, and they have continued to win concessions from the psychiatric establishment.

However, the groups which have been most active in opposing community psychiatry, by and large, represent marginally employed populations and low-income mental health workers. Their isolation from broader political and labour struggles limits both their base of support and their political analysis. They tend to view community psychiatry as the main enemy, leading to distorted theories that psychiatrists run the government in a "therapeutic state." They confine their protests to specific, particularly objectionable practices of community psychiatry, and confine their positive programmes largely to self-improvement through Zen, natural food, and peer support. As a result, a number of their struggles have been easily co-opted or defeated by bureaucratic red tape and the government's ability to pit groups against each other in competition for funding.

Mainstream labour groups have not yet seriously addressed the threat of community psychiatry, largely because the psychiatric programmes directed at workers are well camouflaged. Much of the treatment of workers takes place outside the workplace — in the offices of family doctors and in public mental health centres, mental hospitals, and drug and alcohol treatment programmes. The stigma associated with mental illness, not to mention the threat it poses to employability, keeps workers from discussing their emotional symptoms openly, especially when there are so many places where one can get "help" without others knowing.

Management-run treatment programmes appear on the surface to have little to do with these non-job-related psychiatric treatments (although they are heavily subsidized with public funds and expertise), and so whatever protests workers wage against psychiatric treatment tend to focus only on the local occupational programme. In addition, employers often have been able to slip mental health "services" into a broad occupational health package, and thereby to put workers in the position of accepting them as part of a benefit for which they fought. However, many unions have managed to see through this stratagem:

> The development of multiple issue employee assistance policies (often called "broadbrush" programs) has stirred up considerable union resistance. Such broadbrush programs, encompassing a variety of behavioral problems under one program, are viewed by many union officials as extending management's option to deal with mental health, an area of traditional union suspicion. Such a broadbrush program can be viewed as an open-ended device for management control of practically any form of dissent.[266]

We can expect, however, that as economic conditions deteriorate further, employers will intensify the "maddening" aspects of work — speed-up, job insecurity, occupational hazards, and attacks on wages and benefits. And we can also expect that the government will subsidize further expansions of community psychiatry to counteract both the psychological breakdowns resulting from work pressure and the rising militancy of workers in struggling against those pressures. Battles directly against community psychiatry may well become an arena of struggle in store for workers.

If such a struggle is to be effective, there are several strategic points which emerge from this study as crucial. Firstly, workers need to be clear about what the enemy is and about who their friends are. The "enemy" is no longer just the specific employer, but the entire capitalist class and its State. As community psychiatry now exists, employers can manage quite well without actually running their own private treatment programmes by referring "problem" employees to outside treatment by HMO's (Health Maintenance Organizations), private doctors, and public mental health programmes. They have access to public computer records and publicly funded research and training programmes. To prevent psychiatric social control of workers, effectively, all of these programmes must be attacked.

For friends, workers must ally with a broader population than just the members of their own union locals. In addition to other labour organizations, workers can well cooperate with other populations which are also protesting psychiatric oppression—organized ex-mental patients, mental health workers, women, prisoners, and Third World liberation movements.

Another area of common concern is with parents of school-age children. From the perspective of business, children represent the future labour force, and therefore children tend to be subjected to psychiatric innovations similar to those of their parents. This practice has a long history dating to the early days of the National Committee for Mental Hygiene and the child guidance clinics it organized. Since then, the link between public education and community psychiatry has grown increasingly intimate. Children are exposed to personality and intelligence tests, vocational tracking, "non-directive" counselling (as well as highly directive coercion), and, most recently and perhaps most dangerously, sophisticated behav-

142

iour modification programmes and psychotropic drugs. A detailed analysis of this process is beyond the scope of this study; but as a strategic question, it is important to recognize and fight the powerful tools that these techniques give business in preparing children to become subservient, other-directed, and anti-revolutionary workers.

We might do well to remember that community psychiatry has consistently been a defensive weapon against the power of united labour militancy. Viewed in isolation, community psychiatry's expansion may seem intimidating. But in the context of its direct response to labour unrest, we can see that community psychiatry's development derives largely from the vulnerability of business. Although the weapons of community psychiatry have grown more sophisticated and have spread to treat an ever larger proportion of the world population, the labour force which it addresses also has grown in size, sophistication, and militancy. During this period of economic instability and preparation for war, we can expect community psychiatry to become more extensive and more coercive. But, as in the past, workers can mobilize to fight back effectively, because they are not passive victims but active combatants.

FOOTNOTES

1. Cerletti, V. In L. Bellak (Ed.), *Contemporary European Psychiatry*. New York: Grove Press, 1961, pp. 189-198; Hoff, H., & Arnold, O.H. "Germany and Austria." Same volume, pp. 63-86.
2. Bellak, L. "Some personal reflections on European and American psychiatry." In L. Bellak (Ed.), *Contemporary European Psychiatry*. New York: Grove Press, 1961, pp. ix-x.
3. Hoff & Arnold, *op. cit.*, p. 109.
4. Cloutier, F. "International activities: An integrated overview." In H.P. David (Ed.), *International Trends in Mental Health*. New York: McGraw-Hill, 1966.
5. David, H.P. "Mental health grants: International progress and problems." In H.P. David (Ed.), *International Trends in Mental Health*. New York: McGraw-Hill, 1966; Lin, T-Y. "Evolution of mental health programme in Taiwan." *American Journal of Psychiatry*, 1961, 117, 961-971.
6. Langfeldt, G. "Scandinavia." In L. Bellak (Ed.), *Contemporary European Psychiatry*. New York: Grove Press, 1961., p. 220.
7. Expert Committee on Mental Health. *Report on the First Session, World Health Organization Technical Report Series #9*. Geneva: World Health Organization, 1950; Sangsingkeo, P. "Mental health in developing countries." In H.P. David (Ed.), *International Trends in Mental Health*. New York: McGraw-Hill, 1966.
8. Chisholm, B. "Introductory remarks." *Proceedings of the International Conference on Mental Hygiene* (Vol. 4). In *International Congress on Mental Health*. London: A.K. Lewis and Company, 1948; Expert Committee, *op. cit.*, pp. 8-12.
9. President's Commission on Mental Health. *Task Panel Reports Submitted to the President's Commission on Mental Health* (Vol. 1). Washington: U.S. Government Printing Office, 1978, p. viii.
10. Bellak, L. "Community psychiatry: The third psychiatric revolution." In L. Bellak (Ed.), *Handbook of Community Psychiatry and Community Mental Health*. New York: Grune and Stratton, 1964.
11. Felix, R.H. "The National Mental Health Act: How it can operate to meet a national problem." *Mental Hygiene*, 1947, 31, 363-373, p. 364.
12. Lawson, F.S. "The Saskatchewan Plan." *The Canadian Nurse*, 1967, 63, 28.
13. Goffman, E. *Asylums: Essays on the social situation of mental patients and other inmates*. Garden City, N.Y.: Doubleday, 1961.

14. Burrows, W.G. "Community psychiatry—Another bandwagon?" *Canadian Psychiatric Association Journal*, 1969, 14, 105-114; Citizen's Medical Reference Bureau. *Letter to House Sub-Committee.* U.S. Congress, House Committee on Interstate and Foreign Commerce, 79th Congress, 1st Session, 1945; Frazier, S.H., & Pokerny, A.D. *Report of a Consultation to the Minister of Public Health on the Psychiatric Services of Saskatchewan.* Regina, 1968.

15. Smith, D. "The statistics on mental illness: (What they will not tell us about women and why)." In D.E. Smith & S.J. David (Eds.), *Women Look at Psychiatry.* Vancouver: Press Gang Publishers, 1975.

16. Kouri, D., & Stirling, R. *Unemployment Indexes—The Canadian Context.* Unpublished paper, Sample Survey, University of Regina, 1979.

17. President's Commission, *op. cit.*, pp. 2-10.

18. Brown, B.S. "Foreword." In H.J. Weiner, S.W. Akabas & J.J. Sommer. *Mental Health in the World of Work.* New York: Association Press, 1973, pp. 10-11.

19. McLean, A.A., & Taylor, G.C. *Mental Health in Industry.* New York: McGraw-Hill, 1958, pp. 30-31.

20. Bellak, L. "Community mental health as a branch of public health." In L. Bellak & H.H. Barten (Eds.), *Progress in Community Mental Health* (Vol. 1). New York: Grune and Stratton, 1969, p. 253.

21. Shagass, C. *Modern Problems of Pharmacopsychiatry* (Vol. 6, *The Role of Drugs in Community Psychiatry*). Philadelphia: Karger, Basil, 1971, p. 4.

22. Chu, F.D., & Trotter, S. *The Madness Establishment: Ralph Nader's Study Group report on the National Institute of Mental Health.* New York: Grossman, 1974, p. 6.

23. Magaro, P.A., Gripp, R., & McDowell, D.J. *The Mental Health Industry: A cultural phenomenon.* New York: John Wiley and Sons, 1978, p. 12.

24. Burrows, *op. cit.*, p. 112.

25. Chu & Trotter, *op. cit.*, p. 7.

26. Ehrenreich, B., & Ehrenreich, J. "Medicine and social control." In B.R. Mandell (Ed.), *Welfare in America: Controlling the "dangerous classes".* Englewood Cliffs, N.J.: Prentice-Hall, 1975, p. 140.

27. *Ibid.*, p. 139.

28. Szasz, T.S. *Ideology and Insanity: Essays on the psychiatric dehumanization of man.* Garden City, N.Y.: Doubleday, Anchor, 1970, p. 224.

29. Leifer, R. *In the Name of Mental Health: The social functions of psychiatry*. New York: Science House, 1969, pp. 98-99.
30. *Ibid.*, p. 242.
31. *Ibid.*, p. 99.
32. Brandt, A. *Reality Police: The experience of insanity in America*. New York: William Morrow and Company, 1975, p. 272.
33. Scull, A.T. *Decarceration: Community treatment and the deviant. A radical view*. Englewood Cliffs, N.J.: Prentice-Hall, 1977, pp. 9-10.
34. Cooper, D. "Beyond anti-psychiatry." *State and Mind*, 1979, 7(2), 15-16, p. 15.
35. Latz, J. "Keep left for change." *Madness Network News*, 1979, 5(3), 5, p. 5.
36. D'Arcy, C., & Brockman, J. "Changing public recognition of psychiatric symptoms: Blackfoot revisited," *Journal of Health and Social Behavior*, 1976, 17, 302-310; D'Arcy, C., & Brockman, J. "Public rejection of the ex-mental patient: Are attitudes changing?" *Canadian Review of Sociology and Anthropology*, 1977, 14, 68-80; Turner, C.O., & Spivak, G. "Conceptions of mental illness among low income urban women." *The Forum of the Department of Mental Health Services, Hahneman Medical College and Hospital*, 1974, 3(3), 29-37.
37. Ehrenreich & Ehrenreich (1975), *op. cit.*, p. 141.
38. Navarro, V. "Political power, the state, and their implications in medicine." *The Review of Radical Political Economics*, 1977, 9(1), 61-80, p. 63.
39. Panitch, L. Editor's preface and "The role and nature of the Canadian state." In L. Panitch (Ed.), *The Canadian State: Political economy and political power*. Toronto: University of Toronto Press, 1977, p. 14.
40. Spitzer, S. "Toward a Marxian theory of deviance." *Social Problems*, 1975, 22, 638-651, p. 645.
41. Ehrenreich & Ehrenreich (1975), *op. cit.*, pp. 146-147.
42. Spitzer, *op. cit.*, p. 645.
43. *Ibid.*, p. 648.
44. Ehrenreich & Ehrenreich (1975), *op. cit.*, p. 147.
45. *Ibid.*
46. Miliband, R. *The State in Capitalist Society: The analysis of the Western system of power*. London: Quartet Books, 1969, p. 10.
47. Mclean, D., Smith, S., & Hill, J. *Workmen's Compensation*. Unpublished manuscript, University of Regina, 1975.
48. Piven, F.F., & Cloward, R. *Regulating the Poor*. New York: Random House, 1971.

49. Deaton, R. "The fiscal crisis in the state." In D.I. Roussopoulos (Ed.), *The Political Economy of the State: Québec/Canada/U.S.A.* Montréal: Black Rose Books, 1973, pp. 24-25.

50. Krause, E.A. *Power and Illness: The political sociology of health and medical care.* New York: Elsevier, 1977, pp. 320-321.

51. Cassell, W.A., Smith, C.M., Grunberg, F., Boan, J.A., & Thomas, R.F. "Comparing costs of hospital and community care." *Hospital and Community Psychiatry*, 1972, 23(7), 197-200; Murphy, J.A., & Datel, W.E. "A cost-benefit analysis of community versus institutional living." *Hospital and Community Psychiatry*, 1976, 27(3), 165-170; Scull, *op. cit.*, pp. 144-148.

52. Shatan, C. "Community psychiatry—Stretcher bearer of the social order?" *International Journal of Psychiatry*, 1969, 7, 312-321, p. 319.

53. Scull, *op. cit.*, p. 150.

54. Davies, W. *The Pharmaceutial Industry: A personal study. A medical, economic and political survey of the world-wide pharmaceutical industry.* Oxford: Pergamon, 1967, p. 199.

55. Scull, *op. cit.*

56. *Ibid.*, pp. 143-144.

57. Ehrenreich & Ehrenreich (1975), *op. cit.*, p. 162.

58. Spitzer, *op. cit.*, p. 649.

59. ADAMHA (Alcohol, Drug Abuse, and Mental Health Administration). *Alcohol, Drug Abuse, Mental Health, Research Grant Awards*, Fiscal Year 1974. Rockwille, Md., N.A., 1974.

60. Chrichton, A. *Mental Health and Social Policy in Canada.* Ottawa: Canadian Mental Health Association, 1973; Expert Committee on Mental Health. *The Community Mental Hospital*, World Health Organization Technical Report Series #73. Geneva: World Health Organization, 1953; Fein, R. *Economics of Mental Illness.* (Monograph Series #2: Joint Commission on Mental Illness and Health.) New York: Basic Books, 1958; Joint Commission on Mental Illness and Health. *Action for Mental Health.* New York: Basic Books, 1961; Kennedy, J.F. *Message from the President of the United States Relative to Mental Illness and Mental Retardation*, Document #58. 88th Congress, First Session, U.S. House of Representatives, Feb. 5, 1963, p. 13; Martel, P.G. *A Role of the Federal Government in Mental Health: A report prepared for the Department of National Health and Welfare.* Sherbrooke, Qué.: University of Sherbrooke, 1973; McKerracher, D.G. *Trends in Psychiatric Care.* Royal Commission on Health Services (Hall Commission). Ottawa, 1966; President's Commission, *op. cit.*; Richman, A. *Psychiatric Care in Canada: Extent and results.* Royal Commission on Health Services (Hall Commission). Ottawa: Queen's Printer, 1966; Tyhurst,

J.S., Chalke, F.R., Lawson, F.S., McNeil, B.H., Roberts, C.A., Taylor, G.C., Weil, R.J., & Griffin. *More for the Mind: A study of psychiatric services in Canada.* Toronto: Canadian Mental Health Association, 1963.

61. Tuke, D.H. *The Insane in the United States and Canada.* London: H.K. Lewis, 1885, pp. 8-15.

62. Scull, *op. cit.*, pp. 64-65; Deutsch, A. *The Mentally Ill in America: A history of their treatment from colonial times* (2nd ed.). New York: Columbia University Press, 1949, pp. 230-271.

63. Brenner, M.J. *Mental Illness and the Economy.* Cambridge, Mass.: Harvard University Press, 1973.

64. Bucklow, M. "A new role for the work group." In J. Munro (Ed.), *Classes, Conflict, and Control: Studies in criminal justice management.* Cincinnati: Anderson Publishing Company, 1976, p. 389.

65. Butler, J.L. "Industrial psychiatry and social psychiatry." *Symposium on Preventative and Social Psychiatry, Walter Reed Institute of Research.* Washington: U.S. Government Printing Office, 1957, p. 231.

66. Yolles, S.F. "Mental health at work." In A. McLean (Ed.), *To Work is Human: Mental health and the business community.* New York: Macmillan Company, 1967, p. 47.

67. Lawrence, P.R. "How to live with resistance to change." In E.C. Bursk (Ed.), *Human Relations for Management: The newer perspective.* New York: Harper and Brothers, 1966, p. 343.

68. Brown, *op. cit.*, pp. 10-11.

69. Rubin, L.B. *Worlds of Pain: Life in the working-class family.* New York: Basic Books, 1976, p. 159.

70. Selekman, B.M. *Labor Relations and Human Relations.* New York: McGraw-Hill, 1947, pp. 2-3.

71. Giberson, L.G. "Industrial psychiatry: A wartime survey." *The Medical Clinics of North America,* 1942, 26, 1085-1103, p. 1085.

72. Mayo, E. *The Social Problems of an Industrial Civilization.* Boston: Harvard University Press, 1946, pp. 9-10.

73. Terhune, W.B. "Advances in psychotherapy." In J.C. Flugel (Ed.), *Proceedings of the International Congress on Mental Health,* London, 1948 (Vol. 3). London: H.K. Lewis and Company, 1948, pp. 98-106.

74. Cooper, M.R., Morgan, B.S., Foley, P.M., & Kaplan, L.B. "Changing employee values: Deepening discontent." *Harvard Business Review,* Jan.-Feb., 1979, 117-125.

75. Brecher, J. *Strike!* Boston: South End Press, 1972, pp. 264-293; Roberts, B.C., Okamato, H., & Lodge, G.C. *Collective Bargaining and Employee Participation in Western Europe, North*

America and Japan, Report to the Trilateral Task Force on Industrial Relations of the Trilateral Commission. New York: The Trilateral Commission, 1979, p. 21.

76. Roberts, Okamato & Lodge, *op. cit.*, pp. 85-86.
77. Yolles, S.F. *Community Psychiatry: Alternative to chaos.* Unpublished speech presented at Psychiatric Grand Rounds, University of Utah School of Medicine, Department of Psychiatry. Salt Lake City, Utah, April 11, 1968, pp. 17-18.
78. See Chapters 5 and 6 of this book.
79. Bailey, R., & Brake, M. "Introduction: Social work in the welfare state." In R. Bailey & M. Brake (Eds.), *Radical Social Work.* New York: Pantheon, 1975.
80. Kowaluk, L. "Working in a social agency." In W. Johnson (Ed.), *Working in Canada.* Montréal: Black Rose Books, 1975; Ostrum, E. "On the meaning and measurement of output and efficiency in the provision of urban police services." In J. Munro (Ed.), *Classes, Conflict, and Control: Studies in criminal justice management.* Cincinnati: Anderson, 1976; Patry, B. "Taylorism comes to the social services." *Monthly Review,* 1978, 30(5), 30-37.
81. Santiestevan, H. *Deinstitutionalization: Out of their beds and into the streets.* Washington: American Federation of State, County and Municipal Workers, Dec. 1976, p. 16.
82. Collins, R.T. "Occupational psychiatry." *American Journal of Psychiatry,* 1962, 118, 604-609, p. 608.
83. Salmon, T.W. "Mental hygiene." In M.J. Rosenau (Ed.), *Preventative Medicine and Hygiene* (3rd ed.). New York: Appleton, 1917, pp. 352-353.
84. Brenner, *op. cit.*; Brook, A. "Psychiatric disorders in industry." *British Journal of Hospital Medicine,* 1976, 15(5), 484-492; Buck, V.E. *Working Under Pressure.* New York: Crane, Russak and Company, 1972; Grinker, R.R., & Spiegel, J.P. *Men Under Stress.* New York: Blakiston, 1945; Kohn, M.L., & Schooler, C. "Occupational experience and psychological functioning: An assessment of reciprocal effects." *American Sociological Review,* 1973, 38, 97-118; Schuckit, M.A., & Gunderson, E.K.E. "The association between alcoholism and job type in the U.S. Navy." *Quarterly Journal of Studies in Alcoholism,* 1974, 35, 577-585.
85. Gavin, J.F. "Occupational mental health: Forces and trends." *Personnel Journal,* April 1977, 198-201, p. 198.
86. Eyer, J., & Sterling, P. "Stress-related mortality and social organization." *The Review of Radical Political Economics,* 1977, 9(1), 1-44, pp. 26-27.
87. Garson, B. *All the Livelong Day.* New York: Penguin, 1975, p. 218.

88. Gooding, J. "Blue-collar blues on the assembly line." *Fortune*, 1970, 82(6), 69-71, 112-117, p. 71.
89. Garson, *op. cit.*, pp. 211-212.
90. Hofstadter, R. "Introduction." In R. Hofstadter (Ed.), *The Progressive Movement, 1900-1915.* Englewood Cliffs, N.J.: Prentice-Hall, 1963, pp. 1-2.
91. Rayback, J.G. *A History of American Labor.* New York: Free Press, 1966, pp. 162-174.
92. Jarrett, M.C. "The mental hygiene of industry: Report of progress on work undertaken under the Engineering Foundation of New York City." *Mental Hygiene*, 1920, 4, 867-884.
93. Ford, H., II "The challenge of human engineering." *Advanced Management*, 1946, 11, 48-52, pp. 49-50.
94. Taylor, F.W. *The Principles of Scientific Management.* New York: Norton, 1967, p. 125.
95. Hoxie, R.F. *Scientific Management and Labor.* New York: D. Appleton, 1918, pp. 15-17.
96. Rubin, *op. cit.*, pp. 160-161.
97. I am not suggesting that all cases of these social pathologies are directly work-related. Under capitalism, the quality of social life in general deteriorates, disintegrating families and communities, debasing culture, polluting the environment, and so forth. It is interesting to note that even outside of work, Taylor's principles have been applied. We are now witnessing Taylorization of consumption in the form of self-service banks, gas stations, and restaurants, which require us to labour in rigidly defined ways in return for small price discounts, and which, at the same time, replace or degrade the jobs of people formerly employed in these service industries. Self-service is one of the biggest tools for raising productivity in the service industry.
98. Brown, J.A.C. *The Social Psychology of Industry: Human relations in the factory.* Baltimore: Penguin, 1954, p. 14.
99. Brooks, T.R. *Toil and Trouble: A history of American labor* (2nd ed.). New York: Dell, 1971, pp. xiv-xv.
100. *Ibid.*, p. viii; Rayback, *op. cit.*, p. 304.
101. Drucker, P.F. *The Practice of Management.* New York: Harper and Row, 1954, pp. 285-286.
102. Bernstein, I. *The Lean Years: A history of the American worker 1920-1933.* Baltimore: Penguin, 1960, pp. 159-160.
103. Rockefeller, D., Jr. "The personal relation in industry." An address delivered at Cornell University, Jan. 11, 1917. Reprinted in L. Stern & P. Taft (Eds.), *The Management of Workers: Selected arguments.* New York: Arno and the New York Times, 1971, p. 78.

104. Lewisohn, S.A. *The New Leadership in Industry*. New York: E.P. Dutton and Company, 1926, pp. 24-25.

105. Braverman, H. *Labor and Monopoly Capital: The degradation of work in the twentieth century*. New York: Monthly Review Press, 1974, p. 51.

106. Deutsch, *op. cit.*, pp. 314-315.

107. Bromberg, W. *The Mind of Man*. New York: Harper and Brothers, 1937, p. 217.

108. Southard, E.E. "The modern specialist in unrest: A place for the psychiatrist." *Mental Hygiene*, 1920A, 4, 550-563, p. 557.

109. Giberson, *op. cit.*, p. 1088.

110. Deutsch, *op. cit.*, p. 317.

111. *Ibid.*, pp. 317-320; Southard, *op. cit.*.

112. Southard, E.E. "The movement for a mental hygiene of industry." *Mental Hygiene*, 1920B, 4, 43-64, pp. 47-48.

113. Giberson, *op. cit.*, pp. 1088-1089; Noble, D.F. *America by Design: Science, technology, and the rise of corporate capitalism*. New York: Alfred A. Knopf, 1977, pp. 276-320.

114. Baker, R.S. *The New Industrial Unrest: Reasons and remedies*. Garden City, N.Y.: Doubleday, Page and Company, 1920, pp. 3-25; Hutt, A. *British Trade Unionism: A short history*. London: Lawrence and Wishart, 1975, pp. 84-110.

115. Rayback, *op. cit.*, p. 279.

116. Rennie, T.A.C., Swackhamer, G., & Woodward, L.E. "Toward industrial mental health: An historical review." *Mental Hygiene*, 1947, 31, 66-85, p. 67.

117. Anderson, V.V. *Psychiatry in Industry*. New York: Harper, 1929; Bingham, W.V. "Management's concern with research in industrial psychology." *Harvard Business Review*, 1931, 10(1), 40-53; Giberson, *op. cit.*, pp. 1099-1100; Jarrett, *op. cit.*.

118. Baker, *op. cit.*, p. 67.

119. Bingham, *op. cit.*, p. 52.

120. Edison, T.A. "Editorial." *Industrial Management and Engineering Magazine*, Oct. 1920, p. 4.

121. Jarrett, *op. cit.*, p. 872.

122. Southard, 1920B, *op. cit.*, p. 556.

123. *Ibid.*, p. 558.

124. *Ibid.*, p. 561.

125. Mayo, *op. cit.*, p. 20.

126. *Ibid.*, p. 111.

127. Roethlisberger, F.J. "The foreman: Master and victim of double talk." *Harvard Business Review*, 1945, 23, 283-299, p. 299.

128. Roethlisberger, F.J. *Management and Morale*. Cambridge, Mass.: Harvard University Press, 1941, p. 16.

129. Bramel, D., & Friend, R. *Human Relations in Industry: The famous Hawthorne Experiments.* Unpublished paper, State University of New York at Stony Brook, 1978; Carey A. "The Hawthorne Studies: A radical criticism." *American Sociological Review*, 1967, 32(3), 403-416; Gilbert, M. "Review of Management and the Worker by Roethlisberger and Dickson." *American Journal of Sociology*, 1940, 46(1), 98-101; Landsberger, H.A. *Hawthorne Revisited*. Ithaca, N.Y.: Cornell University Press, 1958; Sykes, A.J.M. "Economic interest and the Hawthorne researches." *Human Relations*, 1965, 18, 253-263.

130. Bramel & Friend, *op. cit.*, p. 12.

131. Jackson, D.C. "Lighting in industry." *Journal of the Franklin Institute*, 1928, 205, 289-302, p. 289.

132. Whyte, W.F. "Human relations theory—A progress report." *Harvard Business Review*, 1956, 34(5), 125-132, p. 125.

133. "Fruitful errors of Elton Mayo." *Fortune*, 1946, 34(5), 181-184, 248, p. 181.

134. Bernstein, *op. cit.*, pp. 164-165.

135. *Ibid.*, p. 169.

136. Mayo, *op. cit.*, pp. 74-75.

137. *Ibid.*, p. 84.

138. *Ibid.*.

139. *Ibid.*, p. 78.

140. *Ibid.*.

141. Roethlisberger, F.J., & Dickson, W.J. *Management and the Worker: An account of a research program conducted by the Western Electric Company, Hawthorne Works, Chicago.* Cambridge, Mass.: Harvard University Press, 1939, p. 267.

142. Marcuse, H. *One-Dimensional Man: Studies in the ideology of advanced industrial society.* Boston: Beacon Press, 1964, pp. 109-111.

143. Bernstein, I. *Turbulent Years: A history of the American worker 1933-1941.* Boston: Houghton Mifflin Company, 1969, p. 791.

144. Zusman, J. "The philosophic basis for a community and social psychiatry." In W.E. Barton & C.J. Sanborn (Eds.), *An Assessment of the Community Mental Health Movement.* Toronto: Lexington Books, 1975, pp. 25-26.

145. Bass, B.M., & Barrett, G.V. *Man, Work and Organizations: An introduction to industrial and organizational psychology.* Boston: Allyn and Bacon, 1972, p. 10.

146. Barkin, S. "A trade unionist appraises management personnel philosophy." In E.C. Bursk (Ed.), *Human Relations for Management: The newer perspective.* New York: Harper and Brothers, 1956, pp. 362-363.

147. Drucker, *op. cit.*, p. 279.

148. Saskatchewan Department of Public Works. *Annual Report for the Fiscal Year Ended April 30, 1933.* Regina: Author, 1933, p. 60.

149. Deutsch, *op. cit.*, p. 449.

150. Kahan, F.H. *Brains and Bricks: A history of the Yorkton Psychiatric Centre.* Regina: White Cross, 1965, p. 21.

151. Rees, T.P. "The changing pattern of mental health services." *Royal Society for the Promotion of Health Journal,* 1959, 79(4), 354-356, p. 355.

152. Giberson, L.G. "Psychiatry and industry." *The Labor Gazette,* April 1938, 401-404, p. 401.

153. Rayback, *op. cit.*, p. 377.

154. Burlingame, C.C. "Psychiatry in industry." *American Journal of Psychiatry,* 1946, 103, 549-553, p. 550.

155. Bramel & Friend, *op. cit.*, p. 25.

156. National Committee for Mental Hygiene. *Annual Report 1941-1942.* New York: Author, 1942, p. 9.

157. National Committee for Mental Hygiene. *Annual Report 1940-1941.* New York: Author, 1941, p. 11.

158. *Ibid.*, pp. 16-17.

159. Yolles, S.F. "Past, present and 1980: Trend projections." In L. Bellak & H.H. Barten (Eds.), *Progress in Community Mental Health.* New York: Grune and Stratton, 1969, p. 10.

160. Bylinsky, G. *Mood Control.* New York: Charles Scribner's Sons, 1978, p. 4.

161. Giberson (1942), *op. cit.*, p. 1097.

162. Foley, H.A. *Community Mental Health Legislation: The formative process.* Lexington, Mass.: Lexington Books, 1975, p. 1.

163. *Ibid.*, p. 4.

164. Brooks, *op. cit.*, p. 210.

165. Selekman, *op. cit.*, p. 5.

166. Finkel, A. "Origins of the welfare state in Canada." In L. Panitch (Ed.), *The Canadian State: Political economy and political power.* Toronto: University of Toronto Press, 1977, p. 361.

167. Greene, F. *What Every American Should Know About Imperialism.* New York: Random House, 1970, pp. 113-114.

154

168. Aldridge, J.F.L. "Emotional illness and the working environment." In P.R. Davis (Ed.), *Proceedings of the Symposium on Performance Under Sub-Optimal Conditions.* London: Taylor & Francis Ltd., 1970, p. 84.

169. Trist, L., & Bamforth, K.W. "Some social and psychological consequences of the longwall method of coal getting." *Human Relations*, 1951, 4, 3-38.

170. Rennie, T.A.C., & Woodward, L.E. *Mental Health in Modern Society.* New York: The Commonwealth Fund, 1948, pp. 286-287; McLean, A.A. "Occupational mental health: Review of an emerging art." In R.T. Collins (Ed.), *Occupational Psychiatry.* Boston: Little, Brown and Company, 1969.

171. Huberman, L., & Sweezy, P.M. "The aim is thought control." *Monthly Review*, 1955, 7(3), 81-90, p. 86.

172. *House of Representatives Report #1445*, 79th Congress, 1st Session. National Mental Health Act. House Reports. 79th Congress, 1st Session (Jan.-Dec. 21, 1945), miscellaneous (Vol. 6). Washington: U.S. Government Printing Office, 1945, p. 3.

173. *Ibid.*, pp. 3-4.

174. Foley, *op. cit.*, p. 4.

175. *Ibid.*, p. 5.

176. *Ibid.*, p. 8.

177. Mindus, E. *Industrial Psychology in Great Britain, the United States, and Canada: A report to the World Health Organization.* Stockholm: Institute of Applied Psychology, University of Stockholm, 1953, p. 19.

178. D'Alonzo, C.A. "Rehabilitation of workers addicted to alcohol." *Industrial Medicine and Surgery*, 1961, 30, 14-15; *Occupational Alcoholism: Problems, programs, and progress.* U.S. Department of Health, Education and Welfare Publication # ADM 75-178. Rockville, Md.: ADAMHA, 1973.

179. Dorgan, J. "Foster home care for the psychiatric patient." *Canadian Journal of Public Health*, 1958, 49(10), 411-419; Fein, R. *Economics of Mental Illness.* (Monograph Series #2: Joint Commission on Mental Illness and Health). New York: Basic Books, 1958; Love, E.J., & Hobbs, G.E. "Changing patterns of mental hospital practice 1940-1962." *Canadian Psychiatric Association Journal*, 1971, 16, 77-81; MacClay, W.S. "Trends in the British mental health service." In *Proceedings of the Third World Congress of Psychiatry* (Vol. 1). Montréal: University of Toronto Press, 1961, 98-102.

180. Hargreaves, G.R. "The next steps in mental health." *Royal Society for the Promotion of Health Journal*, 1959, 79(4), 357-360, p. 358.

181. Richman, *op. cit.*, p. 34.

182. Brown, J.A.C., *op. cit.*, pp. 265-266; Cruickshank, W.M. "Mental hygiene in industry." *Canadian Journal of Public Health*, 1955, 46(12), p. 475; Gadourek, I. "Absenteeism: An unsolved problem." In R.T. Collins (Ed.), *Occupational Psychiatry*. Boston: Little, Brown and Company, 1969, p. 195; Plumb, R.K. "One-third adults upset." *New York Times*, Oct. 13, 1954, p. 21.

183. Kolb, L.C. "The current problem of research involving human beings: The curse of the holy grail." In D.H. Efron, J.O. Cole, J. Levine & J.R. Wittenborn (Eds.), *Psychopharmacology: A review of progress 1957-1967*. Public Health Service Publication #1836. Washington: U.S. Government Printing Office, 1968, p. 335.

184. Levinson, H. "Dilemmas of the occupational physician in mental health programming—Part II." *Journal of Occupational Medicine*, 1960, 2(5), 205-208, p. 207.

185. Mindus, *op. cit.*.

186. Albee, G.W. "The manpower crisis in mental health." In R.H. Felix (Ed.), *Mental Health and Social Welfare*. New York: Columbia University Press, 1961; Fein, *op. cit.*; Kline, N.S. "Pharmaceuticals in the treatment of psychiatric patients." *Mental Hygiene*, 1957, 41, 207-221, p. 208.

187. Collins, R.T. "Industrial psychiatry." *American Journal of Psychiatry*, 1956, 112, 546-549; Gomberg, W. "The use of psychology in industry: A trade union point of view." *Management Science*, 1957, 3, 348-370; "Labor looks at mental health." *The Massachusetts Association for Mental Health Newsletter*, Feb.-Mar. 1954, p. 1; Mindus, *op. cit.*, p. 3; Stagner, R. "The psychologist's function in union-management relations." *Personnel Administration*, 1963, 26(1), 42-46.

188. Silverman, M., & Lee, P.R. *Pills, Profits and Politics*. Berkeley: University of California Press, 1974.

189. Segal, J. (Ed.), *Research in the Service of Mental Health*. Rockville, Md.: National Institute of Mental Health, 1975, p. 329.

190. Evans, W.O., & Kline, N.S. (Eds.), *The Psychopharmacology of the Normal Human*. Springfield, Ill.: Charles C. Thomas, 1969.

191. Bylinsky, *op. cit.*, p. 5.

192. *Ibid.*, pp. 152-154; Caldwell, A.E. *Origins of Psychopharmacology: From CPZ to LSD*. Springfield, Ill.: Charles C. Thomas, 1970, pp. 35, 79.

193. Hersch, C. "The discontent explosion in mental health." *American Psychologist*, 1968, 23, 497-506, p. 504.

194. Laurence, W.L. "Drug found help in schizophrenia." *New York Times*, Feb. 4, 1955, p. 28.

195. Allodi, F., & Kedward, H.B. "The evolution of the mental hospital in Canada." *Canadian Journal of Public Health*, 1977, 68, 219-224, p. 221; Brill, H., & Patton, R.E. "The impact of modern chemotherapy on hospital organization, psychiatric care, and public policies: Its scope and its limits." *Proceedings of the Third World Congress of Psychiatry*. Toronto: University of Toronto Press, 1971, 3, 433-457, p. 434.

196. Gillis, J.S. "Effects of chlorpromazine and thiothixene on acute schizophrenic patients." In K.R. Hammond (Ed.), *Psychoactive Drugs and Social Judgement: Theory and research*. New York: John Wiley and Sons, 1975, p. 183.

197. Vonnegut, Mark. *The Eden Express*. New York: Bantam Books, 1975, pp. 252-253.

198. Evans, W.O. "The psychopharmacology of the normal human: Trends in research strategy." In D.H. Efron, J.O. Cole, J. Levine, & J.R. Wittenborn (Eds.), *Psychopharmacology: A review of progress, 1957-1967*. Public Health Service Publication #1836. Washington: U.S. Government Printing Office, 1968, p. 1007.

199. Bylinsky, *op. cit.*, p. 4.

200. Mintz, M. *By Prescription Only*. Boston: Beacon Press, 1967, pp. 186-295; Silverman & Lee, *op. cit.*, p. 292; Waldron, I. "Increased prescribing of Valium, Librium and other drugs — An example of the influence of economic and social factors on the practice of medicine." *International Journal of Health Services*, 1977, 7(1), 37-62.

201. Robertson, R.L., & Shriver, B.M. "The general practitioner training program of the National Institute of Mental Health: Fiscal Years 1959-1962." *Journal of Medical Education*, 1964, 39, 925-934, p. 926.

202. Muller, C. "The overmedicated society: Forces in the marketplace for medical care." *Science*, 1972, 176, 488-492, p. 488.

203. Lamb, D. " 'Epidemic' of dependency." *Guardian*, May 3, 1978, p. 11.

204. Berger, F.M., & Potterfield, J. "The effect of anti-anxiety tranquilizers on the behavior of normal people." In W.O. Evans & N.S. Kline, *op. cit.*, p. 38; Evans, W.O., & Kline, N.S. (Eds.), *Psychotropic Drugs in the Year 2000*. Springfield, Ill.: Charles C. Thomas, 1971.

205. Kline, N.S. "Pharmaceuticals in the treatment of psychiatric patients." *Mental Hygiene*, 1957, 41, 207-212, p. 208.

206. Baker, E.F., Young, M.P., Gauld, D.M., & Fleming, J.F.R. "A new look at midedial prefrontal leukotomy." *Canadian Medical Association Journal*, 1970, 102, 37-41; Balasubramanian, T.S., Kanaka, B., & Ramamurthi, B. "Surgical treatment of hyper-

157

kinetic and behavior disorders." *International Surgery*, 1970, 54(1), 18-23; Delgado, J.M.R. *Physical Control of the Mind: Toward a psychocivilized society.* New York: Harper and Row, 1969; Kohler, W.C. "Medicine's role in juvenile corrections." *American Journal of Corrections*, 1976, 38(1), 11-16.

207. Eyer & Sterling, *op. cit.*, pp. 34-35.

208. Meany, G. *What Organized Labor Expects of Management.* New York: National Association of Manufacturers, 1956, pp. 10-11.

209. Horowitz, D. *Empire and Revolution: A radical interpretation of contemporary history.* New York: Random House, 1969, p. 232.

210. *Ibid.*, p. 234.

211. Chomsky, N. "The Pentagon Papers and U.S. Imperialism in South East Asia." In (no. Ed.) *Spheres of Influence in the Age of Imperialism.* Nottingham, England: Spokesman, 1972, p. 6.

212. Sweezy, P.M. "Growing wealth, declining power." *Monthly Review*, 1974, 25(10), 1-11, p. 7.

213. Crispo, J. *Industrial Democracy in Western Europe: A North American perspective.* New York: McGraw-Hill, 1978, pp. 8-9.

214. Brecher, *op. cit.*, pp. 264-266.

215. Salpukas, A. "Workers increasingly rebel against boredom on assembly line." *New York Times*, April 2, 1972, p. N34.

216. Follman, J.F., Jr. *Alcoholics and Business: Problems, costs, solutions.* New York: Amacom, 1976, pp. 19, 79; Masi, F.A., & Spencer, G.E. "Alcoholism and employee assistance programs in industry: A new frontier for social work." *Social Thought*, 1977, 3(1), 19-27, p. 20; Ralston, A. "Employee alcoholism: Response of the largest industrials." *The Personnel Administrator*, 1977, 22(6), 50-56, p. 51.

217. Follman, *op. cit.*, pp. 20, 81-82.

218. Scher, J.M. "The impact of the drug abuser in the work organization." In J.M. Scher (Ed.), *Drug Abuse in Industry: Growing corporate dilemma.* Springfield, Ill.: Charles C. Thomas, 1973, p. 8.

219. Special Task Force to the Secretary of Health, Education and Welfare. *Work in America.* Cambridge, Mass.: MIT Press, 1973, p. 86.

220. Foley, *op. cit.*, p. 128.

221. Fleming, J.L. "Industry looks at the emotionally troubled employee." In P.A. Carone, S.N. Kieffer, L.W. Krinsky & S.F. Yolles (Eds.), *The Emotionally Troubled Employee: A challenge to industry.* New York: SUNY Press, 1976, pp. 57-58.

222. Pursch, J.A. "Pursch cites treatment barriers." *NIAAA Information and Feature Service*, Aug. 6, 1979, 62, 3, p. 3.

223. Masi & Spencer, *op. cit.*, p. 22.
224. Myers, J.M. "The psychiatric hospital looks at the emotionally troubled employee." In P.A. Carone, S.N. Kieffer, L.W. Krinsky & S.F. Yolles (Eds.), *The Emotionally Troubled Employee: A challenge to industry.* New York: SUNY Press, 1976, pp. 33-34.
225. Yolles (1968), *op. cit.*.
226. Foley, *op. cit.*, p. 31.
227. Eyer & Sterling, *op. cit.*, p. 1.
228. Foley, *op. cit.*, pp. 35-37, 59-65.
229. Yolles, S.F. "The future of community psychiatry." In W.E. Barton & C.J. Sanborn (Eds.), *An Assessment of the Community Mental Health Movement.* Lexington, Mass.: D.C. Heath and Company, 1975, p. 157.
230. Smith, C.M. "Crisis and aftermath: Community psychiatry in Saskatchewan, 1963-69." *Canadian Psychiatric Association Journal,* 1971, 16, 63-71, p. 68; Stewart, A., LaFave, H.G., Grunberg, F., & Herjanic, H. "The Weyburn experience: Reducing intake as a factor in phasing out a large psychiatric hospital." *American Journal of Psychiatry,* 1968, 125(1), 121-129, p. 123.
231. Smith, C.M. "Measuring some effects of mental illness on the home." *Canadian Psychiatric Association Journal,* 1969, 514, pp. 97-103.
232. Segal, *op. cit.*, pp. 15-21.
233. Yolles (1969), *op. cit.*, p. 5.
234. Laska, E.M., & Bank, R. *Safeguarding Psychiatric Privacy: Computer systems and their uses.* New York: John Wiley and Sons, 1975, p. 42.
235. Editorial: "Mental health programs, trends and prospects." *Canadian Journal of Public Health,* 1970, 61, 93-95, p. 94.
236. Laska & Bank, *op. cit.*, p. 369.
237. Secretary's Advisory Committee on Automated Personal Data Systems. *Records, Computers and the Rights of Citizens.* Boston: Massachusetts Institute of Technology, 1973, pp. 243-244.
238. Obers, D. " 'Tayloring' the social sciences." *State and Mind,* 1979, 7(2), 25-29, p. 28.
239. Laska & Bank, *op. cit.*, p. 18.
240. Ontario Council of Health. *Mental Health Services Personnel: A report of the Ontario Council of Health senior advisory body to the Minister of Health.* Toronto: Author, 1973, pp. 34-37.
241. "The ultimate psychiatrist." *Mental Hospitals,* July 1965, p. 196.

242. Brown, P. *Toward a Marxist Psychology*. New York: Harper and Row, 1974, pp. 647-649; Reissman, F. *New Approaches to Mental Health Treatment for Labor and Low Income Groups*. New York: National Institute of Labor Education, 1964.

243. Altman, L. "Growing use of mind-affection drugs worries F.D.A." *New York Times*, March 14, 1971, p. 1; Balter, M., Levine, J., & Rubinstein, J. *Cross-National Study of the Extent of Anti-Anxiety Sedative*. Psychopharmacology Research Bureau, NIMH. Presented at CJNP Congress, Copenhagen, Aug. 1972; Cooperstock, R. "Some factors involved in the increased prescribing of psychotropic drugs." In R. Cooperstock (Ed.), *Social Aspects of Medical Use of Psychotropic Drugs*. Toronto: Addiction Research Foundation, 1973; Doig, J. "The high cost of tranquility." *The Canadian Magazine*, July 22, 1978, pp. 3-5; President's Commission on Mental Health. *Task Panel Reports Submitted to the President's Commission on Mental Health*, Vol. 2. Washington: U.S. Government Printing Office, 1978, p. 16; Harding, J., & Wolfe, N. *Accounting for Social Environmental Determinants in Developing Alternatives to the Use of Prescribed Mood-Modifying Drugs*. Paper presented at the 13th Annual Conference of the Canadian Addictions Foundation, Calgary, Sept. 24-29, 1978; Waldron, *op. cit.*.

244. Armstrong, B. "Labor relations in mental health: A look at what's happening." *Hospital and Community Psychiatry*, 1976, 27(1), 42-52; McFadden, R.D. "Strike beginning to disrupt state services." *New York Times*, April 2, 1972, p. 1; Santiestevan, H., *op. cit.*.

245. Brown, P., *op. cit.*, pp. 647-648.

246. Miranda, M.R., & Kitano, H. "Mental health services in third world communities." *International Journal of Health Services*, 1976, 5(2), 39-49.

247. Foley, *op. cit.*, pp. 127-133; Segal, *op. cit.*, pp. 21-22.

248. Leopold, R.L. "Toward health maintenance organization." In L. Bellak (Ed.), *A Concise History of Community Psychiatry and Community Mental Health*. New York: Grune and Stratton, 1974, pp. 187-188.

249. Muszynski, S. "Mental health care and treatment: Will health planning make a difference?" *Hospital and Community Psychiatry*, 1976, 27(6), 398-400, p. 399.

250. Brown, P. "The transfer of care: U.S. mental health policy since World War II." *International Journal of Health Services*, 1979, 9(4), 645-662, p. 655.

251. Abramson, M.F. "The criminalization of mentally disordered behavior." *Hospital and Community Psychiatry*, 1972, 23(4) 101-105; Allmand, W. *The General Program for the Development of Psychiatric Services in Federal Correctional Services of Can-*

ada. Ottawa: Information Canada, 1973; Arboleda-Florez, J. "The development of a forensic psychiatric service." *Canadian Journal of Criminology and Corrections,* 1975, 17, 141-145.

252. Hoffer, A. Letter. *Canada's Mental Health,* 1977, 25(4), 34-35; Hoffer, A. *Community Psychiatry.* Unpublished manuscript, Sept. 1979.

253. Brown, P., *op. cit.,* p. 653.

254. Laing, R.D. *Do You Love Me? An entertainment in conversation and verse.* New York: Pantheon Books, 1976, p. 47.

255. Tiffany, D.W., Cavan, J.R., & Tiffany, P.M. *The Unemployed: A social-psychological portrait.* Englewood Cliffs, N.J.: Prentice-Hall, 1970, pp. 14-15.

256. National Committee (1942), *op. cit.,* p. 9.

257. Trice, H.N., Hunt, R.E., & Beyer, J.M. "Alcoholism programs in unionized work settings: Problems and prospects in union-management collaboration." *Journal of Drug Issues,* 1977, 7(2), 103-115.

258. Lehmann, H.E. "Psychoactive drugs and their influence on the dynamics of working capacity." *Journal of Occupational Medicine,* 1960, 2, 523-527, p. 527.

259. Caligari, D. "Lithium: The great pretender." *Madness Network News,* 1979, 5(5), 1, 15-17.

260. O'Connor, R.B. "The impact of emotions on production and safety." *The Menninger Quarterly,* 1958, 13(3), 1-6, p. 1.

261. Smith, G. Taped interview. Regina, Sask., Feb. 16, 1978.

262. Gershon, S., & Shaw, F.H. "Psychiatric Sequelae of chronic exposure to organophosphorous insecticides." *The Lancet,* June 24, 1961, pp. 1371-1374.

263. Kinnersly, P. *The Hazards of Work: How to fight them.* London: Pluto Press, 1973, pp. 95-120.

264. Stellman, J.M., & Daum, S.M. *Work is Dangerous to Your Health: A handbook of health hazards in the work place and what you can do about them.* New York: Random House, 1973; Wallick, F. *The American Worker: An endangered species.* New York: Ballantine Books, 1972.

265. Pilisuk, M., & Ober, L. "Torture and genocide as public health problems." *American Journal of Orthopsychiatry,* 1976, 46(3), 388-392, pp. 389-391.

266. Trice, Hunt & Beyer, *op. cit.,* p. 110.

161

BIBLIOGRAPHY

Abramson, M. F. "The criminalization of mentally disordered behavior: Possible side-effect of a new mental health law." *Hospital and Community Psychiatry*, 1972, *23(4)*, 101-105.

ADAMHA (Alcohol, Drug Abuse, and Mental Health Administration). *Alcohol, drug absue, mental health, research grant awards, Fiscal Year 1974*. Rockville, Md.: Author, 1974.

Ahmed, P.I., & Plog, S.C. "Introduction and an overview of the closing scene." *State Mental Hospitals: What happens when they close?* New York: Plenum Medical Book Company, 1976.

Albee, G.W. *Mental Health Manpower Trends.* (Monograph Series #3: Joint Commission on Mental Illness and Health). New York: Basic Books, 1959.

Albee, G.W. "The manpower crisis in mental health." In R.H. Felix (Ed.), *Mental Health and Social Welfare.* New York: Columbia University Press, 1961.

"Alcoholism: An illness of concern to labor and management." *Oil Chemical and Atomic Union News*, Oct. 1960, p. 5.

Aldridge, J.F.L. "Emotional illness and the working environment." In P.R. Davis (Ed.), *Proceedings of the Symposium on Performance Under Sub-optimal Conditions.* London: Taylor & Francis Limited, 1970.

Alix, J.P., & Boudreau, T.J. *Mental Illness: Some of the Costs.* Ottawa: Canadian Mental Health Association, 1975.

Allen, H.L. "A radical critique of Federal work and manpower programs, 1933-1974." In B.R. Mandell (Ed.), *Welfare in America: Controlling the "dangerous classes."* Englewood Cliffs, N.J.: Prentice-Hall, 1975.

Allen, P. "A consumer's view of California's mental health care system." *Psychiatric Quarterly*, 1974, *48*, 1-13.

Allmand, W. *The general program for the development of psychiatric services in federal correctional services in Canada.* Ottawa: Information Canada, 1973.

Allodi, F., & Kedward, H.B. "The evolution of the mental hospital in Canada." *Canadian Journal of Public Health*, 1977, *68*, 219-224.

Altman, L. "Growing use of mind-affecting drugs worries F.D.A." *New York Times*, March 14, 1971, p. 1.

Amin, S. "In praise of socialism." *Monthly Review*, 1974, *26(4)*, 1-16.

Amin, S. "The class structure of the contemporary imperialist system." *Monthly Review*, 1980, *3(4)*, 9-26.

"Anatomy of the labor force." *Fortune*, 1946, *34(5)*, 128-131.

Anderson, J. "Unsafe nursing homes crackdown needed." *Huron Daily Plainsman*, April 25, 1979, p. 4.

Anderson, J. "U.S. creating 'psychiatric ghettos.'" *The Washington Post*, Feb. 18, 1978, p. E39.

Anderson, V.V. *Psychiatry in Industry*. New York: Harper, 1929.

Appley, M.H., & Rickwood, J. *Psychology in Canada*, (Special study, Number 3). Ottawa: Science Secretariat, 1967.

Arboleda-Florez, J. "The development of a forensic psychiatric service." *Canadian Journal of Criminology and Corrections*, 1975, *17*, 141-145.

Argandona, M., & Kiev, A. *Mental Health in the Developing World: A case study in Latin America*. New York: The Free Press, 1972.

Argyris, C. *Personality and Organization*. New York: Harper, 1957.

Armstrong, B. "Labor relations in mental health: A look at what's happening." *Hospital and Communisty Psychiatry*, 1976, *27(1)*, 45-52.

Armstrong, H. "The labour force and state workers in Canada." In L. Panitch (Ed.), *The Canadian State: Political economy and political power*. Toronto: University of Toronto Press, 1977.

Arnhoff, F.N., Rubinstein, E.A., Shriver, B.M., & Jones, D.R. "The mental health fields: An overview of manpower growth and development." In F.N. Arnhoff, E.A. Rubinstein & J.C. Spiesman (Eds.), *Manpower for Mental Health*. Chicago: Aldine Publishers, 1969.

Aronson, J., & Field, M.G. "Mental health programming in the Soviet Union." *American Journal of Orthopsychiatry*, 1964, *34*, 913-924.

Auster, S.L. "Approaches to industrial mental health." In A. McLean (Ed.), *To Work is Human: Mental health and the business community*. New York: The Macmillan Company, 1967.

Ayllon, T., & Michael, J. "The psychiatric nurse as a behavioral engineer." *Journal of Experimental and Analytical Behavior*, 1959, *2*, 323-334.

Back, K.W. *Beyond Words: The story of sensitivity training and the encounter movement*. Baltimore: Penguin Books, 1972.

Bailey, P., Williams, F.E., & Komora, P.O. "In the United States." In *The Medical Department of the United States Army in the World War* (Vol. 10, Neuropsychiatry). Washington: U.S. Government Printing Office, 1929.

Bailey, R., & Brake, M. Introduction: "Social work in the welfare state." In R. Bailey & M. Brake (Eds.), *Radical Social Work*. New York: Pantheon, 1975.

163

Bakal, Y. "Closing Massachusetts' institutions: A case study." In Y. Bakal (Ed.), *Closing Correctional Institutions: New strategies for youth services.* Toronto: Lexington Books, 1973.

Baker, E.F., Young, M.P., Gauld, D.M., & Fleming, J.F.R. "A new look at midedial prefontal leukotomy." *Canadian Medical Association Journal,* 1970, *102,* 37-41.

Baker, H. *Employee Counseling: A survey of a new development in personnel relations.* Princeton, N.J.: Princeton University Press, 1944.

Baker, R.S. *The New Industrial Unrest: Reasons and remedies.* Garden City, N.Y.: Doubleday, Page and Company, 1920.

Balasubramanian, T.S., Kanaka, B., & Ramamurthi, B. "Surgical treatment of hyperkinetic and behavior disorders." *International Surgery,* 1970, *54(1),* 18-23.

Balter, M., Levine, J., & Rubinstein, J. *Cross-national Study of the Extent of Anti-anxiety Sedative.* Psychopharmacology Research Bureau, NIMH. Presented at C.J.N.P. Congress, Copenhagen, Aug., 1972, 14-17.

Baran, P.A., & Sweezy, P.M. *Monopoly Capital: An essay on the American economic and social order.* New York: Modern Reader Paperbacks, 1966.

Barkin, S. "A trade unionist appraises management personnel philosophy." In E.C. Bursk (Ed.), *Human Relations for Management: The Newer Perspective.* New York: Harper and Brothers, 1956.

Barkin, S. "The third postwar decade (1965-75): Progress, activism, and tension." In S. Barkin (Ed.), *Worker Militancy and Its Consequences, 1965-75.* New York: Praeger, 1975.

Barten, H.H. "The coming of age of the brief psychotherapies." In L. Bellak & H.H. Barten (Eds.), *Progress in Community Mental Health* (Vol. 1). New York: Grune and Stratton, 1969.

Bass, B.M., & Barrett, G.V. *Man, Work and Organizations: An introduction to industrial and organizational psychology.* Boston: Allyn and Bacon, 1972.

Beers, C. *A Mind that Found Itself: An autobiography.* Garden City, N.Y.: Doubleday, Doran and Company, 1908.

"Behavior modification case study: Therapy or management." *The Psych-agitator,* 1979, *5,* 18-22.

"Behavior modification in prisons." *The Psych-agitator,* 1979, *5,* 22-25.

Bell, D. "Exploring factory life." *Commentary,* Jan. 1947, 79-88.

Bell, R.G. "The problem within industry." *American Journal of Public Health,* 1958, *48,* 585-589.

164

Bellak, L. "Some personal reflections on European and American psychiatry." In L. Bellak (Ed.), *Contemporary European Psychiatry*. New York: Grove Press, 1961.

Bellak, L. "Community psychiatry: The third psychiatric revolution." In L. Bellak (Ed.), *Handbook of Community Psychiatry and Community Mental Health*. New York: Grune and Stratton, 1964.

Bellak, L. "Community mental health as a branch of public health." In L. Bellak & H.H. Barten (Eds.), *Progress in Community Mental Health* (Vol. 1). New York: Grune and Stratton, 1969.

Benedetti, G., & Muller, C. "Switzerland." In L. Bellak (Ed.), *Contemporary European Psychiatry*. New York: Grove Press, 1961.

Bennett, D. "Community mental health services in Britain." *American Journal of Psychiatry*, 1973, *130(10)*, 1065-1070.

Bercuson, D. "The Winnipeg General Strike." In I. Abella (Ed.), *On Strike: Six key labour struggles in Canada 1919-1949*. Toronto: James, Lewis and Samuel, 1974.

Berger, F.M., & Potterfield, J. "The effect of anti-anxiety tranquilizers on the behavior of normal people." In W.O. Evans & N.S. Kline (Eds.), *The Psychopharmacology of the Normal Human*. Springfield, Ill.: Charles C. Thomas, 1969.

Berger, P.L. *The Human Shape of Work*. New York: Macmillan and Company, 1964.

Berliner, H.S. "Emerging ideologies in medicine." *The Review of Radical Political Economics*, 1977, *9(1)*, 116-123.

Bernstein, I. *The Lean Years: A history of the American worker 1920-1933*. Baltimore: Penguin Books, 1960.

Bernstein, I. *Turbulent Years: A history of the American worker 1933-1941*. Boston: Houghton Mifflin Company, 1969.

Bingham, W.V. "Management's concern with research in industrial psychology." *Harvard Business Review*, 1931, *10(1)*, 40-53.

Bion, W.R. *Experiences in Groups and Other Papers*. London: Tavistock, 1961.

Bird, R. "Canada and the United Kingdom: Is Canada going down the same road?" *The Canadian Business Review*, Winter 1977, 13-15.

Birnbaum, M. "The right to treatment: Some comments on its development." In F.J. Ayd, Jr. (Ed.), *Medical, Moral and Legal Issues in Mental Health Care*. Baltimore: Williams and Wilkins, 1974.

Bladen, V.W. "Work relationships." *Canadian Journal of Public Health*, 1949, *40(7)*, 283-291.

Blank, R. "Community psychiatry and the psychiatrist in private practice." In L. Bellak (Ed.), *Handbook of Community Psychiatry and Community Mental Health.* New York: Grune and Stratton, 1964.

Block, F. "The stalemate of European Communism: Eurocommunism and the postwar order." *Socialist Review,* 1979, *9(1),* 53-89.

Bloom, B.L. *Community Mental Health: A historical and critical analysis.* Morristown, N.J.: General Learning Press, 1973.

Bordeleau, J.M., & Kline, N.S. "Experience in developing psychiatric services in Haiti." *World Mental Health,* 1962, *14,* 170-182.

Bowles, S., & Gintis, H. *Schooling in Capitalist America: Educational reform and the contradictions of economic life.* New York: Basic Books, 1976.

Braceland, F.J. "Mental hygiene and moral." *Hospital Corps Quarterly.* Washington, 1945, *18,* 51-53.

Braceland, F.J. *Man and his Work: Health maintenance in industry, with special reference to the executive-psychiatric considerations.* Address to the Congress on Industrial Health. Washington, Jan. 25, 1955.

Brady, J.P. "Drugs in behavior therapy." In D.H. Efron, J.O. Cole, J. Levine & J.R. Wittenborn (Eds.), *Psychopharmacology: A review of progress 1957-1967,* Public Health Service Publication #1836.Washington: U.S. Government Printing Office, 1968.

Bramel, D., & Friend, R. *Human Relations in Industry: The famous Hawthorne Experiments.* Unpublished paper, State University of New York at Stony Brook, 1978.

Brandt, A. *Reality Police: The experience of insanity in America.* New York: William Morrow and Company, 1975.

Braverman, H. *Labor and Monopoly Capital: The degradation of work in the twentieth century.* New York: Monthly Review Press, 1974.

Brayfield, A.H., & Crockett, W.H. "Employee attitudes and employee performance." *Psychological Bulletin,* 1955, *52,* 396-424.

Brecher, J. *Strike!* Boston: South End Press, 1972.

Bremer, J. "Community mental health in Norway." *Proceedings of the Third World Congress of Psychiatry.* Montréal: University of Toronto Press, 1961, *3,* 72-75.

Brenner, M.H. *Mental Illness and the Economy.* Cambridge, Mass.: Harvard University Press, 1973.

Brenner, M.H. "Estimating the social costs of national economic policy: Implications for mental and physical health, and criminal aggression." In Joint Economic Committee, Congress of the United States *Achieving the goals of the Employment Act of 1946 — Thirtieth Anniversary Review.* (Vol. 1 — Employment). Washington: U.S. Government Printing Office, Oct. 26, 1976.

Brickman, H.R. "Mental health and social change: An ecological perspective." In H.P. Dreitzel (Ed.), *The Social Organization of Health.* London: Collier-Macmillan Limited, 1971.

Brill, H., & Patton, R.E. "Analysis of 1955-56 population fall in New York state mental hospitals during the first year of large scale use of tranquilizing drugs." *American Journal of Pyshciatry,* 1957, *114,* 509-517.

Brill, H., & Patton, R.E. "Analysis of population reduction in New York state mental hospitals during the first four years of large scale therapy with psychotropic drugs." *American Journal of Insanity,* 1959, *116,* 495-508.

Brill, H., & Patton, R.E. "The impact of modern chemotherapy on hospital organization, psychiatric care, and public health policies: Its scope and its limits." *Proceedings of the Third World Congress of Psychiatry.* Toronto: University of Toronto Press, 1971, *3,* 433-457.

Brody, M. "Dynamics of mental hygiene in industry." *Industrial Medicine,* 1945, *14,* 760-774.

Bromberg, W. *The Mind of Man.* New York: Harper and Brothers, 1937.

Brook, A. "Psychiatric disorders in industry." *British Journal of Hospital Medicine,* 1976, *15(5),* 484-492.

Brooks, T.R. *Toil and Trouble: A history of American labor* (2nd ed.). New York: Dell, 1971.

Brown, B.S. Forward. In H.J. Weiner, S.W. Akabas & J.J. Sommer, *Mental Health in the World of Work.* New York: Association Press, 1973.

Brown, B.S. "Conflict and détente between social issues and clinical practice." *American Journal of Orthopsychiatry,* 1977, *47(3),* 466-475.

Brown, B.S., Wienckowski, L.A., & Bivens, L.W. *Psychosurgery: Perspective on a current issue.* Rockville, Md.: NIMH Alcohol, Drug Abuse and Mental Health Administration, 1973.

Brown, E.R. *Rockefeller Medicine Men: Medicine and capitalism in America.* Berkeley: University of California Press, 1979.

Brown, E.R. "Public health in imperialism: Early Rockefeller programs at home and abroad." *American Journal of Public Health,* 1976, *66(9),* 897-903.

Brown, J.A.C. *The Social Psychology of Industry: Human relations in the factory*. Baltimore: Penguin, 1957.

Brown, L., & Brown, C. *An Unauthorized History of the R.C.M.P.* Toronto: James Lorimer and Company, 1973.

Brown, M.B. "Imperialism in our era." In (no Ed.) *Spheres of Influence in the Age of Imperialism*. Nottingham, England: Spokesman Books, 1972.

Brown, M.E. *Condemnation and Persecution: Social control and the closing of alternatives. A case study*. Unpublished paper. Flushing, N.Y.: Department of Sociology, Queen's College, 1968.

Brown, P. "The transfer of care: U.S. mental health policy since World War II." *International Journal of Health Services*, 1979, *9(4)*, 645-662.

Brown, P. *Toward a Marxist Psychology*. New York: Harper and Row, 1974.

Buck, T. *Canada and the Russian Revolution: The impact of the world's first socialist revolution on labor and politics in Canada*. Toronto: Progress Books, 1967.

Buck, V.E. *Working Under Pressure*. New York: Crane, Russak and Company, 1972.

Bucklow, M. "A new role for the work group." In J. Munro (Ed.), *Classes, Conflict, and Control: Studies in criminal justice management*. Cincinnati: Anderson Publishing Company, 1976.

Bullough, B. "The new militancy in nursing." *Nursing Forum*, 1977, *3*, 273-288.

Bullough, B., & Bullough, V. "The causes and consequences of the differentiation of the nursing role." In P.L. Stewart & M.G. Cantor (Eds.), *Varieties of Work Experience: The social control of occupational groups and roles*. New York: John Wiley and Sons, 1974.

Burlingame, C.C. "Psychiatry in industry." *American Journal of Psychiatry*, 1946, *103*, 549-553.

Burrows, W.G. "Community psychiatry - Another bandwagon?" *Canadian Psychiatric Association Journal*, 1969, *14*, 105-114.

Bursk, E.C. *Human Relations for Management*. New York: Harper and Brothers, 1956.

Butler, J.L. "Industrial psychiatry and social psychiatry." *Symposium on Preventive and Social Psychiatry*, Walter Reed Institute of Research, Washington: U.S. Government Printing Office, 1957.

Bylinsky, G. *Mood Control*. New York: Charles Scribner's Sons, 1978.

Byron, C. "To set the economy right." *Time*, 1979, *114(9)*, 24-36.

Caldwell, A.E. *Origins of Psychopharmacology: From CPZ to LSD.* Springfield, Ill.: Charles C. Thomas, 1970.

Caligari, D. "Amphetamines or more chemical weirdness." *Madness Network News*, 1977, *4(5)*, 12-13.

Caligari, D. "The tricycle "anti-depressants": A medicine for melancholy?" *Madness Network News.* 1978a, *5*, 14-15.

Caligari, D. "The tardive dyskinesia epidemic." *Madness Network News.* 1978b, *5(3)*, 20-21.

Caligari, D. "Lithium: The great pretender." *Madness Network News*, 1979, *5(5)*, 1, 15-17.

Campbell, C.M. *Mental Hygiene in Industry.* New York: National Committee for Mental Hygiene, 1921.

Care, G.P., & Turner, W.D. "The effects of benzedrine sulfate (amphetamine sulfate) on performance in a comprehensive psychometric examination." *Journal of Psychology,* 1939, *8*, 165-216.

Carey, A. "The Hawthorne Studies: A radical criticism." *American Sociological Review,* 1967, *32(3)*, 403-416.

Carnoy, M. *Education and Cultural Imperialism.* New York: David McKay Company, 1974.

Casey, D., & Rabins, P. "Tardive dyskinesia as a life threatening illness." *American Journal of Psychiatry,* 1978, *135(4)*, 486-489.

Cassell, W.A., Smith, C.M., Grunberg, F., Boan, J.A., & Thomas, R.F. "Comparing costs of hospital and community care." *Hospital and Community Psychiatry,* 1972, *23(7)*, 197-200.

Census of Jails and Survey of Jail Inmates, 1978. National Prisoner Statistics Bulletin, #SD-NPS-J-6P, Washington: Law Enforcement Assistance Administration, 1979.

Center for Research on Criminal Justice. *The Iron Fist and the Velvet Glove: An analysis of the U.S. Police* (2nd ed.). Berkeley, California: Author, 1977.

Cerletti, V. In L. Bellak (Ed.), *Contemporary European Psychiatry.* New York: Grove Press, 1961.

Chafetz, M.E. *Alcohol and Health: New knowledge. Second special report to the U.S. congress.* Rockville, Md.: National Institute of Alcohol Abuse and Addiction, 1974.

Chandler, D., & Sallychild, A. *The Use and Misuse of Psychiatric Drugs in California's Mental Health Programs.* Sacramento, Ca.: Assembly Office of Research, June, 1977.

Cherniss, C., Egnatios, E.S., & Wacker, S. "Job stress and career development in new public professionals." *Professional Psychology,* 1976, *7(4)*, 428-436.

Chisholm, B. Introductory remarks. *Proceedings of the International Conference on Mental Hygiene* (Vol. 4). In *International Congress on Mental Health*. London: A.K. Lewis and Company, 1948.

Chomsky, N. "The Pentagon Papers and U.S. imperialism in South East Asia." In (no Ed.) *Spheres of Influence in the Age of Imperialism*. Nottingham, England: Spokesman, 1972.

Chrichton, A. *Mental Health and Social Policy in Canada*. Ottawa: Canadian Mental Health Association, 1953.

Chrichton, A. "Mental health and social policies: An overview." *Canada's Mental Health*, 1975, *23(4)*, supplement.

Chu, F.D., & Trotter, S. *The Madness Establishment: Ralph Nader's Study Group report on the National Institute of Mental Health*. New York: Grossman, 1974.

Citizens Medical Reference Bureau. *Letter to House Sub-Committee*. U.S. Congress, House Committee on Interstate and Foreign Commerce. 79th Congress 1st Session, 1945.

Clarkson, J.G. "Community integration of health and welfare services." *Canadian Journal of Public Health*, 1972, *63*, 203-206.

Clegg, H. *A New Approach to Industrial Democracy*. Oxford: Basil Blackwell, 1960.

Cloutier, F. "International activities: An integrated overview." In H.P. David (Ed.), *International Trends in Mental Health*. New York: McGraw-Hill, 1966.

Cobb, J. *Applications of Psychiatry to Industrial Hygiene*. New York: National Committee for Mental Hygiene, 1919.

Coburn, F.E. "Community psychiatry for a million people." In L.M. Roberts, S.L. Halleck & M.B. Loeb (Eds.), *Community Psychiatry*. Garden City, N.Y.: Doubleday, 1969.

Cochran, T.C. *The Great Depression and World War II: 1929-1945*. Glenview, Ill.: Scott, Foresman and Company, 1968.

Cohen, S. *The Punitive City: Notes on the dispersal of social control*. Unpublished paper, Dep. of Sociology, University of Essex, 1979.

Cole, J., & Pilisuk, M. "Differences in the provision of mental health services by race." *American Journal of Orthopsychiatry*, 1976, *46(3)*, 494-506.

Cole, G.D.H. *A Short History of the British Working-Class Movement* (Revised ed.). London: George Allen & Unwin, 1948.

Colligan, M.J., Smith, M.J., & Hurrell, J.J. "Occupational incidence rates of mental health disorders." *Journal of Human Stress*, 1977, *3(3)*, 34-39.

Colligan, M.J., & Stockton, W. "The mystery of assembly-line hysteria." *Psychology Today*, June, 1978, pp. 93-99, 114.

Collins, R.T. "Occupational psychiatry." *American Journal of Psychiatry*, 1962, *118*, 604-609.

Collins, R.T., & Klem, E.S. "Industrial psychiatry." *American Journal of Psychiatry*, 1956, *112*, 546-549.

Committee on Occupational Psychiatry of the American Psychiatric Association. *The Mentally Ill Employee: His treatment and rehabilitation. A guide for management.* New York: Harper and Row, 1965.

Connell, C. "Twenty percent of cancer deaths may be linked to chemicals at work site." *Huron Daily Plainsman*, Sept. 12, 1978, p. 14.

Connery, R.H. *The Politics of Mental Health: Organizing community mental health in metropolitan areas.* New York: Columbia University Press, 1968.

Cooper, C.L., & Marshall, J. "Occupational sources of stress: a review of the literature relating to coronary heart disease and mental ill health. " *Journal of Occupational Psychology*, 1976, *49*, 11-28.

Cooper, D. *Psychiatry and Anti-Psychiatry.* London: Tavistock Publications, 1967.

Cooper, D. "Beyond anti-psychiatry." *State and Mind*, 1979, *7(2)*, 15-16.

Cooper, M.R., Morgan, B.S., Foley, P.M., & Kaplan, L.B. "Changing employee values: Deepening discontent." *Harvard Business Review*, Jan.-Feb., 1979, 117-125.

Cooper, S. "Reflections on the mental health system." *American Journal of Orthopsychiatry*, 1976, *46(3)*, 393-400.

Cooperstock, R. "Some factors involved in the increased prescribing of psychotropic drugs. " In R. Cooperstock (Ed.), *Social Aspects of the Medical Use of Psychotropic Drugs.* Toronto: Addiction Research Foundation, 1973.

Cooperstock, R. *The Edpidemiology of Psychotropic Drug Use in Canada Today.* Unpublished paper, Toronto: Addiction Research Foundation, 1977.

Cotter, F. "Primary care providers target of HEW training." *NIAAA Information and Feature Service*, National Clearinghouse of Alcohol Information of the National Institute of Alcohol Abuse and Alcoholism, May 4, 1979, *59*, 1.

Crabtree, C.T. *Investigation-apprehension Control and Management System.* Springfield, Va.: National Technical Information Service, 1973.

Crane, G.E. "Clinical psychopharmacology in its 20th year." *Science*, 1973, *181*, 124-128.

Crawford, J.L., Morgan, D.W., & Gianturco, D.C. *Progress in Mental Health Information Systems.* Cambridge, Mass.: Ballinger, 1974.

Crispo, J. *Industrial Democracy in Western Europe: A North American perspective.* New York: McGraw-Hill, 1978.

Crow, H.J., Cooper, R., & Phillips, D.G. "Progressive leucotomy." In J.H. Masserman (Ed.), *Current Psychiatric Therapies.* New York: Grune & Stratton, 1963.

Cruickshank, W.M. "Mental hygiene in industry." *Canadian Journal of Public Health,* 1955, *46(12)*, 475-485.

Cumming, J., Coates, D., & Bunton, P. "Community care services in Vancouver: Initial planning and implementation." *Canada's Mental Health,* 1976, *24(1)*, 28-29.

Cuthbertson, K. "How safe are our medical secrets?" *Regina Leader-Post,* June 9, 1979, pp. 2-3.

Cuthbertson, D.P., & Knox, J.A.C. "The effects of analeptics on the fatigued subject." *Journal of Physiology,* 1947, *106*, 42-59.

D'Alonzo, C.A. "Rehabilitation of workers addicted to alcohol." *Industrial Medicine and Surgery,* 1961, *30*, 14-15.

D'Arcy, C. "The manufacture and obsolescence of madness: Age, social policy, and psychiatric morbidity in a prairie province." *Social Science and Medicine,* 1976a, *10*, 5-13.

D'Arcy, C. *Change and Consequence in a Mental Health System: Theoretical and empirical chapters in a sociology of mental illness.* Unpublished Ph.D. dissertation, University of Toronto, 1976b.

D'Arcy, C. *Patterns in the Delivery of Psychiatric Care in Saskatchewan, 1971-1972.* Service Interface Study, Interim Report. Applied Research Unit, Psychiatric Research Division, University Hospital, Saskatoon, Sask., 1976c.

D'Arcy, C., & Brockman, J. "Changing public recognition of psychiatric symptoms: Blackfoot revisited." *Journal of Health and Social Behavior,* 1976, *17*, 302-310.

D'Arcy, C., & Brockman, J. "Public rejection of the ex-mental patient: Are attitudes changing?" *Canadian Review of Sociology and Anthropology,* 1977, *14*, 68-80.

David, H.P. "Mental health grants: International progress and problems." In H.P. David (Ed.), *International Trends in Mental Health.* New York: McGraw-Hill, 1966.

Davidoff, E., Best, J.L., & McPheeters, H.L. "The effect of Ritalin (methylphendylacitate hpdrochloride) on mildly depressed ambulatory patients." *New York Journal of Medicine,* 1957, *57*, 1753-1755.

172

Davidson, P.O. "Graduate training and research funding for clinical psychology in Canada." *Canadian Psychologist*, 1970, *11*, 101-127.

Davies, W. *The Pharmaceutical Industry: A personal study. A medical, economic and political survey of the world-wide pharmaceutical industry.* Oxford: Pergamon, 1967.

Davis, D.R. "Psychomotor effects of analeptics and their relation to fatigue phenomena in air crews." *British Medical Bulletin*, 1947, *5*, 43-45.

Davis, K. "Mental hygiene and the class structure." *Psychiatry: Journal of the Biology and Pathology of Interpersonal Relations*, 1938, *1*, 55-65.

Davis, K., Arrill, M.B., & Sharfstein, S.S. "Economics of mental health." In E.J. Lieberman (Ed.), *Mental Health: The public health challenge.* Washington: American Public Health Association, 1975.

Deaton, R. "The fiscal crisis of the state." In D.I. Roussopoulos (Ed.), *The Political Economy of the State: Québec/Canada /U.S.A.* Montréal: Black Rose Books, 1973.

"Deinstitutionalization: The continuing crossfire." *Behavior Today*, Jan. 30, 1978, pp. 3-4.

Delgado, J.M.R. *Physical Control of the Mind: Toward a psychocivilized society.* New York: Harper and Row, 1969.

Delgado, J.M.R., Mark, V., Sweet, W., Ervin, F., Weiss, G., Bach-y-rita, G., & Hagiwara, R. "Intracerebral radio stimulation and recording in completely free patients." *The Journal of Nervous and Mental Disease*, 1968, *147(4)*, 329-339.

Derber, M. *The American Idea of Industrial Democracy, 1865-1965.* Chicago: University of Illinois Press, 1970.

Deutsch, A. *The Mentally Ill in America: A history of their treatment from colonial times* (2nd ed.). New York: Columbia University Press, 1949.

DSM-II: *(Diagnostic and statistical manual of mental disorders)* (2nd ed.). Washington: American Psychiatric Association, 1968.

Dingman, P.R. "The alternative care is not there." In P.I. Ahmed & S.C. Plog (Eds.), *State Mental Hospitals: What happens when they close?* New York: Plenum Medical Books, 1976.

Dinitz, S., & Beran, N. "Community mental health as a boundaryless and boundary-busting system." *Journal of Health and Social Behavior*, 1971, *12*, 99-108.

Doig, J. "The high cost of tranquility." *The Canadian Magazine*, July 22, 1978, pp. 3-5.

Doll, W. "Family coping with the mentally ill: An unanticipated problem of deinstitutionalization." *Hospital and Community Psychiatry*, 1976, *27(3)*, 183-185.

Dorgan, J. "Foster home care for the psychiatric patient." *Canadian Journal of Public Health*, 1958, *49(10)*, 411-419.

Douglas, V.I. *The Future of Canadian Psychology.* Ottawa: Canadian Psychological Association, 1971.

Douty, H.M. "The slowdown in real wages: A postwar perspective." *Monthly Labor Review*, Aug. 1977, pp. 7-12.

Dowd, D.F. "Stagflation and the political economy of decadent monopoly capitalism." *Monthly Review*, 1976, *28(5)*, 14-29.

Drucker, P.F. *The Practice of Management.* New York: Harper and Row, 1954.

"Drug found help in schizophrenia." *New York Times*, Feb. 4, 1955, p. 28.

Ducker, H. "Uber die Werkung von Pharmaka auf die geistige Tatigkeit voll leistung fahigh Personen." *Arzneimittel-Forschung*, 1964, *14*, 570-573.

Dunan, M. (Ed.) *Larousse Encyclopedia of Modern History From 1500 to the Present Day.* New York: Harper and Row, 1964.

Edginton, B. *The Political Economy of Mental Illness.* Unpublished Master's thesis, University of Saskatchewan, Regina Campus, 1973.

Edison, T.A. Editorial. *Industrial Management and Engineering Magazine*, Oct. 1920, p. 4.

Editorial: "Mental health programs, trends and prospects." *Canadian Journal of Public Health*, 1970, *61*, 93-95.

Ehrenreich, B., & Ehrenreich, J. *The American Health Empire: Power, profits, and politics.* New York: Random House, 1970.

Ehrenreich, B., & Ehrenreich, J. "Medicine and social control." In B.R. Mandell (Ed.), *Welfare in America: Controlling the "dangerous classes."* Englewood Cliffs, N.J.: Prentice-Hall, 1975.

Ehrenreich, J., & Ehrenreich, B. "Work and consciousness." In P.M. Sweezy & H. Magdoff (Eds.), *Technology, the Labour Process and the Working Class.* New York: Monthly Review Press, 1976.

Elkin, L. *Sociology of Stupidity.* Unpublished doctoral dissertation, University of Saskatchewan, Regina Campus, 1972.

Elliott, J.F. *New Police: A description of a possible form of what the municipal police will evolve into, why they must change, and how this evolution may be accomplished.* Springfield, Ill.: Charles C. Thomas, 1973.

Empey, L.T. "Juvenile justice reform: Diversion, due process, and deinstitutionalization." In L.E. Ohlin (Ed.), *Prisoners in America.* Englewood Cliffs, N.J.: Prentice-Hall, 1973.

Engels, F. "Review of Das Kapital." In W.O. Henderson (Ed.), *Engels: Selected Writings.* Baltimore: Penguin, 1967.

Epstein, L. "Differential use of staff: A method to expand social services." *Social Work,* Oct. 1962, pp. 66-72.

Etzioni, A. *The Semi-Professions and Their Organizations.* New York: The Free Press, 1969.

Evans, W.O. "The psychopharmacology of the normal human: Trends in research strategy." In D.H. Efron, J.O. Cole, J. Levine & J.R. Wittenborn (Eds.), *Psychopharmacology: A review of progress, 1957-1967.* Public Health Service Publication #1836, Washington: U.S. Government Printing Office, 1968.

Evans, W.O. Introduction. In W.O. Evans & N.S. Kline (Eds.), *Psychotropic Drugs in the Year 2000: Use by normal humans.* Springfield, Ill.: Charles C. Thomas, 1971.

Evans, W.O., & Kline, N.S. *The Psychopharmacology of the Normal Human.* Springfield, Ill.: Charles C. Thomas, 1969.

Evans, W.O., & Kline, N.S. (Eds.), *Psychotropic Drugs in the Year 2000.* Springfield, Ill.: Charles C. Thomas, 1971.

Ewalt, J.R. "Psychiatry in industry." *Industrial Medicine and Surgery,* 1960, *29,* 474-479.

Ewalt, J.R. "The birth of the community mental health movement." In W.E. Barton & C.J. Sanborn (Eds.), *An Assessment of the Community Mental Health Movement.* Lexington, Mass.: D.C. Heath and Company, 1975.

Ewing, B.G. *The National Manpower Survey of the Criminal Justice System: Executive summary.* Washington: Law Enforcement Assistance Administration, 1978.

Expert Committee on Mental Health. *Report on the First Session, World Health Organization Technical Report Series* #9. Geneva: World Health Organization, 1950.

Expert Committee on Mental Health. *The Community Mental Hospital, World Health Organization Technical Report Series* #73. Geneva: World Health Organization, 1953.

Extendicare Limited, *Annual Report.* Toronto: Author, 1975.

Ey, H. "Psychiatric therapy in France." In J.H. Masserman (Ed.), *Current Psychiatric Therapies* (Vol. 2). New York: Grune and Stratton, 1962.

Eyer, J., & Sterling, P. "Stress-related mortality and social organization." *The Review of Radical Political Economics*, 1977, *9(1)*, 1-44.

Eysenck, H.J. "The effects of psychotherapy: An evaluation." *Journal of Consulting Psychology*, 1952, *16*, 319-329.

Eysenck, H.J. *Behavior Therapy and the Neuroses.* Oxford: Pergamon Press, 1960.

Facts About Electroshock Therapy. DHEW Publication #(ADM)-74-88. Rockville, Md.: Alcohol, Drug Abuse, and Mental Health Administration, 1972.

Faris, R.E.L., & Dunham, H.W. *Mental Disorders in Urban Areas: An ecological study of schizophrenia and other psychoses* (2nd ed.) Chicago: University of Chicago Press, 1967.

Family Weekly. "Professional burnout—and how to avoid it." *Family Weekly*, Feb. 12, 1978, p. 26.

Fein, R. *Economics of Mental Illness.* (Monograph Series #2: Joint Commission on Mental Illness and Health). New York: Basic Books, 1958.

Felix, R.H. "The National Mental Health Act: How it can operate to meet a national problem." *Mental Hygiene*, 1947, *31*, 363-373.

Felix, R.H. "How to live with job pressure." *Nation's Business*, 1956, *44*, 38-39, 85-87.

Felix, R.H. "A comprehensive community mental health program." In (no Ed.), *Mental Health and Social Welfare.* New York: Columbia University Press, 1961.

Felton, J.S., & Wilner, D.M. "Occupational health and mental health." In S.E. Goldston (Ed.), *Mental Health Considerations in Public Health.* Chevy Chase, Md.: NIMH, 1969.

Ferguson, L.L. "Social scientists in the plant." *Harvard Business Review*, 1964, *42*, 133-143.

Ferster, C.B., & Skinner, B.F. *Schedules of Reinforcement.* New York: Appleton Century-Crofts, 1957.

"Fifteen million dollars granted for mental health." *New York Times*, May 8, 1955, p. 1.

Finkel, A. "Origins of the welfare state in Canada." In L. Panitch (Ed.), *The Canadian State: Political economy and political power.* Toronto: University of Toronto Press, 1971.

Fischer, A., & Weinstein, M.R. "Mental hospitals, prestige, and the image of enlightenment." *Archives of General Psychiatry*, 1971, *25*, 41-48.

Fleming, J.L. "Industry looks at the emotionally troubled employee." In P.A. Carone, S.N. Kieffer, L.W. Krinsky & S.F. Yolles

(Eds.), *The Emotionally Troubled Employee: A challenge to industry*. New York: SUNY Press, 1976.

Foley, H.A. *Community Mental Health Legislation: The formative process*. Lexington, Mass.: Lexington Books, 1975.

Follman, J.F. Jr. *Alcoholics and Business: Problems, costs, solutions*. New York: Amacom, 1976.

Ford, H. II "The challenge of human engineering." *Advanced Management*, 1946, *11*, 48-52.

Foucault, M. *Madness and Civilization: A history of insanity in the age of reason* (R. Howard, trans.). New York: Random House, 1965.

Fountain, C.W. "Labor's place in an industrial mental health program." *Mental Hygiene*, 1945, *29*, 95-101.

Fournet, G.P., Distefano, M.K. Jr., & Pryer, M.W. "Job Satisfaction: Issues and problems." In D.P. Schultz (Ed.), *Psychology and Industry*. London: Collier-Macmillan, 1970.

Franco, S.C. "A company policy on drug abuse." In J.M. Scher (Ed.), *Drug Abuse in Industry: Growing corporate dilemma*. Springfield, Ill.: Charles C. Thomas, 1973.

Fraser, H.F. "Problems resulting from the use of habituating drugs in industry." *American Journal of Public Health*, 1958, *48(5)*, 561-570.

Fraser, R. *The Incidence of Neuroses in Factory Workers*. London: H.M.S.O., 1947.

Frazier, S.H., & Pokerny, A.D. *Report of a Consultation to the Minister of Public Health on the Psychiatric Services of Saskatchewan*. Regina, Sask., 1968.

Freedman, A.M. "The redefinition of psychiatric treatment." In F.J. Ayd (Ed.), *Medical, Moral, and Legal Issues in Mental Health Care*. Baltimore: Williams and Wilkins, 1974.

Friedberg, J. *Shock Treatment is Not Good for Your Brain*. San Francisco: Glide, 1976.

Friedmann, G. *Industrial Society*. Glencoe, Ill.: Free Press, 1955.

Friedson, E. *Profession of Medicine: A study of the sociology of applied knowledge*. New York: Dodd, Mead and Company, 1970.

"Fruitful errors of Elton Mayo." *Fortune*, 1946, *34(5)*, 181-184, 248.

Fulton, J.F. *Frontal Lobotomy and Affective Behavior: A Neurophysiological analysis*. New York: W.W. Norton and Company, 1951.

Furman, B. "New drugs mental case aid." *New York Times*, May 18, 1955, p. 28.

Gadourek, I. "Absenteeism: An unsolved problem." In R.T. Collins (Ed.), *Occupational Psychiatry*. Boston: Little, Brown and Company, 1969.

177

Ganser, L.S. Introduction. In E.J. Lieberman (Ed.), *Mental Health: The public health challenge.* Washington: American Public Health Association, 1975.

Garson, B. *All the Livelong Day.* New York: Penguin, 1975.

Gavin, J.F. "Occupational mental health: Forces and trends." *Personnel Journal,* April 1977, pp. 198-201.

Gay, W.G., & Schack, L. *Improving Patrol Productivity* (2 vols.). Washington: National Institute of Law Enforcement and Criminal Justice, 1977. (Stock #027-000-00560-8.)

Geerds, F. [Relationship between the economy and domestic security from a criminological point of view] (Technassociates, trans.). In *International Summaries: A collection of translations in law enforcement and criminal justice* (Vol. 1). Washington: National Institute of Law Enforcement and Criminal Justice, 1978.

Geller, J. "Forms of capitalist control over the labor process." *Monthly Review,* 1979, *31,* 39-46.

General Accounting Office. *Returning the Mentally Disabled to the Community: Governement needs to do more.* Washington: U.S. Government Printing Office, 1977.

Gershon, S., & Shaw, F.H. "Psychiatric sequelae of chronic exposure to organophoshorus insecticides." *The Lancet,* June 24, 1961, pp. 1371-1374.

Giberson, L.G. "Psychiatry and industry." *The Labor Gazette,* April 1938, pp. 401-404.

Giberson, L.G. "Industrial psychiatry: A wartime survey." *The Medical Clinics of North America,* 1942, *26,* 1085-1103.

Gilbert, M. "Review of *Management and the Worker* by Roethisberger and Dickson." *American Journal of Sociology,* 1940 *46(1),* 98-101.

Gillis, J.S. "Effects of chlorpromazine and thiothixene on acute schizophrenic patients." In K.R. Hammond (Ed.), *Psychoactive Drugs and Social Judgement: Theory and research.* New York: John Wiley and Sons, 1975.

Glasser, M.A. "Psychiatric disability: The UAW response." In A.A. McLean (Ed.), *To Work is Human: Mental health in the business community.* New York: Macmillan, 1967.

Glenn, E.N., & Feldberg, R.L. "Degraded and deskilled: The proletarianization of clerical work." *Social Problems,* 1977, *25,* 52-64.

Glenn, M. (Ed.), *Voices from the Asylum.* New York: Harper and Row, 1974.

Goebel, F. "Issues in mental retardation." In President's Committee on Mental Retardation, *Mental Retardation: Century of decision.* Washington, March 1976.

178

Goffman, E. *Asylums: Essays on the social situation of mental patients and other inmates.* Garden City, N.Y.: Doubleday, 1961.

Goffman, E. *Stigma: Notes on the management of spoiled identity.* Englewood Cliffs, N.J.: Prentice-Hall, 1963.

Gold, D.A., Lo, C.Y.H., & Wright, E.O. "Recent developments in Marxist theories of the capitalist state, Part 2." *Monthly Review,* 1975, *27(6),* 36-51.

Goldberg, D. "The scope and limits of community psychiatry." In C. Shagass (Ed.), *Modern Problems of Pharmacopsychiatry* (Vol. 6, *The Role of Drugs in Community Psychiatry.).* Philadelphia: Karger and Basel, 1971.

Goldman, H. "Conflict, competition and co-existence: The mental hospital as parallel health and welfare systems." *American Journal of Orthopsychiatry,* 1977, *47(1),* 60-65.

Gomberg, W. "The use of psychology in industry: A trade union point of view." *Management Science,* 1957, *3,* 348-370.

Gonick, C.W. *Inflation and Wage Control.* Toronto: Canadian Dimension Publications, 1976.

Gooding, J. "Blue-collar blues on the assembly line." *Fortune,* 1970a, *82, 69-71,* 112-117.

Gooding, J. "The fraying white collar." *Fortune,* 1970b, *82(6),* 78-80, 108-109.

Gordon, D.M. "Capitalist efficiency and socialist efficiency." In (no Ed.), *Technology, the Labor Process, and the Working Class.* New York: Monthly Review Press, 1976a.

Gordon, D.M. "Capitalism, class, and crime in America." In J.L. Munro (Ed.), *Classes, Conflict, and Control: Studies in criminal justice management.* Cincinnati: Anderson, 1976b.

Graf, O. "Increases in efficiency by means of pharmaceutics (stimulants)." In *German Aviation Medicine World War II* (Vol. 2). Washington: U.S. Government Printing Office, 1950.

Gravley, G.G. "Company mental health programs aim to trim absenteeism, turnover." *Wall Street Journal,* March 5, 1963, pp. 1, 20.

Graziano, A.M. "Clinical innovation and the mental health power-structure: A social case history." *American Psychologist,* 1969, *24,* 10-18.

Greenbaum, J. "Division of labor in the computer field." In (no Ed.), *Technology, the Labor Process, and the Working Class.* New York: Monthly Review Press, 1976.

Greenberg, D. "Problems in community corrections." *Issues in Criminology,* 1975, *10(1),* 1-34.

Greenblatt, M. "Historical factors affecting the closing of the hospitals." In P.I. Ahmed & S.C. Plog (Eds.), *State Mental Hospitals: What happens when they close.* New York: Plenum Medical Books, 1976.

Greenblatt, M., & Glazier, E. "Some major issues in the closing of the hospitals." In P.I. Ahmed & S.C. Plog (Eds.), *State Mental Hospitals: What happens when they close.* New York: Plenum Medical Books, 1976.

Greenburg, L.A. "The use of tranquilizers by the worker." *Comprehensive Medicine*, 1957, *9*, 13-15.

Greene, F. *The Enemy: What every American should know about imperialism.* New York: Random House, 1970.

Gregg, A. "Lessons to learn: Psychiatry in World War II." *American Journal of Psychiatry*, 1947, *104*, 217-220.

Greve, R. *Selected and partially annotated bibliography on certain aspects of the quality of working life, with special reference to work organization.* Geneva: International Institute for Labour Studies, 1976.

Grieco, A.L. "New prisons: Characteristics and community reception." *Quarterly Journal of Corrections*, 1979, *2(2)*, 55-59.

Griffin, J.D. "Community mental health services." *Canadian Journal of Public Health*, 1966, *57*, 153-157.

Grinker, R.R., & Spiegel, J.P. *Men Under Stress.* New York: Blakiston, 1945.

Gumbert, E.B., & Spring, J.H. *The Superschool and the Superstate: American education in the twentieth century, 1918-1970.* New York: John Wiley and Sons, 1974.

Habbe, S. "Industry considers mental health." *Journal of Occupational Medicine*, 1960, *2(6)*, 299-301.

Haider, C. *Capital and Labor Under Fascism.* New York: AMS Press, 1968.

Hall, R.H. "Professionalization and bureaucratization." *American Sociological Review*, 1968, *33*, 92-104.

Halsey, G.D. *Supervising People* (2nd ed.). New York: Harper and Row, 1953.

Handbook on Labor Statistics, 1968. (U.S. Department of Labor, Bureau of labor Statistics, Bulletin #1600). Washington: U.S. Government Printing Office, 1968.

Harding, J., & Wolfe, N. *Accounting for social environmental determinants in developing alternatives to the use of prescribed mood-modifying drugs.* Paper presented at the 13th Annual Conference of the Canadian Addictions Foundation, Calgary, Sept. 24-29th, 1978.

Harding, J., Wolfe, N., & Chan, G. *A socio-demographic profile of people prescribed mood-modifiers in Saskatchewan.* Regina, Sask.: Alcoholism Commission of Saskatchewan, 1978.

Hargreaves, G.R. "The next steps in mental health." *Royal Society for the Promotion of Health Journal,* 1959, *79(4),* 357-360.

Hartt, E.P., Lamer, A., Mohr, J.W., & LaForest, G.V. *Mental Disorders* (Reports of the Law Reform Commission of Canada). Ottawa: Information Canada, 1976.

Hauty, G.T. *Methods for the Mitigation of Work Decrement.* U.S. Air Force School of Aviation Medicine, Report #4, Randolf Air Force Base, 1953.

Hauty, G.T., & Payne, R.B. "Effects of analeptic and depressant drugs upon psychological behavior." *American Journal of Public Health,* 1958, *48,* 571-577.

Haythorne, G.V. "Canada: Postwar changes and current ferment." In S. Barkin (Ed.), *Worker Militancy and Its Consequences, 1965-1975.* New York: Praeger, 1975.

Henderson, H.W. "Community mental health: Administrative implications." *Canadian Journal of Public Health,* 1966, *57(4),* 145-157.

Henderson, J., & Cohen, R. "Capital and the work ethic." *Monthly Review,* 1979, *30,* 11-26.

Hersch, C. "The discontent explosion in mental health." *American Psychologist,* 1968, *23,* 497-506.

Hersch, C. "Social history, mental health, and community control." *American Psychologist,* 1972, *27,* 749-754.

Hersh, S.M. *Chemical and Biological Warfare: America's hidden arsenal.* New York: Bobbs-Merrill, 1968.

Herzberg. F., Mausner, B., Peterson, R.O., & Capwell, D.F. *Job Attitudes: Review of research and opinion.* Pittsburgh: Psychological Service of Pittsburgh, 1957.

"HEW's Califano announces new alcohol initiatives." *NIAAA Information and Feature Service,* July 11, 1979, *61,* p. 1.

Hincks, C.M. "Mental hygiene provisions in public health programs." *Canadian Journal of Public Health,* 1945, *36(3),* 8-95.

Hincks, C.M. *A report submitted by the Canadian National Committee on a mental hygiene program for Canada.* Regina, Sask.: Saskatchewan Department of Public Health, 1946.

Hindelang, M.J., Gottfredson, M.R., Dunn, C.S., & Parisi, N. *Sourcebook of Criminal Justice Statistics, 1976.* Washington: Law Enforcement Assistance Administration, 1977.

Hine, C.H. "Biological threshold of impairment drugs in industrial performance." *Activitas Nervosa Superior,* 1973, *15(4),* 266-268.

Hint, J. "The politics of psychosurgery." *The Real Paper,* June 13, 1973, pp. 2-4.

Hirschowitz, R.G., & Levy, B. Introduction. In R.G. Hirschowitz & B. Levy (Eds.), *The Changing Mental Health Scene.* New York: Spectrum, 1976.

Hobbs, G.E., Walkin, J., & Ladd, K.B. "Changing patterns of mental hospital discharges and readmissions in the past two decades." *Canadian Medical Association Journal,* 1965, *93,* 17-20.

Hobbs, N. "Mental health's third revolution." *American Journal of Orthopsychiatry,* 1964, *34,* 822-833.

Hoch, P.H. "New aspects of treatment of mental illness." *Mental Hygiene,* 1957, *41,* 415-419.

Hoff, H., & Arnold, O.H. "Germany and Austria." In L. Bellak (Ed.), *Contemporary European Psychiatry.* New York: Grove Press, 1961.

Hoffer, A. Letter. *Canada's Mental Health,* 1977, *25(4),* 34-35.

Hoffer, A. *Community Psychiatry.* Unpublished manuscript, Sept. 1979.

Hofstadter, R. Introduction. In R. Hofstadter (Ed.), *The Progressive Movement, 1900-1915.* Englewood Cliffs, N.J.: Prentice-Hall, 1963.

Holliday, A.R., & Dillie, J.M. "The effects of meprobamate, chlor-promazine, promaxine, phenobarbital, and a placebo on a behavioral task performed under stress conditions." *Journal of Comparative Physiology and Psychology,* 1958, *51,* 811-815.

Holland, J.G. "Behavior modification for prisoners, patients, and other people as a prescription for the planned society." *Mexican Journal of Behavioral Analysis,* 1975, *1(1),* 81-95.

Hollingstead, A.B., Ellis, R.A., & Kirby, E.C. "Social mobility and mental illness." *American Sociological Review,* 1958, *18,* 163-169.

Hollingstead, A.B., & Redlich, F.C. "Social stratification and psychiatric disorders." *American Sociological Review,* 1953, *18(2),* 163-169.

Hollingstead, A.B., & Redlich, F.C. "Schizophrenia and social structure." *American Journal of Psychiatry,* 1954, *110(9),* 695-701.

Honey, M. "Western drugs and Third World markets." *Manchester Guardian,* Aug. 21, 1977, *117(8),* 1, 5.

Horowitz, D. *Empire and Revolution: A radical interpretation of contemporary history.* New York: Random House, 1969.

Horowitz, D.L. *The Italian Labor Movement.* Cambridge, Mass.: Harvard University Press, 1963.

House of Representatives Report #1445, 79th Congress, 1st Session. National Mental Health Act. *House Reports. 79th Congress, 1st Session, (January-December 21, 1945), miscellaneous* (Vol. 6). Washington: U.S. Government Printing Office, 1945.

Hoxie, R.F. *Scientific Management and Labor.* New York: D. Appleton, 1918.

Huberman, L., & Sweezy, P.M. "The aim is thought control. " *Monthly Review,* 1955, *7(3),* 81-90.

Huberman, L., & Sweezy, P.M. "End of the boom?" *Monthly Review,* 1967, *18(11),* 1-9.

Hughes, E. *Men and Their Work.* Glencoe, Ill.: Free Press, 1958.

Hurd, H.M., Drewry, W.F., Dewey, R., Pilgrim, C.M., Alder, G., Blumer, E., & Burgess, T.J.W. *The Institutional Care of Insane in the United States and Canada* (Vol. 1). Baltimore: The Johns Hopkins Press, 1916.

Hutt, A. *British Trade Unionism: A short history.* London: Lawrence and Wishart, 1975.

Hymer, S. "International politics and international economics: A radical approach." *Monthly Review,* 1978, *29(10),* 15-35.

Iacono, G., & Bellelli, G. "Industrial psychology." In *Encyclopedia of Occupational Health and Safety.* (Vol. II). Geneva: International Labour Organization, 1972.

ICD-7. *International classification of diseases: Manual of the international statistical classification of diseases, injuries, and causes of death* (1955 revision - 7th revision). Geneva: World Health Organization, 1957.

ICD-8. *International classification of diseases adopted for use in the United States* (Eighth revision), Public Health Service publication #1695. Washington: U.S. Government Printing Office, 1965.

Illich, I. *Medical Nemesis: The expropriation of health.* London: McClelland and Stewart, 1975.

Illson, M. "Psychiatry urged in world affairs." *New York Times,* May 4, 1955a, p. 1.

Illson, M. "New help on way for mentally ill: Eventual treatment by the family doctor forecast, tranquillizing drug cited." *New York Times,* May 10, 1955b, p. 2.

Indexes of output per man-hour in selected industries, 1972 edition. U.S. Department of Labor Bulletin #1758. Washington: U.S. Government Printing Office, 1972.

Industrial Relations Committee. *'Big' Labor and Big Strikes: Analyses and recommendations.* New York: National Association of Manufacturers, 1967.

"Industry is the psychiatrist's new patient." *Business Week*, Feb. 15, 1956, pp. 56-59.

International Congress on Mental Health. *Proceedings of the International Conference on Mental Hygiene*, 16-21 Aug., London, 1948. New York: Columbia University Press, 1948.

Ivy, A.C., & Goetzl, F.R. "d-desoxyephedrine: A review." *War Medicine*, 1943, *3*, 60-77.

Jackson, D.C. "Lighting in industry." *Journal of the Franklin Institute*, 1928, *205*, 289-302.

Jaco, E.G. "The social isolation hypothesis and schizophrenia." *American Sociological Review*, 1958, *19*, 567-577.

Jaco, E.G. "Mental illness in response to stress." In S. Levine & N.A. Scotch (Eds.), *Social Stress*. Chicago: Aldine Publishing Company, 1970.

Jacoby, A.J. *Disciplinary Problems of the Navy.* New York: National Committee for Mental Hygiene, 1919.

Jamieson, S.M. *Industrial Relations in Canada.* Ithaca, N.Y.: Cornell University Press, 1957.

Jamieson, S.M. *Times of Trouble: Labour unrest and industrial conflict in Canada, 1900-66.* Task Force on Labour Relations Privy Council Office. Ottawa: Minister of Supply and Services Canada, 1974.

Janke, W., & Debus, G. "Experimental studies on anti-anxiety agents with normal subjects: Methodological considerations and review of the main effects." In D.H. Efron, J.O. Cole, J. Levine & J.R. Wittenborn (Eds.), *Psychoparmacology: A review of progress 1957-1967*, Public Health Service Publication #1836. Washington: U.S. Government Printing Office, 1968.

Jarrett, M.C. *The Psychopathic Employee: A problem of industry.* New York: National Committee for Mental Hygiene, 1917.

Jarrett, M.C. "The mental hygiene of industry: Report of progress on work undertaken under the Engineering Foundation of New York City." *Mental Hygiene*, 1920, *4*, 867-884.

Johnson, J.H., Giannetti, R.D., & Nelson, N.M. "The results of a survey on the use of technology in a mental health centre." *Hospital and Community Psychiatry*, 1976, *27(6)*, 385-391.

Johnson, R.W. "Human relations in modern business." In E.C. Bursk (Ed.), *Human Relations for Management: The newer perspective.* New York: Harper and Brothers, 1950.

184

Joint Commission on Mental Illness and Health. *Action for Mental Health*. New York: Basic Books, 1961.

Joyce, C.R.B. "Psychedelics." In S. Rose (Ed.) *CBW: Chemical and biological warfare*. London: George G. Harrop and Company, 1968.

Kahan, F.H. *Brains and Bricks: A history of the Yorkton Psychiatric Centre*. Regina, Sask.: White Cross, 1965.

Kahan, R.L. "Conflict, ambiguity, and overload: Three elements in job stress." *Occupational Mental Health*, 1973, *3*, 2-9.

Kalinowsky, L.B. "Present status of electroconvulsive therapy." In J.H. Masserman (Ed.), *Current Psychiatric Therapies* (Vol. 1), New York: Grune and Stratton, 1961.

Karpas, M.R. *Mental Disorders: A sociological overview*. Educational Research Monograph #7. Chicago: Juvenile Delinquency Research Projects, 1964.

Katz, D. "Approaches to managing conflict." In R.L. Kahn & E. Boulding (Eds.), *Power and Conflict in Organizations*. New York: Basic Books, 1964.

Kele, M.H. *Nazis and Workers: National socialist appeals to German labor, 1919-1933*. Chapel Hill, N.C.: University of North Carolina Press, 1972.

Kelman, S. "The social nature of the definition problem in health." *International Journal of Health Services*, 1975, *5(4)*, 625-642.

Keniston, K. "How community mental health stamped out the riots (1968-1978)." In S. Wallace (Ed.), *Total Institutions*. New York: Transaction, 1968.

Kennedy, J.F. *Message from the President of the United States relative to mental illness and mental retardation*, Document #58, 88th Congress, First Session, U.S. House of Representatives, Feb. 5, 1963, p. 13.

Kerr, W. "Shift from foreign to domestic sector growth seen at Conference Board." *Globe and Mail*, March 2, 1979, p. 34.

Kets de Vries, M.F.R. "Managers can drive their subordinates mad." *Harvard Business Review*, July-Aug. 1979, pp. 125-134.

Kinnersly, P. *The Hazards of Work: How to fight them*. London: Pluto Press, 1973.

Kline, N.S. "Pharmaceuticals in the treatment of psychiatric patients." *Mental Hygiene*, 1957, *41*, 207-212.

Kline, N.S. "Psychiatry in Indonesia." *American Journal of Psychiatry*, 1963, *119*, 809-815.

Kline, N.S. Presidential address. In D.H. Efron, N.O. Cole, J. Levine & J.R. Wittenborn (Eds.), *Psychopharmacology: A review of progress 1957-1967*, Public Health Service Publication #1836. Washington: U.S. Government Printing Office, 1968.

Kohler, W.C. "Medicine's role in juvenile corrections." *American Journal of Corrections*, 1976, *38(1)*, 11-16.

Kohn, M.L. "Social class and schzophrenia: A critical review." *Journal of Psychiatric Research*, 1968, *6*, 155-173.

Kohn, M.L., & Schooler, C. "Occupational experience and psychological functioning: An assessment of reciprocal effects." *American Sociological Review*, 1973, *38*, 97-118.

Kolb, L.C. "The current problem of research involving human beings: The curse of the holy grail." In D.H. Efron, J.O. Cole, J. Levine & J.R. Wittenborn (Eds.), *Psychopharmacology: A review of progress 1957-1967*, Public Health Service Publication #1836. Washington: U.S. Government Printing Office, 1968.

Korman, A.K. *Industrial and Organizational Psychology*. Englewood Cliffs, N.J.: Prentice-Hall, 1971.

Kornhauser, A. *Mental Health of the Industrial Worker*. New York: John Wiley and Sons, 1965.

Kouri, D., & Stirling, R. *Unemployment Indexes—The Canadian Context*. Unpublished paper, Sample Survey, University of Regina, 1979.

Kovel, J. *The American Mental Health Industry*. Unpublished paper. New York: Albert Einstein Medical School, 1976.

Kowaluk, L. "Working in a social agency." In W. Johnson (Ed.), *Working in Canada*. Montréal: Black Rose Books, 1975.

Kramer, M. "Psychiatric services and the changing institutional scene." In *Research on Disorders of the Mind: Progress and prospects*. Washington: U.S. Government Printing Office, 1977.

Kramer, M., Rosen, B.M., & Willis, L. "Definitions and distributions of mental disorders in a racist society." In C.V. Willie, B.M. Kramer & B.S. Brown (Eds.) *Racism and Mental Health*. Pittsburgh: University of Pittsburgh Press, 1973.

Krause, E.A. *Power and Illness: The political sociology of health and medical care*. New York: Elsevier, 1977.

Kristjanson, K. "Policy initiatives for the period of controls and beyond." *Canadian Personnel and Industrial Relations Journal*, 1977, *24(1)*, 20-23.

Kuznets, S. *Postwar Economic Growth: Four lectures*. Cambridge, Mass.: Harvard University Press, 1964.

"Labor looks at mental health." *The Massachusetts Association for Mental Health Newsletter*, Feb.-March, 1954, p. 1.

Laforest, L. "Facteurs socio-culturels de l'étiologie au Québec: quelques hypothèses de recherche." *Toxicomanies*, Québec, 1968, *1*, 105-110.

186

Laing, R.D. *Do You Love Me? An entertainment in conversation and verse.* New York: Pantheon Books, 1976.

Lamb, D. " 'Epidemic' of dependency." *Guardian,* May 3, 1978, p. 11.

Lamb, H.N., & Goertzel, V. "Discharged mental patients: Are they really in the community." *Archives of General Psychiatry,* 1971, *24,* 29-34.

Lamont, C. "Conform — or lose your job." *Monthly Review,* 1956, *7(10),* 401-407.

Lampkin, P. *Job Enrichment.* Ottawa: Department of Labour, 1975.

Landers, S. "Capitalism and the drug industry." *State and Mind,* 1978, *6,* 28-33.

Landsberger, H.A. *Hawthorne Revisited.* Ithaca, N.Y.: Cornell University Press, 1958.

Langer, E. "United States." In S. Rose (Ed.), *CBW: Chemical and Biological Warfare.* London: George G. Harrap and Company, 1968.

Langfeldt, G. "Scandinavia." In L. Bellack (Ed.), *Contemporary European Psychiatry.* New York: Grove Press, 1961.

Langner, T.S., & Michael, S.T. *Life Stress and Mental Health.* London: Collier-Macmillan, 1963.

Larned, D. "Do you take valium?" *Ms.,* Nov. 1975, pp. 26-35.

Laska, E.M., & Bank, R. *Safeguarding Psychiatric Privacy: Computer systems and their uses.* New York: John Wiley and Sons, 1975.

Laska, E., & Kline, N.S. "Computers at the Rockland Research Center." In N.S. Kline & E. Laska (Eds.), *Computers and Electronic Devices in Psychiatry.* New York: Grune and Stratton, 1968.

Latz, J. "Keep left for change." In *Madness Network News,* 1979, *5(3),* 5.

Lawrence, W.L. "Drug found help in schizophrenia." *New York Times,* Feb. 4, 1955, p. 28.

Lawrence P.R. "How to live with resistance to change." In E.C. Bursk (Ed.), *Human Relations for Management: The newer perspective.* New York: Harper and Brothers, 1956.

Lawson, F.S. "The Saskatchewan Plan." *The Canadian Nurse,* 1967, *63,* 27-29.

Lazarus, R. *Psychological Stress and the Coping Process.* New York: McGraw-Hill, 1966.

Lehmann, H.E. "Psychoactive drugs and their influence on the dynamics of working capacity." *Journal of Occupational Medicine,* 1960, *2,* 523-527.

Leifer, R. "Community psychiatry and social power." *Social Problems,* 1966, *14,* 16-22.

Leifer, R. "Involuntary psychiatric hospitalization and social control." *International Journal of Social Psychiatry*, 1967, *13*, 53-58.

Leifer, R. *In the Name of Mental Health: The social functions of psychiatry*. New York: Science House, 1969.

Lenard, V.A., & More, H.W. *Police Organization and Management* (4th ed.). Mineola, N.Y.: Foundation Press, 1974.

Lenin, V.I. *Imperialism: The highest stage of capitalism*. New York: International Publishers, 1939.

Lenin, V.I. *Karl Marx: A brief biographical sketch with an exposition of Marxism*. Peking: Foreign Languages Press, 1970.

Lenin, V.I. "The state." In V.I. Lenin (Ed.), *Selected Works* (Vol. 3). Moscow: Progress Publishers, 1971.

Lenin, V.I. *Marxism on the State*. Moscow: Progress Publishers, 1972.

Lenin, V.I. *The State and Revolution*. Peking: Foreign Languages Press, 1973.

Lennard, H.L., & Bernstein, A. "Perspectives on the new psychoactive drug technology." In R. Cooperstock (Ed.), *Social Aspects of the Medical Use of Psychotropic Drugs*. Ottawa: Addiction Research Foundation of Ontario, 1973.

Leopold, R.L. "Toward health maintenance organization." In L. Bellak (Ed.), *A Concise History of Community Psychiatry and Community Mental Health*. New York: Grune and Stratton, 1974.

Levine, S., & Scotch, N.A. "Social stress." In S. Levine & N.A. Scotch (Eds.), *Social Stress*. Chicago: Aldine Publishers.

Levinson, H. "Alcoholism in industry." *Menninger Quarterly*, 1957, *11(2)*, entire issue.

Levinson, H. "Dilemmas of the occupational physician in mental health programming — Part II." *Journal of Occupational Medicine*, 1960, *2(5)*, 205-208.

Levinson, H., Price, C.R., Munden, K.J., Mandl, H.J., & Solley, C.M. *Men, Management and Mental Health*. Cambridge, Mass.: Harvard University Press, 1963.

Levy, H. "The military medicinemen." In J. Ehrenreich (Ed.) *The Cultural Crisis of Modern Medicine*. New York: Monthly Review Press, 1978.

Lewin, K. *Dynamic Theory of Personality*. New York: McGraw-Hill, 1935.

Lewin, K. *Principles of Topological Psychology*. New York: McGraw-Hill, 1936.

Lewin, K. *Resolving Social Conflicts*. New York: Harper, 1948.

Lewin, K. *Field Theory in Social Science*. New York: Harper, 1951.

Lewisohn, S.A. *The New Leadership in Industry.* New York: E.P. Dutton and Company, 1926.

Liazos, A. "Class oppression: The functions of juvenile justice." *Insurgent Sociologist,* 1974, *5,* 2-24.

Lieberman, Elliott (Ed.), *Mental Health: The public health challenge.* Washington: American Public Health Association, 1975.

Likert, R. *The Human Organization: Its management and value.* New York: McGraw-Hill, 1967.

Lin, T-Y. "Evolution of mental health programme in Taiwan." *American Journal of Psychiatry,* 1961, *117,* 961-971.

Lindstrom, P.D. "Studies in the technic and effects of ultrasonic irradiation." *Ultraschall in Medicine,* 1959, *7,* 85.

Lindstrom, P.A., Moench, L.G. & Rounanek, A. "Prefrontal sonic treatment." In J.H. Masseman (Ed.), *Current Psychiatric Therapies* (Vol. 4). New York: Grune and Stratton, 1964.

Linn, L.S. "Physician characteristics and attitudes toward legitimate use of psychotropic drugs." *Journal of Health and Social Behavior,* 1971, *12,* 132-140.

Lipton, C. *The Trade Union Movement of Canada 1827-1959.* Toronto: New Canada Press, 1967.

Livant, W.P. *On Statistics: Canada's two sets of books.* Unpublished paper, University of Regina, April 1978.

Livingston, Martha. *The Mass Line and Mental Health Work in New China.* Unpublished Master's Thesis, University of Regina, 1974.

Lopata, H. *Occupation Housewife.* New York: Oxford University Press, 1971.

Lottherhos, J.F., & Waldrop, H. "A historical perspective of employee alcoholism programs." *Inventory,* 1972, *22(1),* 14-18.

Love, E.J., & Hobbs, G.E. "Changing patterns of mental hospital practice 1940-1962." *Canadian Psychiatric Association Journal,* 1971, *16,* 77-81.

Lovelock, C.H., & Young, R.F. "Look to consumers to increase productivity." *Harvard Business Review,* May-June 1979, 168-179.

MacClay, W.S. "Trends in the British mental health service." In *Proceedings of the Third World Congress of Psychiatry* (Vol. 1). Montréal: University of Toronto Press, 1961, 98-102.

MacIver, J. "The impact of psychiatry on American management: A psychiatrist's view." *Industrial Medicine and Surgery,* 1962, *31(11),* 471-475.

MacIver, J. "The epidemiology of mental illness in industry." In R.T. Collins (Ed.), *Occupational Psychiatry.* Boston: Little, Brown and Company, 1969.

189

MacIver, J., McLean, A.A., Herzberg, F., Burling, T., & Roethlisberger, F.J. "Psychiatry and the future of American management." *Industrial Medicine and Surgery*, 1962, *31(11)*, 499-503.

Magaro, P.A., Gripp, R., & McDowell, D.J. *The Mental Health Industry: A cultural phenomenon*. New York: John Wiley and Sons, 1978.

Maguigad, L.C. "Psychiatry in the Philippines." *American Journal of Psychiatry*, 1964, *121*, 21-25.

Mallinson, T.J. "A social psychologist looks at industry." *Canadian Journal of Public Health*, 1957, *48*, 107-108.

Mandell, B.R. "Whose welfare: An Introduction." In B.R. Mandell (Ed.), *Welfare in America: Controlling the "dangerous classes."* Englewood Cliffs, N.Y.: Prentice-Hall, 1975.

Marcuse, H. *One-dimensional Man: Studies in the ideology of advanced industrial society*. Boston: Beacon Press, 1964.

Marquis, D.G., Kelley, E.L., Miller, J.G., Gerard & Rapoport, A. "Experimental studies in behavioral effects of meprobamate on normal subjects." *Annals of the New York Academy of Science*, 1957, *67*, 701-711.

Martel, P.G. *A Role of the Federal Government in Mental Health: A report prepared for the Department of National Health and Welfare*, Sherbrooke, Québec: University of Sherbrooke, 1973.

Martell, G. "The schools, the state and the corporations." In G. Martell (Ed.), *The Politics of the Canadian Public School*. Toronto: James Lewis and Samuel, 1974.

Marx, K. *Wage-labour and Capital*. New York: International Publishers, 1933.

Marx, K. *Wages, Price and Profit*. Peking: Foreign Languages Press, 1965.

Marx, K. *Capital: A critique of political economy*. (Vol. 1: *A Critical Analysis of Capitalist Production*) (3rd ed.). (S. Moore & E. Dulling, trans., F. Engels, Ed.). New York: International Publishers, 1967.

Marx, K. Letter to Engels (Sept. 25, 1857). In K. Marx and F. Engels, *Selected Letters*. Peking: Foreign Languages Press, 1977.

Marx, K., & Engels, F. *Manifesto of the Communist Party*. Peking: Foreign Languages Press, 1972.

Masi, F.A., & Spencer, G.E. "Alcoholism and employee assistance programs in industry: A new frontier for social work." *Social Thought*, 1977 *3(1)*, 19-27.

Maslow, A.H. *Toward a Psychology of Being*. Princeton, N.J.: D. Van Nostrand, 1962.

Matles, J.J., & Higgins, J. *Them and Us: Struggles of a rank-and-file union*. Englewood Cliffs, N.J.: Prentice-Hall, 1974.

Mayo, E. "Civilized unreason." *Harper Magazine*, 1924, *148*, 527-535.

Mayo, E. "Changing methods in industry." *Personality Journal*, 1930, *8*, 326-332.

Mayo, E. *The Human Problems of an Industrial Civilization*. New York: Viking Press, 1933.

Mayo, E. "Psychiatry and sociology in relation to social disorganization." *American Journal of Sociology*, 1937, *42*, 825-831.

Mayo, E. *The Social Problems of an Industrial Civilization*. Boston: Harvard University Press, 1946.

McCallum, P. "Programs aid troubled workers on job." *The Globe and Mail*, April 21, 1979, p. 1.

McFadden, R.D. "Strike beginning to disrupt state services." *New York Times*, April 2, 1972, p. 1.

McGuire, T.F., & Leary, F.J. "Problems resulting from the use of habituating drugs in industry: Tranquilizing drugs and stress tolerance." *American Journal of Public Health*, 1958, *48*, 578-584.

McKerracher, D.G. *Trends in Psychiatric Care*. Royal Commission on Health Services: Hall Commission. Ottawa, 1966.

McLean, A.A. (Ed.) *To Work is Human: Mental health and the business community*. New York: The Macmillan Company, 1967.

McLean, A.A. "Occupational mental health: Review of an emerging art." In R.T. Collins (Ed.), *Occupational Psychiatry*. Boston: Little, Brown and Company, 1969.

McLean, A.A., & Taylor, G.C. *Mental Health in Industry*. New York: McGraw-Hill, 1958.

McLean, A.A., & Wohlking, W. "The impact of psychiatry on American management: A conference presented by the New York State School of Industrial and Labor Relations, Cornell University, New York City, March 1962." *Industrial Medicine and Surgery*, 1962, *31(11)*, 469.

McLean, D., Smith, S., & Hill, J. *Workmen's Compensation*. Unpublished manuscript, University of Regina, 1975.

McMurry, R.N. "Mental illness: Industry's three billion dollar burden." *Advanced Management*, Sept. 1960, pp. 18-20.

McNair, F.E., & Barnes, K.E. "Where is the community mental health center going?" *Canadian Journal of Public Health*, 1970, *61*, 98-103.

McNamara, W.J. "Use of test data in selection and placement." In D.P. Schultz (Ed.), *Psychology and Industry*. Toronto: Collier-Macmillan Limited, 1970.

191

Meany, G. *What Organized Labor Expects of Management.* New York: National Association of Manufacturers, 1956.

Mechanic, D. "Community psychiatry: Some sociological perspectives and implications." In L.M. Roberts, S.L. Halleck & M.B. Loeb, *Community Psychiatry.* Garden City, N.Y.: Doubleday and Company, 1969.

Meissner, M. "The long arm of the job: A study of work and leisure." *Industrial Relations,* 1971, *10*, 239-260.

Meltz, N.M. *Manpower in Canada 1931 to 1961: Historical Statistics of the Canadian Labour Force.* Department of Manpower and Immigration Publication #MP 34-368. Ottawa: Queen's Printer, 1969.

Melzack, R. "The perception of pain." *Scientific American,* 1961, *204(2),* 41-49.

Menninger, W.C. "Lessons from military psychiatry for civilian psychiatry." *Mental Hygiene,* 1946, *30,* 572-576.

Menninger, W.C. "Men, machines, and mental health." *Mental Hygiene,* 1952, *36,* 184-196.

Menninger, W.C., & Levinson, H. "The Menninger Foundation Survey of Industrial Mental Health: Observations and perspectives." *Menninger Quarterly,* 1954, *8,* 1-13.

Menninger, W.C., & Levinson, H. "Psychiatry in industry: Some trends and perspectives." *Personnel,* 1955, *32,* 90-99.

Mental Health Statistics. *Trends in hospital care and patient characteristics, 1955-1963.* Dominion Bureau of Statistics. Ottawa: Queen's Printer, 1966.

"Mental illness traced: Western group blames modern tensions for increase." *New York Times,* Aug. 30, 1955, p. 53.

Meyer, N.G. *Changes in the age, sex and diagnostic composition of first admissions to state and county mental hospitals, United States 1962-72,* Statistical note #97. Office of Program planning and evaluation, biometry branch. Rockville, Md.: NIMH, Sept. 1973.

Migler, B., & Wolpl, J. "Automated self-desensitization: A case report." *Behavior Research and Therapy,* 1967, *5,* 133-135.

Mikulos, W.L. *Behavior Modification.* New York: Harper and Row, 1978.

Miliband, R. *The State in Capitalist Society: The analysis of the Western system of power.* London: Quartet Books, 1969.

Miliband, R. "Reply to Nicos Poulantzas." In R. Blackburn (Ed.), *Ideology in Social Science: Readings in critical social theory.* Glasgow: William Collins Sons and Company, 1972.

Mindus, E. *Industrial Psychology in Great Britain, the United States, and Canada: A report to the World Health Organization.* Stockholm: Institute of Applied Psychology, University of Stockholm, 1953.

Mintz, M. *By Prescription Only.* Boston: Beacon Press, 1967.

Miranda, M.R., & Kitano, H. "Mental health services in third world communities." *International Journal of Mental Health,* 1976, *5(2),* 39-49.

Mishler, E.G., & Scotch, N.A. "Sociocultural factors on the epidemiology of schizophrenia." *International Journal of Psychiatry,* 1965, *1,* 258-293.

Mitchell, L.E. "Nonprofessionals in mental health." In C. Grosser, W.E. Henry & J.G. Kelly (Eds.), *Nonprofessionals in the Human Services.* San Francisco: Jossey-Bass, 1969.

Modlin, H.C. "Put the psychiatrist on the team." *Health and Safety,* Jan.-Feb. 1976, pp. 34-35.

Monahan, J. "The psychiatrization of criminal behavior." In J. Monahan (Ed.), *Community Mental Health and the Criminal Justice System.* New York: Pergamon Press, 1976.

Moody's Industrial Manual, 1960. New York: Moody's Investor's Service, 1960.

Mostow, E., & Newberry, P. "Work role and depression in women: A comparison of workers and housewives in treatment." *American Journal of Orthopsychiatry,* 1975, *45(4),* 538-548.

Mott, P.E., Mann, F.C., McLoughlin, Q., & Warwick, D.P. *Shift Work: The social, psychological, and physical consequences.* Ann Arbor: University of Michigan Press, 1965.

Muller, C. "The overmedicated society: Forces in the marketplace for medical care." *Science,* 1972, *176,* 488-492.

Munden, K.J. "Dilemmas of the occupational physician in mental health prgramming—Part I." *Journal of Occupational Medicine,* 1960, *2(5),* 201-204.

Munro, J.L. (Ed.), *Classes, Conflict, and Control: Studies in criminal justice management.* Cincinnati: Anderson Publishers, 1976.

Münsterberg, H. *Psychology and Industrial Efficiency.* Boston: Houghton Mifflin and Company, 1913.

Murphy, H.B., Pennee, B., & Luchens, D. "Foster Homes: The new back wards?" *Canada's Mental Health,* 1972, Supplement *71,* 1-17.

Murphy, J.A., & Datel, W.E. "A cost-benefit analysis of community versus institutional living." *Hospital and Community Psychiatry,* 1976, *27(3),* 165-170.

Muszynski, S. "Mental health care and treatment: Will health planning make a difference?" *Hospital and Community Psychiatry*, 1976,, *27(6)*, 398-400.

Myers, J.M. "The psychiatric hospital looks at the emotionally troubled employee." In P.A. Carone, S.N. Kieffer, L.W. Krinsky & S.F. Yolles (Eds.), *The Emotionally Troubled Employee: A challenge to industry.* New York: SUNY Press, 1976.

Nationaal Congres voor de Geestilijke Volksgezondheid, Amsterdam, 1947. Handelingen: Zwolle, Tiji, 1947.

National Committee for Mental Hygiene. *Minutes and proceedings of the twelfth annual meeting of the National Committee for Mental Hygiene.* New York: Author, 1921.

National Committee for Mental Hygiene. *Twenty years of mental hygiene, 1909-1929.* New York: Author, 1929.

National Committee for Mental Hygiene. *Annual Report 1939-1940.* New York: Author, 1940.

National Committee for Mental Hygiene. *Annual Report 1940-1941.* New York: Author, 1941.

National Committee for Mental Hygiene. *Annual Report 1941-1942.* New York: Author, 1942.

National Committee for Mental Hygiene. *Annual Report 1944.* New York: Author, 1944.

National Committee for Mental Hygiene. *Bibliography: Mental Hygiene in Industry.* New York: Author, 1945.

Nasatir, A.V. "Mental hygiene and industry in an ailing world." *Industrial Medicine*, 1940, *9*, 583-588.

National Advisory Commission on Criminal Justice Standards and Goals. *Police.* Washington: U.S. Government Printing Office, 1973.

National Manpower Survey of the Criminal Justice System: Executive Summary. Washington: Law Enforcement Assistance Administration, 1978.

Navarro, V. *Medicine Under Capitalism.* New York: Neale Watson Academic Publications, 1976a.

Navarro, V. "Social class, political power and the state, and their implications in medicine." *Social Science and Medicine,* 1976b, *10*, 437-457.

Navarro, V. "The underdevelopment of health of working America: Causes, consequences, and possible solutions." *American Journal of Public Health*, 1976c, *66(6)*, 538-548.

Navarro, V. "Political power, the state, and their implications in medicine." *The Review of Radical Political Economics,* 1977, *9(1)*, 61-80.

Network Against Psychiatric Assault. *Shock Packet*. San Francisco: Author, 1977.

"New drug for anxiety," *New York Times*, Aug. 23, 1955, p. 21.

"New 'mood-lifting' pill drives blues away." *New York Times*, May 4, 1954, p. 16.

Newell, J. "Aggression and brain chemistry." *Liaison*, 1979, *5(6)*, 8-10.

Newman, H.W. "The effect of amphetamine sulfate on performance of normal and fatigued subjects." *Journal of Pharmacological Experimental Therapies*, 1947, *89*, 106-108.

"NIMH Report examines issues in deinstitutionalization, notes trend to moderate views." *Hospital and Community Psychiatry*, 1977, *28(7)*, 552-557.

Noble, D.F. *America by Design: Science, technology, and the rise of corporate capitalism*. New York: Alfred A. Knopf, 1977.

Norbury, F.G. "Evaluation of tranquilizers." *Industrial Medicine and Surgery*, 1957, *26*, 437-439.

Norris, H.S. "Psychiatric drugs in a general hospital." In C. Shagass (Ed.), *Modern Problems of Pharmacopsychiatry* (Vol. 6 *The Role of Drugs in Community Psychiatry*). Philadelphia: Karger, Basil, 1971.

Obers, D. "'Tayloring' the social sciences." *State and Mind*, 1979, *7(2)*, 25-29.

Occupational Alcoholism: Problems, programs, and progress. Department of Health, Education and Welfare Publication #(ADM) 75-178. Rockville, Md.: ADAMHA, 1973.

O'Connor, J. "Summary of the theory of the fiscal crisis." *Kapitalistate*, 1973, *1*, 79-84.

O'Connor, R.B. "The impact of emotions on production and safety." *The Menninger Quarterly*, 1958 *13(3)*, 1-6.

Offe, C. "Advanced capitalism and the welfare state." *Politics and Society*, 1972, *2(4)*, 479-488.

Office of Program Liaison. *Increasing NIMH responsiveness to youth: Programs, problems, and potentials*. Unpublished report of the Office of Program Liaison Youth Team. Chevy Chase, Md.: NIMH, 1969.

Ontario Council of Health. *Mental health services personnel: A report of the Ontario Council of Health, senior advisory body to the Minister of Health*. Toronto: Author, 1973.

Ostrom, E. "On the meaning and measurement of output and efficiency in the provision of urban police services." In J. Munro (Ed.), *Classes, Conflict, and Control: Studies in criminal justice management*. Cincinnati: Anderson, 1976.

Ozarin, L.D. "Recent community mental health legislation: A brief review." *American Journal of Public Health*, 1962, *52(3)*, 436-441.

Paehike, R. "Occupational health policy in Canada." In W. Leiss (Ed.), *Ecology Versus Politics in Canada*. Toronto: University of Toronto Press, 1979.

Paget, N. "Industrial strategy in need of change." *Globe and Mail*, May 19, 1979, p. 24.

Panitch, L. Editor's preface and "The role and nature of the Canadian state." In L. Panitch (Ed.), *The Canadian State: Political economy and political power*. Toronto: University of Toronto Press, 1977.

Paredes, A., Gogerty, J.H. & West, L.J. "Psychopharmacology." In J.H. Masserman (Ed.), *Current Psychiatric Therapies* (Vol. 1). New York: Grune and Stratton, 1961.

Parish, P.A. "What influences have led to increased prescribing of psychotropic drugs?" *Journal of the Royal College of General Practitioners*, 1973, *23* (Supplement 2), 49.

Parisi, N., Gottfredson, M.R., Hindelang, M.J., & Flanagan, T.J. (Eds.), *Sourcebook of Criminal Justice Statistics, 1978*. Washington: Law Enforcement Assistant Administration, 1979.

Patry, B. "Taylorism comes to the social services." *Monthly Review*, 1978, *30(5)*, 30-37.

Pearl, A., & Fiessman, F. *New Careers for the Poor: The nonprofessional in human service*. New York: Free Press, 1965.

Pearlin, L.I. "Alienation from work: A study of nursing personnel." *American Sociological Review*, 1962, *27(3)*, 314-326.

Peck, D.F., & Gathercole, C.E. "Automation techniques in clinical psychology." In R.L. Schwitzgebel & R.K. Schwitzgebel (Eds.), *Psychotechnology: Electronic control of mind and behavior*. New York: Holt, Rinehart and Winston, 1973.

Pekkanen, J. "The impact of promotion on physicians' prescribing patterns." *Journal of Drug Issues*, 1976, *6*, 14-20.

Pelling, H. *A History of British Trade Unionism* (2nd ed.). London: Macmillan, 1972.

Perry, H.J. "Use of psychotropic drugs by U.S. adults." *Public Health Reports*, 1968, *83(10)*, whole report.

Persky, S., & Brunet, M. "How the NDP's Dennis Cocke took the community out of community mental health: And why." *Canadian Dimension*, April 1975, 32-41.

Peterson, P.G. *The United States in the Changing World Economy* (Vol. 2). Washington: U.S. Government Printing Office, 1971.

Pflanz, M., Basder, H.D., & Schwoon, D. "Use of tranquilizing drugs by a middle-aged population in a West German City." *Journal of Health and Social Behavior*, 1977, *18*, 194-205.

Pilisuk, M., & Ober, L. "Torture and genocide as public health problems." *American Journal of Orthopsychiatry*, 1976, *46(3)*, 388-392.

Pinkerton, A. *Strikers, Communists, Tramps and Detectives.* New York: G.W. Carleton and Company, 1878.

Piven, F.F., & Cloward, R. *Regulating the Poor.* New York: Random House, 1971.

Planondon, P. "Transactional analysis cools out prisoners." *Radical Therapist* , 1973, *3(5)*, 11.

Plumb, R.K. "One-third adults upset." *New York Times*, Oct. 13, 1954, p. 21.

Poulantzas, N. "The problem of the capitalist state." In R. Blackburn (Ed.), *Ideology in Social Science: Readings in critical social theory.* Glasgow: William Collins Sons and Company, 1972.

President's Commission on Mental Health. *Task panel reports submitted to the President's Commission on Mental Health* (Vol. 2). Washington: U.S. Government Printing Office, 1978.

Preston, G.H. "The new public psychiatry." *Mental Hygiene*, 1947, *31(2)*, 177-184.

Prewst, C. "Cutbacks in Britain meet resistance." *Guardian*, Aug. 29, 1979, p. 14.

"Proposed legislation on mental health care." *New York Times*, May 16, 1979, p. 12.

Pruette, L., & Fryer, D. *Affective Factors in Vocational Maladjustment.* New York: National Committee for Mental Hygiene, 1923.

Pursch, J.A. "Pursch cites treatment barriers." *NIAAA Information and Feature Service*, Aug. 6, 1969, *62*, 3.

Rabkin, J.G. "Opinions about mental illness: A review of the literature." *Psychological Bulletin*, 1972, *77*, 152-171.

Radloff, L. "Sex differences in depression: The effects of occupation and marital status." *Sex Roles*, 1975, *1(3)*, 249-265.

Ralph, D. "Racism in mental health: A case study." *The Advocate*, 1969, *2(4)*, 1, 4.

Ralph, D. "Shrinking to fit in Saskatchewan." *State and Mind*, 1979, *7(2)*, 21-24.

Ralston, A. "Employee alcoholism: Response of the largest industrials." *The Personnel Administrator*, 1977, *22(6)*, 50-56.

Rayback, J.G. *A History of American Labor.* New York: Free Press, 1966.

Red Star Collective, *Canada's Sick Economy.* Vancouver Author, 1978.

"Red Strip." *Fortune,* 1954, *50(6),* 66, 70.

Rees, T.P. "The changing pattern of mental health services." *Royal Society for the Promotion of Health Journal,* 1959, *79(4),* 354-356.

Rees, T.P. "The world community." In H.P. David (Ed.), *International Trends in Mental Health.* New York: McGraw-Hill, 1966.

Reid, D. "Precipitating proximal factors in the occurence of mental disorders: Epidemiological evidence." *Milbank Memorial Fund Quarterly,* 1961, *39(2),* 229-258.

Reiff, R., & Riessman, F. *The Indigenous Nonprofessional: A strategy of change in community action and community mental health programs.* Washington: NIMH, 1964.

Reiff, R., & Scribner, S. *Issues in the New National Mental Program Relating to Labor and Low Income Groups.* New York: National Institute of Labor Education, 1963.

Rennie, T.A.C., Swackhamer, G., & Woodward, L.E. "Toward industrial mental health: An historical review." *Mental Hygiene,* 1947, *31,* 66-85.

Rennie, T.A.C., & Woodward, L.E. *Mental Health in Modern Society.* New York: The Commonwealth Fund, 1948.

Renshaw, P. *The Wobblies: The story of syndicalism in the United States.* Garden City, N.Y.: Doubleday, 1967.

Repo, M. "The fallacy of community control." *Transformation,* 1971, *1(1),* 11-17, 33-34.

Richman, A. *Psychiatric Care in Canada: Extent and results.* Royal Commission on Health Services (Hall Commission). Ottawa: Queen's Printer, 1966.

Rickels, K. "Drugs in outpatient practice." In C. Shagass (Ed.), *Modern Problems of Pharmacopsychiatry* (Vol. 6, *The Role of Drugs in Community Psychiatry*). Philadelphia: Karger, Basil, 1971.

Riessman, F. *New Approaches to Mental Health Treatment for Labor and Low Income Groups.* New York: National Institute of Labor Education, 1964.

Ritti, R.R., & Hyman, D.W. "The administration of poverty: Lessons from the 'welfare explosion' 1967-1973." *Social Problems,* 1977, *25,* 157-175.

Robbins, E., & Robbins, L. "Charge to the community: Some early effects of a state hospital systems change of policy." *American Journal of Psychiatry,* 1974, *131(6),* 641-645.

Roberts, B.C., Okamato, H., & Lodge, G.C. *Collective bargaining and employee participation in Western Europe, North America and Japan, Report to the Trilateral Task Force on industrial relations to the Trilateral Commission.* New York: The Trilateral Commission, 1979.

Robertson, R.L., & Shriver, B.M. "The general practitioner training program of the National Institute of Mental Health: Fiscal years 1959-1962." *Journal of Medical Education,* 1964, *39*, 925-934.

Robitscher, J. "Moving patients out of hospitals—in whose interests?" In P.I. Ahmed & S.L. Plog (Eds.), *State Mental Hospitals: What happens when they close?* New York: Plenum Medical *Books,* 1976.

Rockefeller, D., Jr. "The personal relation in industry." An address delivered at Cornell University, Jan. 11, 1917. Reprinted in L. Stern & P. Taft (Eds.), *The Management of Workers: Selected arguments.* New York: Arno and *The New York Times,* 1971.

Rockefeller, J.D., Jr. *The Personal Relation in Industry.* New York: Boni and Liveright, 1923.

Roethlisberger, F.J. *Management and Morale.* Cambridge, Mass.: Harvard University Press, 1941.

Roethlisberger, F.J. "The foreman: Master and victim of double talk." *Harvard Business Review,* 1945, *23*, 283-299.

Roethlisberger, F.J., & Dickson, W.J. *Management and the Worker: An account of a research program conducted by the Western Electric Company, Hawthorne Works, Chicago.* Cambridge, Mass.: Harvard University Press, 1939.

Rogers, C.R., & Roethlisberger, F.J. "Barriers and gateways to communication." In E.C. Bursk (Ed.), *Human Relations for Management: The newer perspective.* New York: Harper and Brothers, 1956.

Rogg, S.G., & Pell, S. "Use of psychotropic drugs by employed persons." *Industrial Medicine and Surgery,* 1963, *32(7)*, 255-260.

Ross, W.D. "Mental and emotional health problems in the worker." *Archives of Environmental Health,* 1963, *7*, 473-476.

Ross, W.D., Powles, W.E., & Winslow, W.W. "Secondary-prevention of job description in industry." *Journal of Occupational Medicine,* 1965, *7(7)*, 363-372.

Rostow, W.W. *The World Economy: History and prospect.* Austin: University of Texas Press, 1978.

Rothman, D.J. *The Discovery of the Asylum: Social order and disorder in the New Republic.* Toronto: Little, Brown and Company, 1971.

199

Rothman, D.J. "Of prisons, asylums and other decaying institutions." *The Public Interest*, 1972, *26*, 3-17.

Rothschild, J.H. *Tomorrow's Weapons, Chemical and Biological.* New York: McGraw-Hill and Company, 1964.

Rubin, L.B. *Worlds of Pain: Life in the working-class family.* New York: Basic Books, 1976.

Ruitenbeck, H.M. *The New Group Therapies.* New York: Avon, 1970.

Rushing, W.A. "Occupation, income and mental hospitalization." *Mental Hygiene*, 1971, *55(2)*, 248-252.

Ryan, W. (Ed.), *Distress in the City: Essays on the design and administration of urban mental health services.* Cleveland: Press of Case Western Reserve University, 1969.

Salpukas, A. "Workers increasingly rebel against boredom on assembly line." *New York Times*, April 2, 1972, p. N34.

Sangsingkeo, P. "Mental health in developing countries." In H.P. David (Ed.), *International Trends in Mental Health.* New York: McGraw-Hill, 1966.

Salmon, T.W. "Mental hygiene." In M.J. Rosenau (Ed.), *Preventive Medicine and Hygiene* (3rd ed.). New York: Appleton, 1917.

Salmon, T.W. *Psychiatric Lessons From the War.* New York: National Committee for Mental Hygiene, 1919.

Salutin, L. "Psychiatric involvement in the criminal process." *Canadian Journal of Criminology and Corrections*, 1975, *17*, 236-249.

Santiestevan, H. *Deinstitutionalization: Out of their beds and into the streets.* Washington: American Federation of State, County, and Municipal Workers, Dec. 1976.

Sargent, W., & Blackburn, J.M. "The effect of benzedrine on intelligence scores." *Lancet*, 1936, *231*, 1385-1387.

Saskatchewan Department of Public Works. *Annual Report for the Fiscal Year Ended April 30, 1933.* Regina, Sask.: Author, 1933.

Sass, R. "The underdevelopment of occupational health and safety in Canada." In W. Leiss (Ed.), *Ecology Versus Politics in Canada.* Toronto: University of Toronto Press, 1979.

Sayles, L.R. *Behavior of Industrial Work Groups: Prediction and control.* New York: John Wiley and Sons, 1958.

Schatzkin, A. "Health and labor-power: A theoretical investigation." *International Journal of Health Services*, 1978, *8(2)*, 213-234.

Schecter, S. "Capitalism, class and educational reform in Canada." In L. Panitch (Ed.), *The Canadian State: Political economy and political power.* Toronto: University of Toronto Press, 1977.

Scheff, T.J. "The role of the mentally ill and the dynamics of mental disorder: A research framework." In S.P. Spitzer & N.K. Denzin (Eds.), *The Mental Patient: Studies in the sociology of deviance*. New York: McGraw-Hill, 1968.

Scheff, T.J. "Medical dominance: Psychoactive drugs and mental health policy." *American Behavioral Scientist*, 1976, *19(3)*, 299-317.

Scher, J.M. "The impact of the drug abuser in the work organization." In J.M. Scher (Ed.), *Drug Abuse in Industry: Growing corporate dilemma*. Springfield, Ill.: Charles C. Thomas, 1973.

Schoen, D.R. "Human relations: Boon or boggle?" *Harvard Business Review*, Nov.-Dec. 1957, pp. 91-97.

Schrag, A.R. "Mental health—A community problem." *Canadian Journal of Public Health*, 1956, *47*, 203-205.

Schrag, P. *Mind Control*. New York: Pantheon, 1978.

Schrag, P., & Divoky, D. *The Myth of Hyperactivity and Ohter Means of Child Control*. New York: Dell, 1975.

Schuchman, H. "On confidentiality of health records." *American Journal of Orthopsychiatry*, 1975, *45(5)*, 732-733.

Schuckit, M.A., & Gunderson, E.K.E. "The Association between alcoholism and job type in the U.S. Navy." *Quarterly Journal of Studies in Alcoholism*, 1974, *35*, 577-585.

Schumacher, H.C. "The integration of mental hygiene concepts and practices in a public health program." *Canadian Journal of Public Health*, 1948, *39(9)*, 351-357.

Schwab, J.L., & Schwab, M.E. *Sociocultural Roots of Mental Illness: An epidemiologic survey*. New York: Plenum Book Company, 1978.

Schwarz, B.E., Bickford, R.G., & Rome, H.P. "Reversibility of induced psychosis with chlorpromazine." *Mayo Clinical Proceedings*, 1955, 30, 407-415.

Scobel, D. "Doing away with factory blues." *The Personnel Administrator*, 1977, *22(6)*, 17-19.

Scott, J. *Canadian Workers, American Unions: How the American Federation of Labour took over Canada's Unions*. Vancouver: New Star Books, 1978.

Scrivener, R.C. "Productivity in a modern economy." *The Canadian Business Review*, 1974, *1*, 18-20.

Scull, A.T. *Decarceration: Community treatment and the deviant: A radical view*. Englewood Cliffs, N.J.: Prentice-Hall, 1977.

Secretary's Advisory Committee on Automated Personal Data Systems. *Records, Computers and the Rights of Citizens*. Boston: Massachusetts Institute of Technology, 1973.

Seeman, M. "On the personal consequences of alienation in work." *American Sociological Review*, 1967, *32*, 273-285.

Segal, J. (Ed.), *Research in the Service of Mental Health: Report of the Research Task Force of the National Institute of Mental Health*. Rockville, Md.: National Institute of Mental Health, 1975.

Selekman, B.M. *Labor Relations and Human Relations*. New York: McGraw-Hill, 1947.

Sennett, R. *The Fall of Public Man: On the social psychology of capitalism*. New York: Random House, 1976.

Sennett, R., & Cobb, J. *The Hidden Injuries of Class*. New York: Random House, 1972.

Serrin, W. "Union frets as automation widens at auto assembly plants." *Minneapolis Tribune*, Nov. 11, 1979, p. 6DX.

Shagass, C. Introduction, In C. Shagass (Ed.) *Modern Problems of Pharmacopsychiatry* (Vol. 6. *The Role of Drugs in Community Psychiatry*). Philadelphia: Karger, Basil, 1971.

Shah, S. "Community mental health and the criminal justice system: Some issues and problems." In J. Monahan (Ed.), *Community Mental Health and the Criminal Justice System*. New York: Pergamon Press, 1976.

Sharfstein, S.S., & Nafziger, J.C. "Community care: costs and benefits for a chronic patient." *Hospital and Community Psychiatry*, 1976, *27(3)*, 170-173.

Sharp, L.J., & Nye, F.I. *The Employed Mother in America*. Chicago: Rand McNally, 1963.

Shatan, C. "Community psychiatry—Stretcher bearer of the social order?" *International Journal of Psychiatry*, 1969, *7*, 312-321.

Sheppard, H., & Herrick, N.O. *Where Have All the Robots Gone? Worker dissatisfaction in the seventies*. New York: The Free Press, 1972.

Shelly, W.F. "The general practitioner's contribution to community psychiatry." In L. Bellack (Ed.), *Handbook of Community Psychiatry and Community Mental Health*. New York: Grune and Stratton, 1964.

Shorter, E., & Tilly, C. *Strikes in France, 1830-1968*. Cambridge: Cambridge University Press, 1974.

Silverman, M., & Lee, P.R. *Pills, Profits and Politics*. Berkeley: University of California Press, 1974.

Sinclair, V. *The Jungle*. New York: New American Library, 1905.

Singer, H.A. "The management of stress." *Advanced Management*, Sept. 1960, pp. 11-13.

Skinner, B.F. *Beyond Freedom and Dignity*. New York: Knopf, 1971.

Skinner, B.F., & Lindsley, O.R. *Studies in Behavior Therapy, Status Reports II and III.* Washington: Office of Navy Research, 1954.

Slack, C.B. *The Automatic Interview Machine: A system for reinforcing verbal behavior in the absence of an interviewer.* Mimeographed report. Cambridge, Mass.: Harvard Center for Research in Personality, 1960.

Sligh, C.R., Jr. *What Management Expects of Organized Labor.* New York: National Association of Manufacturers, 1956.

Slotkin, E.J., Levy, L., Wetmore, E., & Runk, F.N. *Mental Health Related Activities of Companies and Unions: A survey based on the Metropolitan Chicago Area.* New York: Behavioral Publications, 1971.

Smith, C.M. "Crisis and aftermath: Community psychiatry in Saskatchewan, 1963-69." *Canadian Psychiatric Association Journal,* 1971, *16,* 63-71.

Smith, C.M. *Mental Health Services in Canada—System or nonsystem? A report for the Sachverständigen-Kommission.* Regina, Sask.: Psychiatric Services Branch, March 14, 1974.

Smith, D.E. "The statistics on mental illness: (What they will not tell us about women and why)" In D.E. Smith & S.J. David (Eds.), *Women Look at Psychiatry.* Vancouver: Press Gang Publishers, 1975.

Smith, G. Taped interview. Regina, Sask.. Feb. 16, 1978.

Smith, H. *Psychology of Industrial Behavior* (2nd ed.). New York: McGraw-Hill, 1964.

Sobey, F. *The Nonprofessional Revolution in Mental Health.* New York: Columbia University Press, 1970.

Southard, E.E. "The movement for a mental hygiene of industry." *Mental Hygiene,* 1920a, *4,* 43-64.

Southard, E.E. "The modern specialist in unrest: A place for the psychiatrist." *Mental Hygiene,* 1920b, *4,* 550-563.

Spargo, J. "On child labor." In R. Hofstadter, *The Progressive Movement 1900-1915.* Englewood Cliffs, N.J.: Prentice-Hall, 1963.

Special Task Force to the Secretary of Health, Education, and Welfare. *Work in America.* Cambridge, Mass.: MIT Press, 1973.

Spitzer, R.L., & Wilson, P.T. "A guide to the new nomenclature." In *DSM-II: Diagnostic and Statistical Manual of Mental Disorders (2nd ed.).* Washington: American Psychiatric Association, 1968.

Spitzer, S. "Toward a Marxian theory of deviance." Social Problems, 1975, *22,* 638-651.

Spitzer, S., & Scull, A.T. "Privatization and capitalist development." *Social Problems*, 1977, *25*, 18-29.

Spivak, J. "Fighting mental ills: Kennedy to push drive for big U.S. aid for treatment, prevention." *Wall Street Journal*, January 15, 1963, p. 23.

Spriegel, W.R. "Emotions can be dangerous." *Supervisory Management*, Nov. 1956, pp. 17-22.

Spring, J.H. "Education and the rise of the corporate state." *Socialist Revolution*, 1972, *2(8)*, 73-101.

Srole, L., Langner, T.S., Michael, S.T., Kopler, M., & Rennie, T.A.C. *Mental Health in the Metropolis: The Midtown Manhattan study.* New York: McGraw-Hill, 1962.

Stagner, R. "The psychologist's function in union-management relations." *Personnel Administration*, 1963, *26(1)*, 24-29.

Stephanson, H. "Evaluating human relations training." *Personnel Administration*, 1966, *29*, 34-39.

Steinhart, M.J. "The selling of community mental health." *Psychiatric Quarterly*, 1973, *47*, 325-340.

Stellman, J.M., & Daum, S.M. *Work is Dangerous to Your Health: A handbook of health hazards in the work place and what you can do about them.* New York: Randon House, 1973.

Stewart, A., LaFave, H.G., Grunberg, F., & Herjanic, H. "The Weyburn Experience: Reducing intake as a factor in phasing out a large psychiatric hospital." *American Journal of Psychiatry*, 1968, *125(1)*, 121-129.

Stewart, P.L., & Cantor, M.G. *Varieties of Work Experience: The social control of occupational groups and roles.* New York: John Wiley and Sons, 1974.

Stogdill, C.G. "Progress of mental hygiene programs in public health in Canada." *Canadian Journal of Public Health*, 1949, *40*, 497-507.

Stone, K. "The origin of job structures in the steel industry." *Radical America*, 1973, *7(6)*, 19-59.

Stotland, E., Walsh, M., & Weinberg, M. *Investigation of White Collar Crime: A manual for law enforcement agencies.* Washington: U.S. Government Printing Office, 1977.

Super, D.E., & Crites, J.O. *Appraising Vocational Fitness by Means of Psychological Tests* (2nd ed.) New York: Harper and Brothers, 1962.

Sutton, W.L. "Psychiatric disorders in industrial toxicology." In R.T. Collins (Ed.), *Occupational Psychiatry*. Boston: Little, Brown and Company, 1969.

Swann, L.J. "A survey of a boarding-home program for former mental patients." *Hospital and Community Psychiatry*, 1973, *24(7)*, 485-486.

Swartz, D. "The politics of reform: Conflict and accommodation in Canadian health policy." In L. Panitch (Ed.), *The Canadian State: Political economy and political power.* Toronto: University of Toronto Press, 1977.

Sweezy, P.M. *The Theory of Capitalist Development: Principles of Marxian political economy.* New York: Oxford University Press, 1942.

Sweezy, P.M. "Growing wealth, declining power." *Monthly Review,* 1974, *25(10),* 1-11.

Sweezy, P.M. "On the new global disorder." *Monthly Review,* 1979, *30(11),* 1-9.

Sweezy, P.M., & Magdoff, H. "Productivity slowdown: A false alarm." *Monthly Review,* 1979, *31(2),* 1-12.

Sykes, A.J.M. "Economic interest and the Hawthorne researches." *Human Relations,* 1965, *18,* 253-263.

Szasz, T.S. "The myth of mental illness." *American Psychologist,* 1960, *15,* 113-118.

Szasz, T.S. *Ideology and Insanity: Essays on the psychiatric dehumanization of man.* Garden City, N.Y.: Doubleday, Anchor, 1970.

Szasz, T.S. *The Myth of Psychotherapy: Mental healing as religion, rhetoric, and repression.* Garden City, N.Y.: Doubleday, Anchor, 1978.

Talbott, J.A. *The Death of the Asylum: A critical study of state hospital management, services, and care.* New York: Grune and Stratton, 1978.

Tallman, F. "Mental and psychological problems relative to industrial employment." *Journal of the Michigan Medical Society,* 1943, *42,* 710-715.

Tallman, F. "Absenteeism and doctor: Place of psychiatry on reducing absenteeims." *Ohio Medical Journal,* 1944a, *40,* 419-427.

Tallman, F. "Organization of industrial mental health." In D.E. Cameron and H.G. Ross (Eds.), *Human Behavior and Its Relations to Industry.* Montréal: McGill University, 1944b.

Tannenbaum, A.S. *Social Psychology of the Work Organization.* London: Tavistock Publishers, 1966.

Task Force on Privacy and Computers. *Privacy and Computers: A report of a task force established jointly by the Department of Communications and the Department of Justice.* Ottawa: Information Canada, 1972.

Tatham, L.E. *The Efficiency Experts: An impartial survey of management consultancy.* London: Business Publications Limited, 1964.

Taube, C.A., & Redick, R.W. *Provisional data on patient care episodes in mental health facilities, 1975. Mental health statistical note #139*. Rockville, Md.: NIMH, Aug. 1977.

Taylor, F.W. *Scientific Management*. New York: Harper, 1911.

Taylor, F.W. *Scientific management, comprising shop management, the principles of scientific management, and testimony before the special house committee*, 3 vols. Westport, Conn.: Greenwood, 1947.

Taylor, F.W. *The Principles of Scientific Management*. New York: Norton, 1967.

Taylor, G.W. *Government Regulation of Industrial Relations*. New York: Prentice-Hall, 1948.

Taylor, L., & Taylor, I. "We are all deviants now — Some comments on crime." *International Socialism*, 1968, *34*, 29-32.

Tead, O. *Instincts in Industry: A study of working-class psychology*. New York: Houghton Mifflin Company, 1918.

Teed, G. "Burnout: How to work in human services and survive as a person." *Focus: Social and Preventive Medicine*. Publication of the Community Health Services Association, Saskatoon, Sask., Nov. 1979, pp. 3-6.

Terhune, W.B. "Advances in psychotherapy." In J.C. Flugel (Ed.), *Proceedings of the International Congress on Mental Health, London, 1948* (Vol. 3). London: H.K. Lewis and Company, 1948, pp. 98-106.

"The labor situation." *Fortune*, 1946, *34(5)*, 121-126, 280-286.

"The resistable rise (and fall?) of behaviorism — A brief history." *The Psych-agitator*, 1977, *4*, 4-10.

"The ultimate psychiatrist." *Mental Hospitals*, July 1965, p. 196.

"Thirty years of labor peace: How of necessity Standard Oil Company (New Jersey) evolved a unique relationship with its workers. This relationship still baffles the C.I.O." *Fortune*, 1946, *34(5)*, 166-171, 206-211.

Thomson, G. *Capitalism and After: The rise and fall of commodity production*. London: China Policy Study Group, 1973.

Tiffany, D.W., Cavan, J.R., & Tiffany, P.M. *The Unemployed: A social-psychological portrait*. Englewood Cliffs, N.J.: Prentice-Hall, 1970.

Traves, T. *The State and Enterprise: Canadian manufacturers and the Federal Government, 1917-1931*. Toronto: University of Toronto Press, 1979.

Trice, H.M., Hunt, R.E., & Beyer, J.M. "Alcoholism programs in unionized work settings: Problems and prospects in union-management collaboration." *Journal of Drug Issues*, 1977, *7(2)*, 103-115.

Trist, E.L., & Bamforth, K.W. "Some social and psychological consequences of the longwall method of coal getting." *Human Relations*, 1951, *4*, 3-38.

Troxele, J.P. "ELements of job satisfaction." *Personnel*, 1954, *31*, 199-205.

Tuke, D.H. *The Insane in the United States and Canada.* London: H.K. Lewis, 1885.

Turner, C.O., & Spivak, G. "Conceptions of mental illness among low income urban women." *The Forum of the Department of Mental Health Sciences, Hahneman Medical College and Hospital*, 1974, *3(3)*, 29-37.

Tyhurst, J.S., Chalke, F.R., Lawson, F.S., McNeil, B.H., Roberts, C.A., Taylor, G.C., Weil, R.J., & Griffin. *More for the Mind: A study of psychiatric services in Canada.* Toronto: Canadian Mental Health Association, 1963.

U.S. Bureau of the Census. *Statistical Abstract of U.S.—1973.* Washington: U.S. Government Printing Office, 1973.

U.S. Bureau of the Census. *Historical Statistics of the United States: Colonial times to 1970*, (Bicentennial ed.) Part I. Washington: U.S. Government Printing Office, 1975.

Vorenberg, E.W., & Vorenberg, J. "Early diversion from the criminal justice system: Practice in search of a theory." In L.E. Ohlen (Ed.), *Prisoners in America.* Englewood Cliffs, N.J.: Prentice-Hall, 1973.

Wade, L.J. "Needed: A closer look at industrial medical programs." *Harvard Business Review*, 1956, *39(2)*, 81-90.

Wagenfeld, M.O., & Robin, S.S. "Boundary busting in the role of the community mental health worker." *Journal of Health and Social Behavior*, 1976, *17(2)*, 111-121.

Waldron, I. "Increased prescribing of Valium, Librium, and other drugs—An example of the influence of economic and social factors on the practice of medicine." *International Journal of Health Services*, 1977, *7(1)*, 37-62.

Wall, L.R. "A study of employer problems." *Personnel Practices Bulletin* 1959, *15(4)*, 33-37.

Wallick, F. *The American Worker an Endangered Species.* New York: Ballantine Books, 1972.

Ward, B. *Progress for a Small Planet.* New York: W.W. Norton and Company, 1979.

Wasserman, R. (Ed.) *Terrorismus contra Reichtstaat.* Darmstaat, West Germany: Hermann Luchterhand Verlag, Zweignieder lassung, 1976.

Watkins, M. "The trade union movement in Canada." In R.M. Laxer (Ed.), *Canada, Ltd.: The political economy of dependency.* Toronto: McClelland and Stewart, 1973.

207

Weaver, W. "New drugs in psychiatric therapy." *New York Times,* Jan. 9, 1955, p. 79.

Weiman, C.G. "A study of occupational stress and the incidence of disease/risk." *Journal of Occupational Medicine,* 1977, *19(2),* 119-122.

Weiner, H.J. "Labor-management relations and mental health." In A. McLean (Ed.), *To Work is Human: Mental health and the business community.* New York: Macmillan Company, 1967.

Weiner, H.J., Akabas, S.H., & Sommer, J.J. *Mental Health Care in the World of Work.* New York: Association Press, 1973.

Weitz, D. "The history of shock treatment." *State and Mind,* 1979, *7(22),* 42-43.

Whitehead, T.N. *The Industrial Worker: A statistical study of human relations in a group of manual workers* (Vol. 2). Cambridge, Mass.: Harvard University Press, 1938.

Whitney, L.H. "Dilemmas of the occupational physician in mental health programming—Part III." *Journal of Occupational Medicine,* 1960, *6,* 209-210.

Whyte, W.F. "Human relations theory—A progress report." *Harvard Business Review,* 1956, *34(5),* 125-132.

Wilcock, R.C. "Industrial management's policies toward unionism." In M. Derber & E. Young (Eds.), *Labor and the New Deal.* Madison: The University of Wisconsin Press, 1961.

Wilensky, J.L., & Wilensky, H.L. "Personnel counseling: The Hawthorne case." *American Journal of Sociology,* 1951, *57,* 265-280.

Willard, J.W. *Mental Health Services in Canada.* Ottawa: Dept. of National Health and Welfare, 1957.

Willie, C.V., Kramer, B.M., & Brown, B.S. (Eds.), *Racism and Mental Health.* Pittsburgh: University of Pittsburgh Press, 1973.

Willis, F.R. *Europe in the Global Age: 1939 to the present.* New York: Dodd, Mead and Company, 1968.

Wilson, H.H., & Glickman, H. *The Problem of Internal Security in Great Britain,* 1948-1953. Baltimore: Doubleday and Company, 1954.

Winston, E. "Reducing the number of patients in mental hospitals by providing non-institutional care for the aging." *Mental Hygiene,* 1958, *42,* 544-549.

Wolfe, D. "The state and economic policy in Canada 1968-75." In L. Panitch (Ed.), *The Canadian State: Political economy and political power.* Toronto: University of Toronto Press, 1977.

Wolpe, J. *The Practice of Behavior Therapy*. New York: Pergamon Press, 1969.

World Health Organization. *The Future of Mental Hospitals*. Copenhagen: Regional Office for Europe, World Health Organization, 1978.

Yolles, S.F. "Mental health at work." In A. McLean (Ed.) *To Work is Human: Mental health and the business community*. New York: Macmillan Company, 1967.

Yolles, S.F. *Community Psychiatry: Alternative to chaos*. Unpublished speech presented at Psychiatric Grand Rounds, University of Utah School of Medicine, Dept. of Psychiatry. Salt Lake City, Utah, April 11, 1968.

Yolles, S.F. "Past, present and 1980: Trend projections." In L. Bellak & H.H. Barten (Eds.), *Progress in Community Mental Health*. New York: Grune and Stratton, 1969.

Yolles, S.F. "The future of community psychiatry." In W.E. Barton & C.J. Sanborn (Eds.), *An Assessment of the Community Mental Health Movement*. Lexington, Mass.: D.C. Heath and Company, 1975.

Young, A.F. *Social Service in British Industry*. London: Routledge and Kegan Paul, 1968.

Zaleznik, A., Kets de Vries, M.F.R., & Howard, J. "Stress reactions in organizations: Syndromes, causes and consequences." *Behavioral Science*, 1977, *22*, 151-162.

Zola, I.K. "Medicine as an institution of social control." In J. Ehrenreich (Ed.), *The Cultural Crises of Modern Medicine*. New York: Monthly Review Press, 1978.

Zusman, J. "The philosophic bases for a community and social psychiatry." In W.E. Barton & C.J. Sanborn (Eds.), *An Assessment of the Community Mental Health Movement*. Toronto: Lexington Books, 1975.

INDEX

211

ACKNOWLEDGEMENTS

Bill Livant's creative, ground-breaking insights into dialectical-materialism and its application to a variety of social phenomena gave me the conceptual tools for this analysis. He is gifted in his ability to see the crucial division of a problem, and many times, when my analysis not tangled, Bill helped to resolve the confusion.

Stan Rands' contribution was extensive. In addition to providing very helpful critical reaction to this study, Stan did everything from on-the-spot proofreading, running library errands, lending me his office, putting me up at his house whenever I needed a place to stay, baby-sitting my son, and generally provided unlimited tender loving care. His personal example of humble wisdom, courage and generosity has meant a great deal to me.

Joe Roberts' wealth of knowledge about international labour history, theories of the state, and political trends was invaluable. In a confusing sea of conflicting perspectives, Joe has been a balanced, accessible, and friendly navigator.

Bob Stirling spent two years of painstaking effort trying to help me gain access to a uniquely useful data file. I appreciate his patience and kindness.

Steeve Heeren and Lorne Elkin each made helpful editorial suggestions and referred me to useful sources of information.

Ruth Ralph, my mother, is a skillful general semanticist who taught me clear, simple writing principles and thoroughly edited my drafts. In the process, we transcended the mother-daughter relationship and became even closer friends. Doris Rands, my dear friend, has been an emotional buoy for me throughout the long process of writing. At times I would have given up if it hadn't been for her support and ready smile.

David Lethbridge's editing improved the book's readability and his gentle "humour" cured me forever of a bad case of "inappropriate quotation-markitis."

I especially want to thank David Hein and Ted Hein for giving me the emotional support to complete this study. Otto

Dreidger, Bonnie Jeffery, Kim Collier and Graham Riches gave me encouragement and practical help.

The people of Canada generously financed this study through Canada Council Doctoral Fellowships and through University of Regina Graduate Scholarships. I hope that they will find it useful.

216

THE MODERN STATE

An Anarchist Analysis
by Frank Harrison

This work raises basic questions about the nature of social organization, the capacities of individuals and groups for autonomous self-directed activity, and the conditions which promote or retard this process.

Harrison's philosophical reflections and analysis focus on how contemporary societies, East and West, have resolved this problem and how social theories, liberal and Marxist alike, have interpreted these developments.

The centralized state as the solution to order is not only a *de facto* reality but has become an ideological reality within the tradition of orthodox socialist theory. The theory and practice of state socialism is premised on a denial of basic human aspirations towards autonomy.

Against the background of the philosophical traditions of individualism and anarchism and the historical context of the Russian revolution, Harrison is able to show how absolutist ideas and practices distorted and silenced the populist sentiments of autonomous social groups.

In an imaginative and readable text, the reader is able to make connections between controversies and disputes within the First International and the crushing of the Makhnovist movement in post-revolutionary Russia, between the philosophical ideas of anarchism, the aspirations of the early soviets and the Kronstadt uprising as well as the contemporary Polish situation. Most of all we become aware of the necessity for a broader, less dogmatic view of history and social change.

This is a timely and insightful analysis of the repressive nature of the state apparatus which looks for a solution neither to the East nor to the West but to the historical experiences of grassroots social movements for change.

Frank Harrison teaches political science at St. Francis-Xavier University. A Bakunin scholar, he has studied in England, Russia and Canada.

227 pages
Publication date: May 1983
Paperback ISBN 0-919619-17-7   **$12.95**
Hardcover ISBN 0-919619-19-3   **$22.95**
BLACK ROSE BOOKS No. L78

Printed by
the workers of
Editions Marquis, Montmagny, Québec
for
Black Rose Books Ltd.